Poetry

OF THE NEW ENGLAND

RENAISSANCE

1790–1890

Poetry

OF THE NEW ENGLAND

RENAISSANCE

1790–1890

EDITED WITH AN INTRODUCTION

BY GEORGE F. WHICHER

NEW YORK   *Rinehart & Co., Inc.*   TORONTO

Fifth Printing, April 1960

Introduction copyright, 1950, by George F. Whicher
Typography and Cover Design by Stefan Salter
Printed in the United States of America

INTRODUCTION TO

POETRY OF THE NEW ENGLAND RENAISSANCE

In spite of all that may be alleged in depreciation of puritan-
ism, Victorian sentiment, and the genteel tradition, poetry by
New England writers remains one of the chief glories of American literature. From Anne Bradstreet and Edward Taylor in
the seventeenth century to Edwin Arlington Robinson and
Robert Frost in the twentieth, the nation's singing strength has
been concentrated mainly in the northeastern corner. No one
would wish to deny that the South also has fostered a succession
of fine poets, and in Poe and Lanier has produced two who
challenge comparison with the best. Whitman and Melville,
though slightly touched by New England influences, belong by
birth and habit of mind to New York. But apart from these
bright particular stars, New England may lay claim to almost
the entire galaxy of poets whose works illuminate nineteenth
century America.

Though a notable outburst of creative energy occurred in the
three decades before the Civil War, it is misleading to think of
"the flowering of New England" as confined to that brief period.
The region blossomed early and late as well. It shared with the
rest of the Atlantic seaboard the fervor of nationalistic feeling
generated by the Revolutionary War and the attainment of
American independence. The impact of the French Revolution,
following closely after our own, likewise was felt in spite of the
Federalists' veiling wings. The unstable condition of Europe
until after 1848 helped to sustain visions of man's liberation
from traditional forms of bondage and to encourage hopes of
unlimited progress. To Americans of the second quarter of the

century it seemed that all things were possible. "There is more day to dawn," wrote Thoreau at the end of *Walden*. "The sun is but a morning star!"

A happy confidence in the future was inspired by the rapid increase in the country's wealth. The opening of roads and canals, the beginnings of steamboat traffic on the rivers, and finally the construction of railways made it profitable to ship crops to market. New inventions such as the cotton gin multiplied the potential gains of agriculture. The establishment of the textile industry and other forms of manufacture in New England supplemented the income derived from lumbering, shipbuilding, fisheries, whaling, and overseas commerce. Though temporary setbacks occurred, the country as a whole was prospering. It had the riches of an unpre-empted continent to exploit. While New England possessed fewer natural advantages than other sections, Yankee ingenuity and enterprise were successful in securing a considerable share of the national wealth. Not without reason did Whittier celebrate in prose the rising importance of the Lowell mills and glorify in rhyme the achievements of workingmen in his *Songs of Labor*.

The first effects of the industrial revolution, moreover, coincided with the westward expansion of the United States, in which men and women from New England played a prominent part. Jefferson's Louisiana Purchase was but the first recognition of a latent and irresistible sense of "manifest destiny." As the settlements advanced westward, land values automatically increased. Americans did not need to be industrious or frugal or wise in order to prosper. They were the natural beneficiaries of unearned increment. A happy-go-lucky frontier optimism, consequently, became a deeply ingrained trait in the national character, even east of the Hudson.

Such cultural influences as reached the United States from abroad intensified rather than diminished the tendency to hopefulness. English liberals were laying down specifications for a millennium of material progress. Germany and France were at the high tide of the Romantic Movement. All these forces conspired to produce a dynamic of the spirit favorable to literature.

If poetic impulses were made articulate in New England more readily than elsewhere, the explanation may be found in conditions peculiar to the region. One of these was a long-standing tradition of literacy, resulting from the fact that instruments of culture were more fully developed in New England than in other parts of America. The church, the school, the college, the town meeting, the local newspaper, and the lyceum were well established vehicles of expression and communication. From earliest colonial times New Englanders had set great store on the leadership of highly educated men and had taken pains to assure a supply of learned ministers and magistrates. The cultivation of poetry was an inevitable by-product of a literary education. Cotton Mather at the close of the seventeenth century could advise young scholars to lighten their theological studies with "a little recreation of poetry." A hundred years later the desire to produce imaginative literature had become a vocation which John Quincy Adams most unwillingly abandoned for the more profitable study of law, and which the young Henry Wadsworth Longfellow insisted on pursuing in spite of parental admonitions. Every village newssheet had its "poet's corner," and it was as a newspaper poet that John Greenleaf Whittier first attracted notice. Emily Dickinson, when she needed a companionship which her world could not supply, turned to poetry as "my only playmate."

Such were the reasons for the pre-eminence of nineteenth century New England poets in the effort to "get the United States stated." Though they all manifestly belong to the region, the fourteen representative writers selected for this anthology do not constitute a school or coterie. A majority of them lived in the vicinity of Boston, flourished in the second and third quarters of the century, contributed to the same magazines, and were warm personal friends. Yet even these are roughly divisible into two groups, with Emerson as a common element between the two, and Whittier standing a little apart from both. Barlow and Brownell were Connecticut men, Bryant, Tuckerman, and Emily Dickinson were associated with western Massachusetts, and none of them was connected with either Cambridge or Concord. When all allowances are made for individual disparities, however, the poets of the region did have something in common. New England was a state of mind, recognizably different from the mind of other sections of the country. Furthermore the culture inherited from puritan times culminated between 1830 and 1860 in an extraordinary vigor of thought and expression. The ensuing intensification of productiveness has given the literary history of the period an organizing principle. It was the age of a rebirth of idealism. The poets included in this volume, accordingly, have been chosen because each in his way made a distinct contribution to the New England Renaissance.

Joel Barlow, for example, may be considered as a representative precursor. Like his friends John Trumbull, Timothy Dwight, and several others of the Hartford Wits, he was a graduate of Yale, where he was imbued with standard eighteenth century ways of thought. After serving as a chaplain during the Revolution, he became in later life a lawyer, man of affairs, and diplomat. While on a mission to Napoleon's government he died of exposure at the time of the retreat of the French army from Moscow.

Barlow's *Columbiad*, a pretentious epic based on an early poem called *The Vision of Columbus*, can no longer be taken seriously, except as a monument of American typography. Its wooden couplets give no indication of the flexibility of mind which its author possessed. While his literary contemporaries were settling down to careers of placid respectability, Barlow went abroad, fell in with Tom Paine and other radicals, and presently expressed his sympathy with the French Revolution in a subversive poem, *The Conspiracy of Kings*, and an even more devastating prose tract, *Advice to the Privileged Orders*. These works caused him to be branded as a renegade in the land of steady habits.

His best claim to remembrance is based on *The Hasty Pudding*, a playful piece written in the mock-heroic vein of Pope's *Rape of the Lock*. But aside from its facetiousness the poem presents a series of realistic pictures of corn-raising, country mirth, and hearthside scenes which anticipate the Yankee pastoral strain of Whittier. No doubt Barlow had his tongue in his cheek when he celebrated, quite literally, "the meal in the firkin, the milk in the pan." A later generation was to ask the meaning of these things in serious earnest.

William Cullen Bryant, as a youth of sixteen, was writing the first version of his "Thanatopsis" in the year of Barlow's death. He was the son of an enlightened country doctor in the town of Cummington among the Berkshire hills. Though Dr. Peter Bryant was proud of his son's literary talents, he could not afford to send him for more than one year to Williams College. Thereafter the young poet reluctantly turned to the law for a livelihood. Not until he had passed his thirtieth birthday and had published a good share of the poems on which his reputation rests did Bryant leave his native uplands to commence his distinguished career as a newspaper editor in New York. His poetic outpourings dwindled in later life to a scanty trickle.

In his own person Bryant exemplified the transition from old attitudes to new. Reared as an orthodox Congregationalist, a convinced Federalist, and an admirer of Popean poetry, he passed through deism to a mild allegiance to the Unitarian creed, became a stanch Jeffersonian Democrat opposed to the extension

of slavery, and found the literary inspiration of his life in
Wordsworth. Like his model, Bryant took nature for a principal
subject, yet his approach remained different from that of the
English poet. While Wordsworth wrote as a mystic with pan-
theistic leanings, Bryant was always a moralist, even when most
touched by the charm of mountains and skies. He never outgrew
the sententious frame of mind induced by his early familiarity
with Cowper, Gray, Young, and other late Augustan poets. His
lyrics on natural objects, such as "The Yellow Violet" and "To
a Waterfowl," come to moral conclusions quite in the fashion
of Burns. Though he may be given credit, together with the
painters of the Hudson River school, for teaching his countrymen to value picturesque scenery, Bryant seldom failed to link
the natural with the human. A mystical appreciation of the external world as the counterpart of the soul of man became the
special subject of Ralph Waldo Emerson and the lesser transcendentalists.

This group, however, may best be left for later consideration.
Though Emerson was several years older than the poets associated with Cambridge, he was slower than they in publishing
his work. In 1847, when Emerson's *Poems* first appeared in book
form Longfellow had five books to his credit, the first collection
of witty occasional verse by Oliver Wendell Holmes was already
ten years old, and even young James Russell Lowell had published two early volumes, and was gathering his forces for the
extraordinary output of four new books in 1848.

The three poets last named may be grouped together because
all three were connected with Harvard College and shared alike
the virtues and shortcomings of cultivated Bostonians of their
day. Though Longfellow was born in Portland, Maine, and educated at Bowdoin College, he became completely acclimated to
Cambridge soon after his appointment as a Harvard professor
of modern languages, while his second marriage allied him with

one of the leading families of Boston. Holmes and Lowell were both born members of what the former playfully denominated as the "Brahmin" class. An aura of kid gloves surrounded the members of this group. It has been sometimes supposed that their minds were likewise insulated from sordid realities. But this supposition is not entirely well founded. Holmes at least was an uninhibited reader and a candid scientist, and Lowell, years before he became an ambassador, was an agitator for unpopular reforms.

But perhaps it is impossible to think of either Longfellow or Lowell as eager young men. Both are firmly established in the public mind as bearded patriarchs inhabiting the spacious houses in Cambridge where they passed their later years, greatly reverenced and beloved. Neither one was called upon to risk all he possessed for poetry's sake like Keats, or to endure long years of poverty and neglect like E. A. Robinson. They were reasonably content with the measure of success that came to them easily; and consequently what one misses in their work is the authority of what is indubitably first rate. In this respect Holmes comes off slightly better than either of his colleagues. As a professor of anatomy in the Medical School he stood at the top of his profession. His writing was purely an avocation. Yet as a gifted amateur he held his own with most professional authors of his time.

There is no doubt, however, that these three New England gentlemen earned the admiration of their contemporaries. They made themselves the accepted spokesmen of received ideals. Readers saw their own features reflected in the poets' placid mentalities. Yet Longfellow did more than embody in fresh images the moral conventions and domestic sentiments of the age. He became the myth-maker extraordinary to the American people, creating a throng of figures to fill the popular imagination. Evangeline and her lover, Miles Standish and Priscilla the puritan maiden, Hiawatha, Paul Revere—these are but the best known. And like Washington Irving, Longfellow ransacked European literatures for Old World souvenirs that he might bring home and display before his countrymen. His explorations ranged from Lapland to Palestine. Through· his efforts Americans could feel a connection with a richer past than the brief history of white settlers in the New World afforded and could blend yesterday's news of the schooner *Hesperus* with immemorial legends of the Middle Ages.

Both Holmes and Lowell were more notable as writers of prose than as poets. Yet the graceful and well-turned society verse of the one and the vigorous political satire in stage-Yankee dialect of the other left an impression not easily effaced. Furthermore, in his "Ode Recited at the Harvard Commemoration" Lowell produced the finest American example of poetry written for a public occasion. Both poets in fact needed the sense of an immediate audience before them in order to write their best.

As a political poet John Greenleaf Whittier had no equal in his generation. He was a plain farmer from north of Boston, untypical only in his devotion to the Quaker creed of his family. He had little education beyond what he could acquire in newspaper offices and by eager reading. With all his honest heart he believed in the promises of democracy, and in the struggle to realize them for even the lowliest of mankind he made himself the incandescent conscience of the American people. For nearly thirty years he served the antislavery cause with the full power of his pen. After that cause was won, though by means he would never have chosen, he returned in the long Indian summer of his days to idealized memories of New England scenes and local legends. In numerous ballads and idylls he joined Longfellow in creating a romantic sense of the American past. The most famous of his poems, *Snow-Bound*, published when he was nearly sixty, is a picture in terms of his boyhood home of the self·

reliant New England household at its best. Whittier was not unaware, however, as the "Prelude" to *Among the Hills* testifies, of the drabber and more desolate aspects of the life about him. Nevertheless he had faith in the gradual meliorization of the human lot. And in a sheaf of deeply felt religious poems he made himself pre-eminently the poet of faith in the immanence of a Divine Being and the power of His sustaining hand.

A special niche in the history of American poetry belongs to Henry Howard Brownell, born in Providence, Rhode Island, but brought up in East Hartford, Connecticut, and educated at Trinity College. As a lawyer with a literary flair he had published a volume of now forgotten verse a decade before the Civil War, but the heat of the great conflict quickly brought him into prominence as, in Holmes's phrase, "Our Battle-Laureate." While attached to Admiral Farragut's staff, he was a witness of at least one hard-fought naval engagement, which he described in "The Bay Fight" in stanzas pulsing with the excitement of the moment. His graphic power is well shown in "Night-Quarters." But altogether the most effective piece that he ever wrote is "Abraham Lincoln," a tribute penned in the immediate aftermath of the president's death and charged with the conflicting emotions of triumph and sorrow. Though uneven in execution and far too long (it has been abridged to half its length for quotation in this anthology), it should be linked with Whitman's "When Lilacs Last in the Dooryard Bloom'd" and Lowell's "Commemoration Ode" as among the finest expressions of northern feelings inspired by the loss of a great leader at the moment of victory.

In most respects the poets hitherto discussed took the world of the nineteenth century as they found it. The reforms they advocated were not calculated to shatter the scheme of things entire, but merely to effect some slight alterations for the better. They accepted a rationally determined set of values, believed in

a simple personal code of right and wrong sanctioned by re-
ligion, and were confident that the civilized portion of the
human race was making fairly steady progress toward a millennium of material prosperity. As literary craftsmen they depended
on a rhetoric of direct communication, a homiletic style sug-
gestive of pulpit eloquence, only modified now and then by a
slight tendency toward romantic vagueness. Unanalyzed con-
cepts such as justice, freedom, truth, and the like were often
the ultimate bases of their thought. Of the complexities and
dilemmas which the twentieth century associates with the names
of Darwin, Marx, Freud, and Einstein, they were happily ignorant. But not all contemporaries of Longfellow and Whittier
were unaware of disturbing paradoxes. It is startling to turn
from banalities such as

> Truth crushed to earth will rise again;
> The eternal years of God are hers;

or

> Lives of great men all remind us
> We can make our lives sublime,

to foreshadowings of our modern world (almost literally in the
conception of curved space!) in the following passage, which is
not as familiar to American readers as it deserves to be.

> Line in nature is not found;
> Unit and universe are round;
> In vain produced, all rays return;
> Evil will bless, and ice will burn.

This quotation is taken from a poem called "Uriel," to which
Robert Frost allows one of his characters in *The Masque of
Reason* to refer obliquely as "the greatest Western poem yet."

Its author, Ralph Waldo Emerson, was the chief literary voice
of the transcendentalist movement. Descended from generations
of clergymen on his father's side and from generations of mer-
chants on his mother's, Emerson combined in his own person
the spirituality and the hard sense implicit in the puritan tradition. Like three of his brothers he was graduated from Harvard. In due time he finished a course at the Divinity School,
became the colleague-pastor of an important Boston church,
and married the ethereal daughter (soon to die) of a prosperous
businessman. So far his career was entirely conventional. But
before he was thirty Emerson resigned his pulpit to devote himself to independent thinking and writing. This he was enabled
to do because a small inheritance from his wife's estate made
it possible for him to live frugally in the country village of
Concord. There he married a second time and had children.
On a trip to Europe in 1832–1833 he met Coleridge, Wordsworth, and Carlyle, of whom the last became a lifelong friend
and correspondent. After three years of quiet meditation Emerson published the tiny anonymous book *Nature*, which condensed into less than one hundred pages the essence of the
transcendental revolt from rationalism. The explosive force of
his doctrine was soon felt in the Harvard Phi Beta Kappa address, "The American Scholar," in 1837, and still more in the
words he spoke the following year to the graduating class at the
Divinity School. During the 1840's Emerson collected the first
and second series of his *Essays* and a volume of *Poems*. He was
also winning attention as an inspiring lyceum lecturer. It had
seemed conceivable about 1840 that he might become the leader
of a semireligious revival, a "Saturnalia of faith," as Jonathan
Edwards had been a century earlier. But the great surge of popu-
lation to the West and the excitements of the Mexican War
absorbed the energies of the country. Emerson came to see
clearly that

> Things are in the saddle
> And ride mankind.

There was little he could do but state his position and wait for the world to come round to him.

What Emerson inaugurated in his own poetry and fostered in the poetry of others was a break with the rationalistic rhetoric which had been basic since the time of Dryden. In this he was a continuator of the literary revolution effected in England by Wordsworth and Coleridge. Meanwhile young and ardent clergymen in the neighborhood of Boston, such men as Frederick Henry Hedge, Orestes A. Brownson, George Ripley, and Theodore Parker, were conducting a parallel religious movement to transcend Locke's philosophy of sensation and its institutional formulation in Unitarianism. They were seeking justification for spiritual experiences which had no place in any rational system of thought, but which were intensely real and all-important to them. In part their movement may be described as a resurgence of native puritan mysticism, but it quickly found support in the popularizations of Kant and other German idealists by Victor Cousin in France and Thomas Carlyle in England. In his efforts to make poetry a vehicle for the expression of dynamic intuitions and vital instincts not demonstrable to the plodding understanding Emerson laid foundations on which poets of our own time have built.

He did not, however, carry the process very far. His training in pulpit eloquence was too deep-seated to be easily modified to suit the exigencies of symbolic expression. Perhaps the little poem called "Days" represents the most perfect realization of the new poetic method that he was ever to attain. But as often happens with experimental tendencies in literature, poets not much in favor with conventional readers of their own day were able to follow up new directions better than widely accepted

writers. Newness flourishes in holes and corners. So we we find
the implications of the new poetry variously developed by the
mad poet Jones Very, the youthful iconoclast Henry Thoreau,
and the eccentric William Ellery Channing, II. And for a conscious celebration of the poetry of the unconscious, a forerunner
of Archibald MacLeish's "Ars Poetica," we must turn to
"Gnosis" by the dilettantish Christopher Pearse Cranch.

> Thought is deeper than all speech,
>   Feeling deeper than all thought;
> Souls to souls can never teach
>   What unto themselves was taught. . . .
>
> Only when our souls are fed
>   By the Fount which gave them birth,
> And by inspiration led,
>   Which they never drew from earth,
>
> We like parted drops of rain
>   Swelling till they meet and run,
> Shall be all absorbed again
>   Melting, flowing into one.

Two poets who gave themselves utterly to seclusion may be
cited, finally, as the ones who exploited to the limits of nineteenth century capacity the possibilities of a poetry of the inner
life. They were Frederick Goddard Tuckerman of Greenfield
and Emily Dickinson of Amherst, both residents of western
Massachusetts.

In their antecedents the two were as different as possible.
Tuckerman came of a literary family, attended Harvard College
for one year and completed a course at the Law School, and
while still conversant with the world visited Tennyson and other

writers in England. He issued a book of *Poems* in 1860 which went through several reprintings. The death of his wife in childbirth shattered his personal life and deepened a tendency to melancholy which was manifest even in his earliest writing. In five series of sonnets marked by highly unorthodox handling of rhyme schemes and brilliantly original imagery Tuckerman attempted to analyze and objectify his grief. Since his real subject could be stated only in indirect terms, he was driven to search for means of expression through the device that T. S. Eliot has called the "objective correlative," or by the implications conveyed through metaphors that sometimes attain the dignity of symbols. Though much of his early poetry lacked assurance, his sonnets reached moments of sheer loveliness such as one associates with sophisticated and slightly decadent poets like Edward Fitzgerald or Ernest Dowson. Tuckerman strikes us today as a strange exotic in the Connecticut Valley. Here, for example, in the last seven lines of a sonnet he describes a view of the ocean which he had last seen in company with his wife while she was still living. He makes the details of visible things stand as an almost perfect analogy for the distress and the high hope that mingle in his heart, ending the poem boldly with a truncated and irregular line.

> Again I hear the drenching of the wave;
> The rocks rise dark, with wall and weedy cave;
> Her voice is in mine ears, her answer yet:
> Again I see, above the froth and fret,
> The blue loft standing like eternity!
> And white feet flying from the surging surf
> And simmering suds of the sea!

Emily Dickinson, unlike Tuckerman, was quintessentially native to the region and completely innocent of literary sophistication. As a daughter of the leading lawyer of Amherst, she might normally have married a young minister or lawyer from the college he served as treasurer, but this fulfillment was denied to her. To compensate for her disaster of the heart she seems to have turned to poetry, and in single-minded concentration on what most concerned her to have immured herself behind the hemlock hedges of the Dickinson house. There she secretly recorded day after day her vivid awarenesses of both outer and inner weather. Only after her death was the extent of her achievement known, and only slowly and with many vexatious delays was the evidence of it laid before the public. Impressions of the seasons, aspects of the day and night, changes of climate, the world of small living things, and garden or household incidents she noted with an extreme objectivity which led Amy Lowell to claim her as a forerunner of the Imagists. But her greater distinction lies in her lyrics of psychological perception, her dramatizations of a heart's longings, and her flashes of intuitive wisdom shaped at a white heat of intensity. These things she wrought in verbal patterns implanted in her mind by the hymns she sang as a girl in church, but with a free and masterly handling of rhythm and hinted rhyme. She supposed her work might be odd, "a kangaroo among the beauty," but it was at least her own and she could not make it otherwise to suit the advice of such mentors as Thomas Wentworth Higginson. Few writers have ever guarded more carefully than she the integrity of the imagination. The greatest of her brief poems are as fresh now as on the day they were written. Of all the New England poets she most perfectly developed the language of intuition which was to be the poetic idiom of the future.

In the century which saw their fullest flowering, therefore, New England poets deepened three main channels of expression. In reaction from colonial subservience to British models they exalted the native strain, both by picturing homely local

scenes, as in the poems of Barlow and Whittier, and by finding
appropriate means of stating the ideal of an inviolable American
Union as this theme was voiced pre-eminently by Lowell and
Brownell. They also assimilated two chief aspects of the Ro-
mantic Movement: the cult of nature as variously displayed by
Bryant, Emerson, Very, Channing, Thoreau, and Emily Dickin-
son; and the revival of the past as this was effected mainly by
Whittier and Longfellow. Most significantly, perhaps, they trans-
muted into poetry the spiritual questionings of sensitive New
Englanders who watched with dismay the progressive cheapen-
ing of the American dream by an ever more crass acquisitiveness.
The chief exponents of the inner life and its dilemmas in the
modern world were Emerson, Thoreau, Tuckerman, and Emily
Dickinson.

The New England Renaissance witnessed likewise some basic
changes in poetic technique. At the beginning of the century
the prevailing style was that of the late Augustans, Barlow con-
tinuing the mock-heroic tradition of Pope, Bryant the senten-
tiousness of Cowper and Wordsworth, and Holmes somewhat
later the exquisite polish of Georgian *vers de société*. Under the
promptings of the naturists, next, there developed a faculty of
close realistic observation, which was manifest in the descriptive
lyrics of Bryant, Whittier, Longfellow, Emerson, and Thoreau.
The Cambridge poets, especially Longfellow, brought verse
craftsmanship to such a pitch of dexterity that there was nothing
for succeeding poets to do but to invent free verse. More radical
experiments in poetic expression were made by Emerson and the
lesser transcendentalists, by Tuckerman, and by Emily Dickinson in their efforts to discover a language for the psychological
experiences which they were concerned to make known. In the
work of these last named poets we may find early efforts to use
words as a plastic medium, or in other terms, the first glimmer-
ings of the perception that language may be used symbolically

to transmit values that cannot be directly stated. From poetry equated to a Newtonian universe the imagination of New England writers ventured out into the unknown, seeking new ways of adjustment in order to surmount the successive waves of disillusionment which overtook sensitive thinkers after the middle of the nineteenth century. In Emily Dickinson we recognize the most advanced precursor of the modern mind, a poet who candidly admits that when she undertakes to organize experience her "little force explodes," and who therefore confines herself to brief and fragmentary insights, some of them startlingly akin to our own.

GEORGE F. WHICHER

Amherst, Massachusetts,
June, 1950

BIBLIOGRAPHICAL AND TEXTUAL NOTE

Apart from general histories of American literature there is no book that discusses the poetry of New England in regional terms and none that deals with American poetry of the nineteenth century as a distinct period. Useful anthologies are Harry H. Clark, *Major American Poets*, 1936 and Louis Untermeyer, *An Anthology of the New England Poets from Colonial Times to the Present Day*, 1948. Critical treatments of several of the poets included in this book may be found in Edmund Clarence Stedman, *Poets of America*, 1885, and in Henry W. Wells, *The American Way of Poetry*, 1943. A profound study of New England sensibility at the mid-nineteenth century is Francis O. Matthiessen, *American Renaissance*, 1941. Perry Miller has compiled a masterly selection from documents illustrating the religious and philosophical thought of the pre-Civil War decades in *The Transcendentalists*, 1950.

In the individual author bibliographies which follow I have marked with an asterisk the sources of the texts reprinted in this volume.

Joel Barlow

Barlow was one of the four main contributors to *The Anarchiad*, 1786–1787. His principal poems, which have never been collected, were issued as follows: *The Vision of Columbus*, 1787, later revised as *The Columbiad*, 1807; *The Conspiracy of Kings*, 1792; * *The Hasty-Pudding*, 1796. The most accessible modern reprint of much of this material is Vernon L. Parrington, *The Connecticut Wits*, 1926.

Among early studies of Barlow which still have value may be mentioned Moses C. Tyler, *Three Men of Letters*, 1895, and Charles B. Todd,* *Life and Letters of Joel Barlow*, 1886. More

Poems, 1838, and *Lays of My Home*, 1843. Later titles include *Ballads and Other Poems*, 1844; *Voices of Freedom*, 1846; *Poems*, 1849 (the first collected edition); *Songs of Labor*, 1850; *The Chapel of the Hermits*, 1853; *The Panorama*, 1856; *Home Ballads*, 1860; *In War Time*, 1864; *National Lyrics*, 1865; *Snow-Bound*, 1866; *The Tent on the Beach*, 1867; *Among the Hills*, 1869; *Miriam*, 1871; *The Pennsylvania Pilgrim*, 1872; and *The Vision of Echard*, 1878.

Under the poet's supervision Horace E. Scudder edited *The Writings of John Greenleaf Whittier*, 7 vols., 1888–1889, which remains the standard library edition. The same editor later produced the one-volume Cambridge Edition of * *The Complete Poetical Works*, 1894.

Samuel T. Pickard, *Life and Letters of John Greenleaf Whittier*, 2 vols., 1894, is a sound but pedestrian biography. It may be supplemented by the same author's *Whittier-Land*, 1904. The most recent and authoritative life is John A. Pollard's *John Greenleaf Whittier, Friend of Man*, 1949. Invaluable is the volume of special studies edited by Howard H. Brinton, *Byways in Quaker History*, 1944.

OLIVER WENDELL HOLMES

After *Poems*, 1836, Holmes published no verse for a decade. His *Poems* were issued with additional material in 1846 and 1849, and finally attained the dignity of *The Poetical Works of Oliver Wendell Holmes*, 1852. Many of his best known pieces first appeared in the *Autocrat* or later essays. Subsequent titles are *Songs in Many Keys*, 1862; *Humorous Poems*, 1865; *The Iron Gate*, 1880; and *Before the Curfew*, 1888.

The Riverside Edition of *The Writings*, 13 vols., 1891, was followed by the standard *Works*, 13 vols., 1892, each including one volume of poems. Horace E. Scudder edited the Cambridge Edition of * *The Complete Poetical Works*, 1895.

The most authoritative biography is that by Ralph L. Rusk, 1949. Other important lives are those by George W. Cooke, 1881; James E. Cabot, 2 vols., 1887; George E. Woodbury, 1907; and Oscar W. Firkins, 1915. Bliss Perry, *Emerson Today*, 1931, contains an extremely sympathetic treatment of the poems.

HENRY WADSWORTH LONGFELLOW

The publication of Longfellow's poems began with *Voices of the Night*, 1839, and included some thirty separate items before his death. Among the more important titles are *Ballads and Poems*, 1842; *Evangeline*, 1847; *The Seaside and the Fireside*, 1850; *The Song of Hiawatha*, 1855; *The Courtship of Miles Standish*, 1858; *Tales of a Wayside Inn*, 1863; *Flower-de-Luce*, 1867; *The Masque of Pandora*, 1875; *Kéramos and Other Poems*, 1878; and *Ultima Thule*, 1880.

The Riverside Edition of the *Complete Poetical and Prose Works*, 11 vols., 1866, and *Works*, 14 vols., 1886–1891, are standard. * *The Complete Poetical Works*, in the one-volume Cambridge Edition supervised by Horace E. Scudder, 1893, is an easily available text.

The Life of Henry W. Longfellow by Samuel W. Longfellow, the poet's brother, was the first of many biographies. The most recent is *Young Longfellow*, 1807–1843, by Lawrance Thompson, 1938. Worth consulting also are William P. Trent, *Longfellow and Other Essays*, 1908; Bliss Perry, *Park Street Papers*, 1908; Oliphant Smeaton, *Longfellow and His Poetry*, London, 1919; and James T. Hatfield, *New Light on Longfellow*, 1933.

JOHN GREENLEAF WHITTIER

Whittier's first book was the journalistic prose and verse *Legends of New England*, 1831. He becomes important with recent and complete information is contained in Theodore A. Zunder, *The Early Days of Joel Barlow*, 1934, and Leon Howard, *The Connecticut Wits*, 1943. Short essays are included in Henry A. Beers, *The Connecticut Wits*, 1920, and John Dos Passos, *The Ground We Stand On*, 1941.

WILLIAM CULLEN BRYANT

Bryant's first slight gathering of eight *Poems* was printed in 1821. Later and greatly augmented collections with the same title were issued in 1832, 1834, 1836, 1839, 1854, 1871, and 1875. He also wrote *The Fountain and Other Poems*, 1842; *The White-Footed Deer and Other Poems*, 1844; *Thirty Poems*, 1864; *The Flood of Years*, 1878. His translation of Homer's *Iliad* appeared in 1870, of the *Odyssey* in 1871–1872.

* *The Poetical Works of William Cullen Bryant*, 1876, was the last supervised by the poet himself. *The Poetical Works*, 2 vols., edited by Parke Godwin, 1883, contains some additional pieces. Other useful texts are the Roslyn Edition, edited by H. C. Sturges and R. H. Stoddard, 1903; the Oxford Edition, 1914; and *William Cullen Bryant: Representative Selections*, edited by Tremaine McDowell, 1935.

Parke Godwin's *A Biography of William Cullen Bryant*, 2 vols., 1883, is still the standard life. A shorter book is John Bigelow, *William Cullen Bryant*, 1890, in the original American Men of Letters. For a competent brief sketch of Bryant's life, see the article by Allan Nevins in DAB.

RALPH WALDO EMERSON

Only two volumes of Emerson's poetry were published during his lifetime: *Poems*, 1847, and *May-Day and Other Pieces*, 1867. Much material has been added in * *Poems*, Vol. IX of *The Complete Works*, Centenary Edition, edited by his son Edward Waldo Emerson, 1903–1904.

The official *Life and Letters*, 2 vols., 1896, is by John T. Morse. An excellent brief sketch is Mark A. DeWolfe Howe, *Holmes of the Breakfast-Table*, 1939.

JONES VERY

Only one book, *Essays and Poems*, 1839, appeared during Very's lifetime. It was reissued as * *Poems and Essays*, 1886, greatly enlarged, with a sketch of the author by James Freeman Clarke. An important critical study and a brief selection from the poems are contained in Yvor Winters, *Maule's Curse*, 1938. Unpublished material is presented in William I. Bartlett, *Jones Very: Emerson's "Brave Saint,"* 1942.

CHRISTOPHER PEARSE CRANCH

Cranch published * *Poems*, 1844; *The Aeneids of Virgil*, 1872; * *The Bird and the Bell*, 1875; and * *Ariel and Caliban*, 1887. His poems have never been collected. A *Life and Letters*, 1917, has been written by Leonora Cranch Scott.

HENRY DAVID THOREAU

None of Thoreau's poetry was collected in book form during his lifetime. A few pieces, mainly from *The Dial*, were included in *Excursions*, 1863, but there was no adequate gathering before Henry S. Salt and Frank B. Sanborn edited *Poems of Nature*, 1895. The standard collection is Carl Bode, * *Complete Poems of Henry Thoreau*, 1943. The only competent discussion of Thoreau as a poet is by Henry W. Wells, "An Evaluation of Thoreau's Poetry," *American Literature*, XVI, 99–109.

Biographies of Thoreau begin with Emerson's short appreciation in *Lectures and Biographical Sketches* (*Complete Works*, Vol. X), and end with Joseph W. Krutch's recent study in the new American Men of Letters series. Along the way are Brooks Atkinson, *Henry Thoreau, Cosmic Yankee*, 1927; Henry S.

Canby, *Thoreau*, 1939; and George F. Whicher, *Walden Revisited*, 1945. Not to be missed is the section on Thoreau in Francis O. Matthiessen, *American Renaissance*, 1941.

WILLIAM ELLERY CHANNING, II

Channing's volumes of poetry include * *Poems*, 1843; * *Poems, Second Series*, 1847; *The Woodman and Other Poems*, 1849; *The Wanderer*, 1871; *Eliot, a Poem*, 1885. His writings have not been collected. Poe attacked Channing with savage rancor in a review of *Poems*. No adequate rejoinder has ever appeared. For an account of his life, consult DAB.

JAMES RUSSELL LOWELL

Lowell's publication of poems extended for nearly half a century, from *A Year's Life*, 1841, to *Heartsease and Rue*, 1888. His great year, however, was 1848, when his *Poems*, 1844, was supplemented by a second volume, and *A Fable for Critics*, the first series of *The Biglow Papers*, and *The Vision of Sir Launfal* all made their appearance. Subsequently he published the *Ode Recited at the Harvard Commemoration*, 1865; *The Biglow Papers, Second Series*, 1867; *Under the Willows*, 1869; *The Cathedral*, 1870, and *Three Memorial Poems*, 1877.

The Elmwood Edition of *The Complete Writings of James Russell Lowell*, 16 vols., 1904, edited by Charles Eliot Norton, contains four volumes of poetry. Horace E. Scudder edited the Cambridge Edition of * *The Complete Poetical Works*, 1917.

The best introduction to Lowell is through his *Letters*, variously published. There are also Horace E. Scudder, *James Russell Lowell*, 2 vols., 1901; Ferris Greenslet, *James Russell Lowell*, 1905, in the American Men of Letters; and Richmond C. Beatty, *James Russell Lowell*, 1942. For criticism, see the Introduction to Harry H. Clark and Norman Foerster, *James Russell Lowell: Representative Selections*, 1947.

HENRY HOWARD BROWNELL

Brownell wrote *Poems*, 1847; *Ephemeron, a Poem*, 1853; *Lyrics of a Day*, 1864; * *War-Lyrics and Other Poems*, 1866. Only the last two are important. Selections appeared as *Poems*, 1867, and *Lines of Battle*, 1912. The Introduction to the last named, by Mark A. DeWolfe Howe, is the best available biographical and critical sketch.

FREDERICK GODDARD TUCKERMAN

* *Poems*, 1860, and subsequent reprintings; *The Sonnets*, edited by Witter Bynner, 1931; and *The Cricket*, 1950: these comprise the complete bibliography of this retiring poet. An essay by Walter Prichard Eaton in the *Forum*, January, 1909; the Introduction to Bynner's edition of *The Sonnets*; and an essay by Yvor Winters in the *Hudson Review* [forthcoming], include all that has been written in his praise. The facts of his life are given in DAB.

EMILY DICKINSON

No more than five of her poems were printed during Emily Dickinson's lifetime. Beginning in 1890 appeared three series of *Poems*, edited by Mabel Loomis Todd with the assistance of Thomas Wentworth Higginson; then after a long interval *The Single Hound*, 1914; *Further Poems*, 1929; and *Unpublished Poems*, 1935, edited by Martha Dickinson Bianchi with the assistance of Alfred Leete Hampson; finally came *Bolts of Melody*, 1945, edited by Mabel Loomis Todd and Millicent Todd Bingham. The first six volumes named above are collected as *Poems by Emily Dickinson*, edited by Bianchi and Hampson. The poems quoted in this anthology are chosen from * *Poems*, 1890, and * *Poems: Second Series*, 1891.

Emily Dickinson's *Letters*, 1931, edited by Mabel Loomis Todd, are the best commentary on her poems. They may be supplemented by George F. Whicher, *This Was a Poet*, 1938.

CONTENTS

Page

INTRODUCTION   v

JOEL BARLOW

The Hasty Pudding   1

WILLIAM CULLEN BRYANT

Thanatopsis   13
The Yellow Violet   15
Inscription for the Entrance to a Wood   17
To a Waterfowl   18
Spain   19
To a Mosquito   20
The Death of the Flowers   23
The Past   24
The Prairies   26
The Planting of the Apple-Tree   30
Robert of Lincoln   33
The Poet   35

RALPH WALDO EMERSON

Two Early Poems
    Thought   38
    To-day   38
The Apology   39
The Rhodora   40

Contents

Each and All	40
Concord Hymn	42
The Problem	43
From Woodnotes, I	
A Forest Seer	45
A Charméd Day	46
The Humble-Bee	48
The Snow-Storm	50
The Bohemian Hymn	51
Grace	51
The Informing Spirit	52
Compensation	52
Experience	53
Mottoes for Nature	54
Music	55
Forbearance	55
The Visit	56
Ode to Beauty	57
Uriel	60
Mithridates	62
To J. W.	63
Hamatreya	64
Suum Cuique	66
Ode Inscribed to W. H. Channing	66
Give All to Love	70
Merlin, I	71
Merlin, II	74
Bacchus	76
Threnody	78
Days	86
Waldeinsamkeit	87
Brahma	89
Two Rivers	90

From Voluntaries
    "In an age of fops and toys"   90
Considerations by the Way   91
Terminus   92

HENRY WADSWORTH LONGFELLOW

The Skeleton in Armor   94
Mezzo Camin   99
Seaweed   100
To the Driving Cloud   101
From Evangeline
    The Forest Primeval   103
In the Churchyard at Cambridge   104
The Warden of the Cinque Ports   105
The Jewish Cemetery at Newport   107
The Golden Mile-Stone   109
My Lost Youth   111
The Children's Hour   114
Snow-Flakes   116
From Tales of a Wayside Inn
    The Landlord's Tale—Paul Revere's Ride   116
    Interlude   121
    The Musician's Tale—The Saga of King Olaf   122
The Cumberland   174
Divina Commedia   175
From The Golden Legend
    The Flight into Egypt   179
Chaucer   181
The Sound of the Sea   182
Boston   182
A Dutch Picture   183
The Leap of Roushan Beg   185

Contents

Kéramos   188
The Three Silences of Molinos   201
The Cross of Snow   201
The Tide Rises, the Tide Falls   202

JOHN GREENLEAF WHITTIER

Proem   203
Cassandra Southwick   204
Massachusetts to Virgina   210
Ichabod   214
First-Day Thoughts   216
My Namesake   217
Skipper Ireson's Ride   223
The Old Burying-Ground   226
Telling the Bees   230
For Righteousness' Sake   232
My Playmate   233
Monadnock from Wachuset   235
Laus Deo!   237
Snow-Bound   239
Abraham Davenport   262
From Among the Hills
     Prelude   264
My Triumph   269
The Brewing of Soma   272
Sunset on the Bearcamp   275
The Dead Feast of the Kol-Folk   278
At Last   280

OLIVER WENDELL HOLMES

The Ballad of the Oysterman   282
Old Ironsides   283

Contents

The Last Leaf 284
My Aunt 286
A Song for the Centennial Celebration of Harvard College 287
The Deacon's Masterpiece; or, the Wonderful "One-Hoss Shay" 289
The Chambered Nautilus 293
Brother Jonathan's Lament for Sister Caroline 294
The Moral Bully 296
A Sun-Day Hymn 298
Bill and Joe 298
Dorothy Q. 301
At the "Atlantic" Dinner 303
To John Greenleaf Whittier 305

JONES VERY

Next mk

To the Canary Bird 307
The Tree 307
The Presence 308
The Dead 308
Thy Brother's Blood 309
The Call 309
The Prayer 310
Yourself 311
The Hand and Foot 311
The Lost 312
The Absent 313
The Created 313
How Long? 314
The Lament of the Flowers 315
The Falling Leaf 316
Ship Rock 318

Contents

CHRISTOPHER PEARSE CRANCH

The Flower and the Bee 320
In the Garden 321
The Pines and the Sea 321
December 322
Gnosis 323
So Far, So Near 324
Human Helpers 325

HENRY DAVID THOREAU

Prayer 327
Smoke in Winter 327
Haze 328
Low-Anchored Cloud 329
Light-Wingéd Smoke 329
When Winter Fringes Every Bough 330
Men Say 331
What's the Railroad 331
The Respectable Folks 332
To the Maiden in the East 333
The Offer 334
Conscience 335
Though All the Fates Should Prove Unkind 336
Rumors from an Æolian Harp 337
Man's Little Acts 338
Epigrams
    "I'm contented you should stay" 338
    "Die and be buried who will" 339
    "Upon the lofty elm tree sprays" 339
    "Thy deeds of king and meanest hedger" 339
    "My life has been the poem I would have writ" 339

The Atlantides	339
My Love Must Be as Free	340
Friendship	341
The Inward Morning	343
My Books I'd Fain Cast Off	345
Sic Vita	346
Love	348
Independence	348
Indeed Indeed, I Cannot Tell	350
From Inspiration	350
A Winter and Spring Scene	352

WILLIAM ELLERY CHANNING

A Poet's Hope	355
The River	357
The Poor	358
For a Wood Scene in Winter	359
From Sonnets	
"Thou art like that which is most sweet and fair"	360
"In those bright, laughing days that pierce the fall"	360
The Lonely Road	361
The Glade	363
Hymn of the Earth	363
Flight of the Wild Geese	364

JAMES RUSSELL LOWELL

Remembered Music	368
To the Spirit of Keats	368
Hebe	369
From The Biglow Papers, *First Series*	
Hosea Biglow and the Recruiting Sergeant	370

From The Biglow Papers, *Second Series*

The Courtin'   375
Mr. Hosea Biglow to the Editor of the Atlantic
    Monthly   379
Ode Recited at the Harvard Commemoration   385
Auspex   398

HENRY HOWARD BROWNELL

The Burial of the Dane   400
Night-Quarters   402
From Abraham Lincoln   403

FREDERICK GODDARD TUCKERMAN

Sonnets, Part I
    "Sometimes, when winding slow by brook and
      bower"   414
    "Wherefore, with this belief, held like a blade"   414
    "And borne with theirs, my proudest thoughts do
      seem"   415
    "Nor looks that backward life so bare to me"   415
    "And so the day drops by; the horizon draws"   416
    "Not sometimes, but—to him that heeds the whole"   416
    "Dank fens of cedar; hemlock-branches gray"   417
    "As when, down some broad River dropping, we"   417
    "Yet wear we on; the deep light disallowed"   418
    "An upper chamber in a darkened house"   418
    "What profits it to me, though here allowed"   419
    "Tall, stately plants, with spikes and forks of gold" 419
    "As one who walks and weeps by alien brine"   420
    "Not proud of station, nor in worldly pelf"   420
    "And she—her beauty never made her cold"   421

Contents

"Yet Nature, where the thunder leaves its trace" 421
"All men,—the preacher saith—whate'er or whence" 422
"Perchance his own small field some charge demands" 422
"Yet vain, perhaps, the fruits our care applaud" 423
"Still craves the spirit: never Nature solves" 423
"O Father, God! to whom, in happier days" 424
"The morning comes; not slow, with reddening gold" 424
"Shall I not see her? Yes: for one has seen" 425
"Perhaps a dream; yet surely truth has beamed" 425
"By this low fire I often sit to woo" 426
"For Nature daily through her grand design" 426
"So, to the mind long brooding but on it" 427
"Not the round natural world, not the deep mind" 427

EMILY DICKINSON

"This is my letter to the world" 428
"I'm nobody! Who are you?" 428
"The soul selects her own society" 428
"Some keep the Sabbath going to church" 429
"The heart asks pleasure first" 429
"I taste a liquor never brewed" 430
Success 430
"Some things that fly there be" 431
"Much madness is divinest sense" 431
"The brain within its groove" 432
"I asked no other thing" 432
"Is Heaven a physician" 432
"To fight aloud is very brave" 433
"I took my power in my hand" 433
"For each ecstatic instant" 434

"Pain has an element of blank"   434
"Remorse is memory awake"   434
"I had no time to hate"   435
"He ate and drank the precious words"   435
"He preached upon 'breadth' "   435
Belshazzar   436
"Surgeons must be very careful"   436
"Faith is a fine invention"   436
"Prayer is the little implement"   436
"A shady friend for torrid days"   437
"Just lost when I was saved"   437
"I never lost as much but twice"   438
"I held a jewel in my fingers"   438
"There came a day at summer's full"   439
"Of all the souls that stand create"   440
"If you were coming in the fall"   440
"Going to him! Happy letter!"   441
"Wild nights! Wild nights!"   442
"I like a look of agony"   442
"If I should die, and you should live"   443
"I dreaded that first robin so"   443
"A bird came down the walk"   444
The Hummingbird   445
"The grass so little has to do"   445
"The mushroom is the elf of plants"   446
The Snake   447
"I think the hemlock likes to stand"   448
"I started early, took my dog"   449
The Locomotive   450
"How happy is the little stone"   450
"It sounded as if the streets were running"   451
"The leaves, like women, interchange"   451
The Crickets   451

Contents

"These are the days when birds come back" 452
"The sky is low, the clouds are mean" 453
"The gentian weaves her fringes" 453
"There's a certain slant of light" 454
"I never saw a moor" 454
"Safe in their alabaster chambers" 455
"The bustle in a house" 455
"Because I could not stop for Death" 456
"If I shouldn't be alive" 456
"I died for beauty" 457
"One need not be a chamber to be haunted" 457
"After a hundred years" 458

Poetry

OF THE NEW ENGLAND
RENAISSANCE

1790–1890

Joel Barlow

1754–1812

THE HASTY PUDDING *

CANTO I

Ye Alps audacious, through the heavens that rise,
To cramp the day and hide me from the skies;
Ye Gallic flags, that o'er their heights unfurled,
Bear death to kings and freedom to the world,
I sing not you. A softer theme I choose,
A virgin theme, unconscious of the muse,
But fruitful, rich, well suited to inspire
The purest frenzy of poetic fire.

Despise it not, ye bards to terror steeled,
Who hurl your thunders round the epic field;
Nor ye who strain your midnight throats to sing
Joys that the vineyard and the stillhouse bring;
Or on some distant fair your notes employ,
And speak of raptures that you ne'er enjoy.
I sing the sweets I know, the charms I feel,
My morning incense, and my evening meal,—
The sweets of Hasty Pudding. Come, dear bowl,
Glide o'er my palate, and inspire my soul.
The milk beside thee, smoking from the kine,
Its substance mingled, married in with thine,
Shall cool and temper thy superior heat,
And save the pains of blowing while I eat.

Oh! could the smooth, the emblematic song
Flow like the genial juices o'er my tongue,
Could those mild morsels in my numbers chime,
And, as they roll in substance, roll in rime,

* Written while the author was living in Savoy.

1

No more thy awkward, unpoetic name
Should shun the muse or prejudice thy fame;
But, rising grateful to the accustomed ear,
All bards should catch it, and all realms revere!
　Assist me first with pious toil to trace
Through wrecks of time, thy lineage and thy race;
Declare what lovely squaw, in days of yore,
(Ere great Columbus sought thy native shore)
First gave thee to the world; her works of fame
Have lived indeed, but lived without a name.
Some tawny Ceres, goddess of her days,
First learned with stones to crack the well-dried maize,
Through the rough sieve to shake the golden shower,
In boiling water stir the yellow flour:
The yellow flour, bestrewed and stirred with haste,
Swells in the flood and thickens to a paste,
Then puffs and wallops, rises to the brim,
Drinks the dry knobs that on the surface swim;
The knobs at last the busy ladle breaks,
And the whole mass its true consistence takes.
　Could but her sacred name, unknown so long,
Rise, like her labors, to the son of song,
To her, to them I'd consecrate my lays,
And blow her pudding with the breath of praise.
If 'twas Oella whom I sang before,
I'd here ascribe her one great virtue more.
Nor through the rich Peruvian realms alone
The fame of Sol's sweet daughter should be known,
But o'er the world's wide climes should live secure,
Far as his rays extend, as long as they endure.
　Dear Hasty Pudding, what unpromised joy
Expands my heart, to meet thee in Savoy!
Doomed o'er the world through devious paths to roam,
Each clime my country, and each house my home,
My soul is soothed, my cares have found an end;

I greet my long-lost, unforgotten friend.
For thee through Paris, that corrupted town,
How long in vain I wandered up and down,
Where shameless Bacchus, with his drenching hoard
Cold from his cave, usurps the morning board.
London is lost in smoke and steeped in tea;
No Yankee there can lisp the name of thee;
The uncouth word, a libel on the town,
Would call a proclamation from the crown.
For climes oblique, that fear the sun's full rays,
Chilled in their fogs, exclude the generous maize;
A grain whose rich, luxuriant growth requires
Short, gentle showers, and bright, ethereal fires.
But here, though distant from our native shore,
With mutual glee, we meet and laugh once more.
The same! I know thee by that yellow face,
That strong complexion of true Indian race,
Which time can never change, nor soil impair,
Nor Alpine snows, nor Turkey's morbid air;
For endless years, through every mild domain,
Where grows the maize, there thou art sure to reign.
But man, more fickle, the bold licence claims,
In different realms to give thee different names.
Thee the soft nations round the warm Levant
Polanta call; the French, of course, *Polante*.
E'en in thy native regions, how I blush
To hear the Pennsylvanians call thee *Mush!*
On Hudson's banks, while men of Belgic spawn
Insult and eat thee by the name *Suppawn*.
All spurious appellations, void of truth;
I've better known thee from my earliest youth:
Thy name is *Hasty Pudding!* thus my sire
Was wont to greet thee fuming from his fire;
And while he argued in thy just defense
With logic clear he thus explained the sense:

"In haste the boiling caldron, o'er the blaze,
Receives and cooks the ready powdered maize;
In haste 'tis served, and then in equal haste,
With cooling milk, we make the sweet repast.
No carving to be done, no knife to grate
The tender ear and wound the stony plate;
But the smooth spoon, just fitted to the lip,
And taught with art the yielding mass to dip,
By frequent journeys to the bowl well stored,
Performs the hasty honors of the board."
Such is thy name, significant and clear,
A name, a sound to every Yankee dear,
But most to me, whose heart and palate chaste
Preserve my pure, hereditary taste.

There are who strive to stamp with disrepute
The luscious food, because it feeds the brute;
In tropes of high-strained wit, while gaudy prigs
Compare thy nursling, man, to pampered pigs;
With sovereign scorn I treat the vulgar jest,
Nor fear to share thy bounties with the beast.
What though the generous cow gives me to quaff
The milk nutritious: am I then a calf?
Or can the genius of the noisy swine,
Though nursed on pudding, claim a kin to mine?
Sure the sweet song I fashion to thy praise,
Runs more melodious than the notes they raise.

My song, resounding in its grateful glee,
No merit claims: I praise myself in thee.
My father loved thee through his length of days!
For thee his fields were shaded o'er with maize;
From thee what health, what vigor he possessed,
Ten sturdy freemen from his loins attest;
Thy constellation ruled my natal morn,
And all my bones were made of Indian corn.
Delicious grain, whatever form it take,

To roast or boil, to smother or to bake,
In every dish 'tis welcome still to me,
But most, my Hasty Pudding, most in thee.
  Let the green succotash with thee contend;
Let beans and corn their sweetest juices blend;
Let butter drench them in its yellow tide,
And a long slice of bacon grace their side;
Not all the plate, how famed soe'er it be,
Can please my palate like a bowl of thee.
Some talk of hoe-cake, fair Virginia's pride!
Rich johnny-cake this mouth has often tried;
Both please me well, their virtues much the same,
Alike their fabric, as allied their fame,
Except in dear New England, where the last
Receives a dash of pumpkin in the paste,
To give it sweetness and improve the taste.
But place them all before me, smoking hot,
The big, round dumpling, rolling from the pot;
The pudding of the bag, whose quivering breast,
With suet lined, leads on the Yankee feast;
The charlotte brown, within whose crusty sides
A belly soft the pulpy apple hides;
The yellow bread whose face like amber glows,
And all of Indian that the bakepan knows,—
You tempt me not; my favorite greets my eyes,
To that loved bowl my spoon by instinct flies.

CANTO II

  To mix the food by vicious rules of art,
To kill the stomach and to sink the heart,
To make mankind to social virtue sour,
Cram o'er each dish, and be what they devour;
For this the kitchen muse first framed her book,
Commanding sweats to stream from every cook;

Children no more their antic gambols tried,
And friends to physic wondered why they died.

Not so the Yankee: his abundant feast,
With simples furnished and with plainness dressed,
A numerous offspring gathers round the board,
And cheers alike the servant and the lord;
Whose well-bought hunger prompts the joyous taste,
And health attends them from the short repast.

While the full pail rewards the milkmaid's toil,
The mother sees the morning caldron boil;
To stir the pudding next demands her care;
To spread the table and the bowls prepare;
To feed the household as their portions cool
And send them all to labor or to school.

Yet may the simplest dish some rules impart,
For nature scorns not all the aids of art.
E'en Hasty Pudding, purest of all food,
May still be bad, indifferent, or good,
As sage experience the short process guides,
Or want of skill, or want of care presides.
Whoe'er would form it on the surest plan,
To rear the child and long sustain the man;
To shield the morals while it mends the size,
And all the powers of every food supplies,—
Attend the lessons that the muse shall bring,
Suspend your spoons, and listen while I sing.

But since, O man! thy life and health demand
Not food alone, but labor from thy hand,
First, in the field, beneath the sun's strong rays,
Ask of thy mother earth the needful maize;
She loves the race that courts her yielding soil,
And gives her bounties to the sons of toil.

When now the ox, obedient to thy call,
Repays the loan that filled the winter stall,

Pursue his traces o'er the furrowed plain,
And plant in measured hills the golden grain.
But when the tender germ begins to shoot,
And the green spire declares the sprouting root,
Then guard your nursling from each greedy foe,
The insidious worm, the all-devouring crow.
A little ashes sprinkled round the spire,
Soon steeped in rain, will bid the worm retire;
The feathered robber with his hungry maw
Swift flies the field before your man of straw,
A frightful image, such as schoolboys bring
When met to burn the Pope or hang the King.

Thrice in the season, through each verdant row,
Wield the strong plowshare and the faithful hoe;
The faithful hoe, a double task that takes,
To till the summer corn and roast the winter cakes.

Slow springs the blade, while checked by chilling rains,
Ere yet the sun the seat of Cancer gains;
But when his fiercest fires emblaze the land,
Then start the juices, then the roots expand;
Then, like a column of Corinthian mold,
The stalk struts upward and the leaves unfold;
The bushy branches all the ridges fill,
Entwine their arms, and kiss from hill to hill.
Here cease to vex them; all your cares are done:
Leave the last labors to the parent sun;
Beneath his genial smiles, the well-dressed field,
When autumn calls, a plenteous crop shall yield.

Now the strong foliage bears the standards high,
And shoots the tall top-gallants to the sky;
The suckling ears their silky fringes bend,
And pregnant grown, their swelling coats distend;
The loaded stalk, while still the burden grows,
O'erhangs the space that runs between the rows;

High as a hop-field waves the silent grove,
A safe retreat for little thefts of love,
When the fledged roasting-ears invite the maid
To meet her swain beneath the new-formed shade;
His generous hand unloads the cumberous hill,
And the green spoils her ready basket fill;
Small compensation for the twofold bliss,
The promised wedding, and the present kiss.

  Slight depredations these; but now the moon
Calls from his hollow tree the sly raccoon;
And while by night he bears his prize away,
The bolder squirrel labors through the day.
Both thieves alike, but provident of time,
A virtue rare, that almost hides their crime.
Then let them steal the little stores they can,
And fill their granaries from the toils of man;
We've one advantage where they take no part—
With all their wiles, they ne'er have found the art
To boil the Hasty Pudding; here we shine
Superior far to tenants of the pine;
This envied boon to man shall still belong,
Unshared by them in substance or in song.

  At last the closing season browns the plain,
And ripe October gathers in the grain;
Deep-loaded carts the spacious corn-house fill;
The sack distended marches to the mill;
The laboring mill beneath the burden groans,
And showers the future pudding from the stones;
Till the glad housewife greets the powdered gold,
And the new crop exterminates the old.
Ah, who can sing what every wight must feel,
The joy that enters with the bag of meal.
A general jubilee pervades the house,
Wakes every child and gladdens every mouse.

CANTO III

The days grow short; but though the falling sun
To the glad swain proclaims his day's work done,
Night's pleasing shades his various tasks prolong,
And yield new subjects to my various song.
For now, the corn-house filled, the harvest home,
The invited neighbors to the husking come;
A frolic scene, where work, and mirth, and play,
Unite their charms to chase the hours away.

Where the huge heap lies centered in the hall,
The lamp suspended from the cheerful wall,
Brown, corn-fed nymphs, and strong, hard-handed beaux,
Alternate ranged, extend in circling rows,
Assume their seats, the solid mass attack;
The dry husks rustle, and the corncobs crack;
The song, the laugh, alternate notes resound,
And the sweet cider trips in silence round.

The laws of husking every wight can tell;
And sure no laws he ever keeps so well:
For each red ear a general kiss he gains,
With each smut ear she smuts the luckless swains;
But when to some sweet maid a prize is cast,
Red as her lips and taper as her waist,
She walks the round and culls one favored beau,
Who leaps the luscious tribute to bestow.
Various the sport, as are the wits and brains
Of well-pleased lasses and contending swains;
Till the vast mound of corn is swept away,
And he that gets the last ear wins the day.

Meanwhile, the housewife urges all her care,
The well-earned feast to hasten and prepare.
The sifted meal already waits her hand,

The milk is strained, the bowls in order stand,
The fire flames high; and as a pool—that takes
The headlong stream that o'er the milldam breaks—
Foams, roars, and rages with incessant toils,
So the vexed caldron rages, roars, and boils.

First with clean salt she seasons well the food,
Then strews the flour, and thickens all the flood.
Long o'er the simmering fire she lets it stand;
To stir it well demands a stronger hand;
The husband takes his turn: and round and round
The ladle flies; at last the toil is crowned;
When to the board the thronging huskers pour,
And take their seats as at the corn before.

I leave them to their feast. There still belong
More useful matters to my faithful song.
For rules there are, though ne'er unfolded yet,
Nice rules and wise, how pudding should be eat.

Some with molasses line the luscious treat,
And mix, like bards, the useful with the sweet.
A wholesome dish, and well deserving praise,
A great resource in those bleak wintry days,
When the chilled earth lies buried deep in snow,
And raging Boreas dries the shivering cow.

Blest cow! thy praise shall still my notes employ,
Great source of health, the only source of joy;
Mother of Egypt's god,—but sure, for me,
Were I to leave my God, I'd worship thee.
How oft thy teats these pious hands have prest!
How oft thy bounties proved my only feast!
How oft I've fed thee with my favorite grain!
And roared, like thee, to see thy children slain!

Ye swains who know her various worth to prize,
Ah! house her well from winter's angry skies.
Potatoes, pumpkins, should her sadness cheer,
Corn from your crib, and mashes from your beer;

When spring returns, she'll well acquit the loan,
And nurse at once your infants and her own.
Milk then with pudding I should always choose;
To this in future I confine my muse,
Till she in haste some further hints unfold,
Well for the young, nor useless to the old.
First in your bowl the milk abundant take,
Then drop with care along the silver lake
Your flakes of pudding; these at first will hide
Their little bulk beneath the swelling tide;
But when their growing mass no more can sink,
When the soft island looms above the brink,
Then check your hand; you've got the portion due;
So taught my sire, and what he taught is true.

There is a choice in spoons. Though small appear
The nice distinction, yet to me 'tis clear.
The deep-bowled Gallic spoon, contrived to scoop
In ample draughts the thin, diluted soup,
Performs not well in those substantial things,
Whose mass adhesive to the metal clings;
Where the strong labial muscles must embrace
The gentle curve, and sweep the hollow space.
With ease to enter and discharge the freight,
A bowl less concave, but still more dilate,
Becomes the pudding best. The shape, the size,
A secret rests, unknown to vulgar eyes.
Experienced feeders can alone impart
A rule so much above the lore of art.
These tuneful lips that thousand spoons have tried,
With just precision could the point decide,
Though not in song; the muse but poorly shines
In cones, and cubes, and geometric lines;
Yet the true form, as near as she can tell,
Is that small section of a goose-egg shell,
Which in two equal portions shall divide

The distance from the center to the side.
　　Fear not to slaver; 'tis no deadly sin.
Like the fine Frenchman, from your joyous chin
Suspend the ready napkin; or, like me,
Poise with one hand your bowl upon your knee;
Just in the zenith your wise head project,
Your full spoon, rising in a line direct,
Bold as a bucket, heeds no drops that fall;
The wide-mouthed bowl will surely catch them all!

William Cullen Bryant

1794-1878

THANATOPSIS *

To him who in the love of Nature holds
Communion with her visible forms, she speaks
A various language; for his gayer hours
She has a voice of gladness, and a smile
And eloquence of beauty, and she glides
Into his darker musings, with a mild
And healing sympathy, that steals away
Their sharpness, ere he is aware. When thoughts
Of the last bitter hour come like a blight
Over thy spirit, and sad images
Of the stern agony, and shroud, and pall,
And breathless darkness, and the narrow house,
Make thee to shudder, and grow sick at heart;—
Go forth, under the open sky, and list
To Nature's teachings, while from all around—
Earth and her waters, and the depths of air—
Comes a still voice.—

          Yet a few days, and thee
The all-beholding sun shall see no more
In all his course; nor yet in the cold ground,
Where thy pale form was laid, with many tears,
Nor in the embrace of ocean, shall exist
Thy image. Earth, that nourished thee, shall claim
Thy growth, to be resolved to earth again,
And, lost each human trace, surrendering up
Thine individual being, shalt thou go

* The title is coined from two Greek words put together to mean "a view of death."

To mix for ever with the elements,
To be a brother to the insensible rock
And to the sluggish clod, which the rude swain
Turns with his share, and treads upon. The oak
Shall send his roots abroad, and pierce thy mould.

    Yet not to thine eternal resting-place
Shalt thou retire alone, nor couldst thou wish
Couch more magnificent. Thou shalt lie down
With patriarchs of the infant world—with kings,
The powerful of the earth—the wise, the good,
Fair forms, and hoary seers of ages past,
All in one mighty sepulchre. The hills
Rock-ribbed and ancient as the sun,—the vales
Stretching in pensive quietness between;
The venerable woods—rivers that move
In majesty, and the complaining brooks
That make the meadows green; and, poured round all,
Old Ocean's gray and melancholy waste,—
Are but the solemn decorations all
Of the great tomb of man. The golden sun,
The planets, all the infinite host of heaven,
Are shining on the sad abodes of death,
Through the still lapse of ages. All that tread
The globe are but a handful to the tribes
That slumber in its bosom.—Take the wings
Of morning, pierce the Barcan wilderness,
Or lose thyself in the continuous woods
Where rolls the Oregon, and hears no sound,
Save his own dashings—yet the dead are there:
And millions in those solitudes, since first
The flight of years began, have laid them down
In their last sleep—the dead reign there alone.
So shalt thou rest, and what if thou withdraw
In silence from the living, and no friend

Take note of thy departure? All that breathe
Will share thy destiny. The gay will laugh
When thou art gone, the solemn brood of care
Plod on, and each one as before will chase
His favorite phantom; yet all these shall leave
Their mirth and their employments, and shall come
And make their bed with thee. As the long train
Of ages glides away, the sons of men,
The youth in life's green spring, and he who goes
In the full strength of years, matron and maid,
The speechless babe, and the gray-headed man—
Shall one by one be gathered to thy side
By those, who in their turn shall follow them.

So live, that when thy summons comes to join
The innumerable caravan, which moves
To that mysterious realm, where each shall take
His chamber in the silent halls of death,
Thou go not, like the quarry-slave at night,
Scourged to his dungeon, but, sustained and soothed
By an unfaltering trust, approach thy grave,
Like one who wraps the drapery of his couch
About him, and lies down to pleasant dreams.

THE YELLOW VIOLET

When beechen buds begin to swell,
    And woods the blue-bird's warble know,
The yellow violet's modest bell
    Peeps from the last year's leaves below.

Ere russet fields their green resume,
    Sweet flower, I love, in forest bare,

To meet thee, when thy faint perfume
　　Alone is in the virgin air.

Of all her train, the hands of Spring
　　First plant thee in the watery mould,
And I have seen thee blossoming
　　Beside the snow-bank's edges cold.

Thy parent sun, who bade thee view
　　Pale skies, and chilling moisture sip,
Has bathed thee in his own bright hue,
　　And streaked with jet thy glowing lip.

Yet slight thy form, and low thy seat,
　　And earthward bent thy gentle eye,
Unapt the passing view to meet,
　　When loftier flowers are flaunting nigh.

Oft, in the sunless April day,
　　Thy early smile has stayed my walk;
But midst the gorgeous blooms of May,
　　I passed thee on thy humble stalk.

So they, who climb to wealth, forget
　　The friends in darker fortunes tried.
I copied them—but I regret
　　That I should ape the ways of pride.

And when again the genial hour
　　Awakes the painted tribes of light,
I'll not o'erlook the modest flower
　　That made the woods of April bright.

INSCRIPTION FOR THE ENTRANCE TO A WOOD

Stranger, if thou hast learned a truth which needs
No school of long experience, that the world
Is full of guilt and misery, and hast seen
Enough of all its sorrows, crimes, and cares,
To tire thee of it, enter this wild wood
And view the haunts of Nature. The calm shade
Shall bring a kindred calm, and the sweet breeze
That makes the green leaves dance, shall waft a balm
To thy sick heart. Thou wilt find nothing here
Of all that pained thee in the haunts of men,
And made thee loathe thy life. The primal curse
Fell, it is true, upon the unsinning earth,
But not in vengeance. God hath yoked to guilt
Her pale tormentor, misery. Hence, these shades
Are still the abodes of gladness; the thick roof
Of green and stirring branches is alive
And musical with birds, that sing and sport
In wantonness of spirit; while below
The squirrel, with raised paws and form erect,
Chirps merrily. Throngs of insects in the shade
Try their thin wings and dance in the warm beam
That waked them into life. Even the green trees
Partake the deep contentment; as they bend
To the soft winds, the sun from the blue sky
Looks in and sheds a blessing on the scene.
Scarce less the cleft-born wild-flower seems to enjoy
Existence, than the wingèd plunderer
That sucks its sweets. The mossy rocks themselves,
And the old and ponderous trunks of prostrate trees
That lead from knoll to knoll a causey rude
Or bridge the sunken brook, and their dark roots,
With all their earth upon them, twisting high,

Breathe fixed tranquillity. The rivulet
Sends forth glad sounds, and tripping o'er its bed
Of pebbly sands, or leaping down the rocks,
Seems, with continuous laughter, to rejoice
In its own being. Softly tread the marge,
Lest from her midway perch thou scare the wren
That dips her bill in water. The cool wind,
That stirs the stream in play, shall come to thee,
Like one that loves thee nor will let thee pass
Ungreeted, and shall give its light embrace.

TO A WATERFOWL

Whither, midst falling dew,
While glow the heavens with the last steps of day,
Far, through their rosy depths, dost thou pursue
    Thy solitary way?

Vainly the fowler's eye
Might mark thy distant flight to do thee wrong,
As, darkly seen against the crimson sky,
    Thy figure floats along.

Seek'st thou the plashy brink
Of weedy lake, or marge of river wide,
Or where the rocking billows rise and sink
    On the chafed ocean-side?

There is a Power whose care
Teaches thy way along that pathless coast—
The desert and illimitable air—
    Lone wandering, but not lost.

All day thy wings have fanned,
At that far height, the cold, thin atmosphere,
Yet stoop not, weary, to the welcome land,
   Though the dark night is near.

And soon that toil shall end;
Soon shalt thou find a summer home, and rest,
And scream among thy fellows; reeds shall bend,
   Soon, o'er thy sheltered nest.

Thou'rt gone, the abyss of heaven
Hath swallowed up thy form; yet, on my heart
Deeply has sunk the lesson thou hast given,
   And shall not soon depart.

He who, from zone to zone,
Guides through the boundless sky thy certain flight,
In the long way that I must tread alone,
   Will lead my steps aright.

SPAIN

Aye, wear the chain—ye who for once have known
The sweets of freedom—yet could crouch again
In blind and trembling worship of a throne;
Aye wear—for ye are worthy—wear the chain
And bow, till ye are weary, to the yoke
      Your patriot fathers broke.

Degenerate Spaniards! let the priestly band
Possess your realm again; and let them wake
The fires of pious murder in your land,

And drag your best and bravest to the stake,
And tread down truth, and in the dungeon bind
    The dreaded strength of mind.

Give up the promise of bright days that cast
A glory on your nation from afar;
Call back the darkness of the ages past
To quench that holy dawn's new-risen star;
Let only tyrants and their slaves be found
    Alive on Spanish ground.

Yet mark! ye cast the gift of heaven away,
And your best blood for this shall yet be shed;
The fire shall waste your borders, and the way
Be covered with its heaps of festering dead,
And vultures of the cliff on every plain
    Feast high upon the slain.

The spirit that of yore had slept so long,
Then woke, and drove the Moors to Afric's shore,
Lives, and repressed, shall rise one day more
    strong—
Rise and redeem your shackled race once more,
And crush, mid showers of blood and shrieks and
    groans,
    Mitres and stars and thrones.

TO A MOSQUITO

Fair insect! that, with threadlike legs spread out,
    And blood-extracting bill and filmy wing,
Dost murmur, as thou slowly sail'st about,
    In pitiless ears full many a plaintive thing,

And tell how little our large veins would bleed,
Would we but yield them to thy bitter need.

Unwillingly, I own, and, what is worse,
   Full angrily men hearken to thy plaint;
Thou gettest many a brush, and many a curse,
   For saying thou art gaunt, and starved, and faint;
Even the old beggar, while he asks for food,
Would kill thee, hapless stranger, if he could.

I call thee stranger, for the town, I ween,
   Has not the honor of so proud a birth,—
Thou com'st from Jersey meadows, fresh and green,
   The offspring of the gods, though born on earth;
For Titan was thy sire, and fair was she,
The ocean-nymph that nursed thy infancy.

Beneath the rushes was thy cradle swung,
   And when at length thy gauzy wings grew strong,
Abroad to gentle airs their folds were flung,
   Rose in the sky and bore thee soft along;
The south wind breathed to waft thee on the way,
And danced and shone beneath the billowy bay.

Calm rose afar the city spires, and thence
   Came the deep murmur of its throng of men,
And as its grateful odors met thy sense,
   They seemed the perfumes of thy native fen.
Fair lay its crowded streets, and at the sight
Thy tiny song grew shriller with delight.

At length thy pinions fluttered in Broadway—
   Ah! there were fairy steps, and white necks kissed
By wanton airs, and eyes whose killing ray
   Shone through the snowy veils like stars through mist;

And fresh as morn, on many a cheek and chin,
Bloomed the bright blood through the transparent skin.

Sure these were sights to touch an anchorite!
    What! do I hear thy slender voice complain?
Thou wailest when I talk of beauty's light,
    As if it brought the memory of pain;
Thou art a wayward being—well—come near,
And pour thy tale of sorrow in my ear.

What sayst thou—slanderer!—rouge makes thee sick?
    And China bloom at best is sorry food?
And Rowland's Kalydor, if laid on thick,
    Poisons the thirsty wretch that bores for blood?
Go! 'twas a just reward that met thy crime—
But shun the sacrilege another time.

That bloom was made to look at, not to touch;
    To worship, not approach, that radiant white;
And well might sudden vengeance light on such
    As dared, like thee, most impiously to bite.
Thou shouldst have gazed at distance and admired,
Murmured thy adoration, and retired.

Thou'rt welcome to the town; but why come here
    To bleed a brother poet, gaunt like thee?
Alas! the little blood I have is dear,
    And thin will be the banquet drawn from me.
Look round—the pale-eyed sisters in my cell,
Thy old acquaintance, Song and Famine, dwell.

Try some plump alderman, and suck the blood
    Enriched by generous wine and costly meat;
On well-filled skins, sleek as thy native mud,
    Fix thy light pump and press thy freckled feet.

Go to the men for whom, in ocean's halls,
The oyster breeds, and the green turtle sprawls.

There corks are drawn, and the red vintage flows
    To fill the swelling veins for thee, and now
The ruddy cheek and now the ruddier nose
    Shall tempt thee, as thou flittest round the brow.
And when the hour of sleep its quiet brings,
No angry hand shall rise to brush thy wings.

THE DEATH OF THE FLOWERS

The melancholy days are come, the saddest of the year,
Of wailing winds, and naked woods, and meadows brown and
        sere;
Heaped in the hollows of the grove, the autumn leaves lie dead;
They rustle to the eddying gust, and to the rabbit's tread;
The robin and the wren are flown, and from the shrubs the jay,
And from the wood-top calls the crow through all the gloomy
        day.

Where are the flowers, the fair young flowers, that lately sprang
        and stood
In brighter light and softer airs, a beauteous sisterhood?
Alas! they all are in their graves, the gentle race of flowers
Are lying in their lowly beds, with the fair and good of ours.
The rain is falling where they lie, but the cold November rain
Calls not from out the gloomy earth the lovely ones again.

The wind-flower and the violet, they perished long ago,
And the brier-rose and the orchis died amid the summer glow;
But on the hills the golden-rod, and the aster in the wood,
And the yellow sunflower by the brook in autumn beauty stood,

Till fell the frost from the clear cold heaven, as falls the plague
    on men,
And the brightness of their smile was gone, from upland, glade,
    and glen.

And now, when comes the calm mild day, as still such days will
    come,
To call the squirrel and the bee from out their winter home;
When the sound of dropping nuts is heard, though all the trees
    are still,
And twinkle in the smoky light the waters of the rill,
The south wind searches for the flowers whose fragrance late
    he bore,
And sighs to find them in the wood and by the stream no more.

And then I think of one* who in her youthful beauty died,
The fair meek blossom that grew up and faded by my side.
In the cold moist earth we laid her, when the forests cast the
    leaf,
And we wept that one so lovely should have a life so brief:
Yet not unmeet it was that one, like that young friend of ours,
So gentle and so beautiful, should perish with the flowers.

THE PAST

Thou unrelenting Past!
Strong are the barriers round thy dark domain,
    And fetters, sure and fast,
Hold all that enter thy unbreathing reign.

    Far in thy realm withdrawn,
Old empires sit in sullenness and gloom,

* The author's sister.

And glorious ages gone
Lie deep within the shadow of thy womb.

Childhood, with all its mirth,
Youth, Manhood, Age that draws us to the ground,
And last, Man's Life on earth,
Glide to thy dim dominions, and are bound.

Thou hast my better years;
Thou hast my earlier friends, the good, the kind,
Yielded to thee with tears—
The venerable form, the exalted mind.

My spirit yearns to bring
The lost ones back—yearns with desire intense,
And struggles hard to wring
Thy bolts apart, and pluck thy captives thence.

In vain; thy gates deny
All passage save to those who hence depart;
Nor to the streaming eye
Thou giv'st them back—nor to the broken heart.

In thy abysses hide
Beauty and excellence unknown; to thee
Earth's wonder and her pride
Are gathered, as the waters to the sea;

Labors of good to man,
Unpublished charity, unbroken faith,
Love, that midst grief began,
And grew with years, and faltered not in death.

Full many a mighty name
Lurks in thy depths, unuttered, unrevered;

With thee are silent fame,
Forgotten arts, and wisdom disappeared.

Thine for a space are they—
Yet shalt thou yield thy treasures up at last:
    Thy gates shall yet give way,
Thy bolts shall fall, inexorable Past!

All that of good and fair
Has gone into thy womb from earliest time,
    Shall then come forth to wear
The glory and the beauty of its prime.

They have not perished—no!
Kind words, remembered voices once so sweet,
    Smiles, radiant long ago,
And features, the great soul's apparent seat.

All shall come back; each tie
Of pure affection shall be knit again;
    Alone shall Evil die,
And Sorrow dwell a prisoner in thy reign.

And then shall I behold
Him, by whose kind paternal side I sprung,
    And her, who, still and cold,
Fills the next grave—the beautiful and young.

THE PRAIRIES

These are the gardens of the Desert, these
The unshorn fields, boundless and beautiful,
For which the speech of England has no name—

The Prairies. I behold them for the first,
And my heart swells, while the dilated sight
Takes in the encircling vastness. Lo! they stretch
In airy undulations, far away,
As if the Ocean, in his gentlest swell,
Stood still, with all his rounded billows fixed
And motionless forever.—Motionless?—
No—they are all unchained again. The clouds
Sweep over with their shadows, and, beneath,
The surface rolls and fluctuates to the eye;
Dark hollows seem to glide along and chase
The sunny ridges. Breezes of the South!
Who toss the golden and the flame-like flowers,
And pass the prairie-hawk that, poised on high,
Flaps his broad wings, yet moves not—ye have played
Among the palms of Mexico and vines
Of Texas, and have crisped the limpid brooks
That from the fountains of Sonora glide
Into the calm Pacific—have ye fanned
A nobler or a lovelier scene than this?
Man hath no part in all this glorious work:
The hand that built the firmament hath heaved
And smoothed these verdant swells, and sown their slopes
With herbage, planted them with island-groves,
And hedged them round with forests. Fitting floor
For this magnificent temple of the sky—
With flowers whose glory and whose multitude
Rival the constellations! The great heavens
Seem to stoop down upon the scene in love,—
A nearer vault, and of a tenderer blue,
Than that which bends above our eastern hills.

As o'er the verdant waste I guide my steed,
Among the high rank grass that sweeps his sides,
The hollow beating of his footstep seems

A sacrilegious sound. I think of those
Upon whose rest he tramples. Are they here—
The dead of other days?—and did the dust
Of these fair solitudes once stir with life
And burn with passion? Let the mighty mounds
That overlook the rivers, or that rise
In the dim forest crowded with old oaks,
Answer. A race, that long has passed away,
Built them; a disciplined and populous race
Heaped, with long toil, the earth, while yet the Greek
Was hewing the Pentelicus to forms
Of symmetry, and rearing on its rock
The glittering Parthenon. These ample fields
Nourished their harvests, here their herds were fed,
When haply by their stalls the bison lowed,
And bowed his manèd shoulder to the yoke.
All day this desert murmured with their toils,
Till twilight blushed, and lovers walked, and wooed
In a forgotten language, and old tunes,
From instruments of unremembered form,
Gave the soft winds a voice. The red-man came—
The roaming hunter-tribes, warlike and fierce,
And the mound-builders vanished from the earth.
The solitude of centuries untold
Has settled where they dwelt. The prairie-wolf
Hunts in their meadows, and his fresh-dug den
Yawns by my path. The gopher mines the ground
Where stood their swarming cities. All is gone;
All—save the piles of earth that hold their bones,
The platforms where they worshipped unknown gods,
The barriers which they builded from the soil
To keep the foe at bay—till o'er the walls
The wild beleaguerers broke, and, one by one,
The strongholds of the plain were forced, and heaped
With corpses. The brown vultures of the wood

Flocked to those vast uncovered sepulchres,
And sat, unscared and silent, at their feast.
Haply some solitary fugitive,
Lurking in marsh and forest, till the sense
Of desolation and of fear became
Bitterer than death, yielded himself to die.
Man's better nature triumphed then. Kind words
Welcomed and soothed him; the rude conquerors
Seated the captive with their chiefs; he chose
A bride among their maidens, and at length
Seemed to forget—yet ne'er forgot—the wife
Of his first love, and her sweet little ones
Butchered, amid their shrieks, with all his race.

Thus change the forms of being. Thus arise
Races of living things, glorious in strength,
And perish, as the quickening breath of God
Fills them, or is withdrawn. The red-man, too,
Has left the blooming wilds he ranged so long,
And, nearer to the Rocky Mountains, sought
A wilder hunting-ground. The beaver builds
No longer by these streams, but far away,
On waters whose blue surface ne'er gave back
The white man's face—among Missouri's springs,
And pools whose issues swell the Oregon—
He rears his little Venice. In these plains
The bison feeds no more. Twice twenty leagues
Beyond remotest smoke of hunter's camp,
Roams the majestic brute, in herds that shake
The earth with thundering steps—yet here I meet
His ancient footprints stamped beside the pool.

Still this great solitude is quick with life.
Myriads of insects, gaudy as the flowers
They flutter over, gentle quadrupeds,

And birds, that scarce have learned the fear of man,
Are here, and sliding reptiles of the ground,
Startlingly beautiful. The graceful deer
Bounds to the wood at my approach. The bee,
A more adventurous colonist than man,
With whom he came across the eastern deep,
Fills the savannas with his murmurings,
And hides his sweets, as in the golden age,
Within the hollow oak. I listen long
To his domestic hum, and think I hear
The sound of that advancing multitude
Which soon shall fill these deserts. From the ground
Comes up the laugh of children, the soft voice
Of maidens, and the sweet and solemn hymn
Of Sabbath worshippers. The low of herds
Blends with the rustling of the heavy grain
Over the dark brown furrows. All at once
A fresher wind sweeps by, and breaks my dream,
And I am in the wilderness alone.

THE PLANTING OF THE APPLE–TREE

Come, let us plant the apple-tree.
Cleave the tough greensward with the spade;
Wide let its hollow bed be made;
There gently lay the roots, and there
Sift the dark mould with kindly care,
    And press it o'er them tenderly,
As, round the sleeping infant's feet,
We softly fold the cradle-sheet;
    So plant we the apple-tree.

What plant we in this apple-tree?
Buds, which the breath of summer days
Shall lengthen into leafy sprays;
Boughs where the thrush, with crimson breast,
Shall haunt and sing and hide her nest;
   We plant, upon the sunny lea,
A shadow for the noontide hour,
A shelter from the summer shower,
   When we plant the apple-tree.

What plant we in this apple-tree?
Sweets for a hundred flowery springs
To load the May-wind's restless wings,
When, from the orchard-row, he pours
Its fragrance through our open doors;
   A world of blossoms for the bee,
Flowers for the sick girl's silent room,
For the glad infant sprigs of bloom,
   We plant with the apple-tree.

What plant we in this apple-tree?
Fruits that shall swell in sunny June,
And redden in the August noon,
And drop, when gentle airs come by,
That fan the blue September sky,
   While children come, with cries of glee,
And seek them where the fragrant grass
Betrays their bed to those who pass,
   At the foot of the apple-tree.

And when, above this apple-tree,
The winter stars are quivering bright,
And winds go howling through the night,
Girls, whose young eyes o'erflow with mirth,

Shall peel its fruit by cottage-hearth,
   And guests in prouder homes shall see,
Heaped with the grape of Cintra's vine
And golden orange of the line,
   The fruit of the apple-tree.

The fruitage of this apple-tree
Winds and our flag of stripe and star
Shall bear to coasts that lie afar,
Where men shall wonder at the view,
And ask in what fair groves they grew;
   And sojourners beyond the sea
Shall think of childhood's careless day,
And long, long hours of summer play,
   In the shade of the apple-tree.

Each year shall give this apple-tree
A broader flush of roseate bloom,
A deeper maze of verdurous gloom,
And loosen, when the frost-clouds lower,
The crisp brown leaves in thicker shower.
   The years shall come and pass, but we
Shall hear no longer, where we lie,
The summer's songs, the autumn's sigh,
   In the boughs of the apple-tree.

And time shall waste this apple-tree.
Oh, when its aged branches throw
Thin shadows on the ground below,
Shall fraud and force and iron will
Oppress the weak and helpless still?
   What shall the tasks of mercy be,
Amid the toils, the strifes, the tears
Of those who live when length of years
   Is wasting this little apple-tree?

"Who planted this old apple-tree?"
The children of that distant day
Thus to some aged man shall say;
And, gazing on its mossy stem,
The gray-haired man shall answer them:
    "A poet of the land was he,
Born in the rude but good old times;
'Tis said he made some quaint old rhymes,
    On planting the apple-tree."

ROBERT OF LINCOLN

Merrily swinging on brier and weed,
    Near to the nest of his little dame,
Over the mountain-side or mead,
    Robert of Lincoln is telling his name:
            Bob-o'-link, bob-o'-link,
            Spink, spank, spink;
Snug and safe is that nest of ours,
Hidden among the summer flowers.
                    Chee, chee, chee.

Robert of Lincoln is gayly drest,
    Wearing a bright black wedding-coat;
White are his shoulders and white his crest,
    Hear him call in his merry note:
            Bob-o'-link, bob-o'-link,
            Spink, spank, spink;
Look, what a nice new coat is mine,
Sure there was never a bird so fine.
                    Chee, chee, chee.

Robert of Lincoln's Quaker wife,
   Pretty and quiet, with plain brown wings,
Passing at home a patient life,
   Broods in the grass while her husband sings:
      Bob-o'-link, bob-o'-link,
      Spink, spank, spink.
Brood, kind creature; you need not fear
Thieves and robbers while I am here.
         Chee, chee, chee.

Modest and shy as a nun is she;
   One weak chirp is her only note.
Braggart and prince of braggarts is he,
   Pouring boasts from his little throat:
      Bob-o'-link, bob-o'-link,
      Spink, spank, spink;
Never was I afraid of man;
Catch me, cowardly knaves, if you can!
         Chee, chee, chee.

Six white eggs on a bed of hay,
   Flecked with purple, a pretty sight!
There as the mother sits all day,
   Robert is singing with all his might:
      Bob-o'-link, bob-o'-link,
      Spink, spank, spink;
Nice good wife, that never goes out,
Keeping house while I frolic about.
         Chee, chee, chee.

Soon as the little ones chip the shell,
   Six wide mouths are open for food;
Robert of Lincoln bestirs him well,
   Gathering seeds for the hungry brood.
      Bob-o'-link, bob-o'-link,

Spink, spank, spink;
This new life is likely to be
Hard for a gay young fellow like me.
                    Chee, chee, chee.

Robert of Lincoln at length is made
    Sober with work, and silent with care;
Off is his holiday garment laid,
    Half forgotten that merry air:
            Bob-o'-link, bob-o'-link,
                Spink, spank, spink;
Nobody knows but my mate and I
Where our nest and our nestlings lie.
                    Chee, chee, chee.

Summer wanes; the children are grown;
    Fun and frolic no more he knows;
Robert of Lincoln's a humdrum crone;
    Off he flies, and we sing as he goes:
            Bob-o'-link, bob-o'-link,
                Spink, spank, spink;
When you can pipe that merry old strain,
Robert of Lincoln, come back again.
                    Chee, chee, chee.

THE POET

Thou, who wouldst wear the name
    Of poet mid thy brethren of mankind,
And clothe in words of flame
    Thoughts that shall live within the general mind!
Deem not the framing of a deathless lay
The pastime of a drowsy summer day.

But gather all thy powers,
    And wreak them on the verse that thou dost weave.
And in thy lonely hours,
    At silent morning or at wakeful eve,
While the warm current tingles through thy veins,
Set forth the burning words in fluent strains.

No smooth array of phrase,
    Artfully sought and ordered though it be,
Which the cold rhymer lays
    Upon his page with languid industry,
Can wake the listless pulse to livelier speed,
Or fill with sudden tears the eyes that read.

The secret wouldst thou know
    To touch the heart or fire the blood at will?
Let thine own eyes o'erflow;
    Let thy lips quiver with the passionate thrill;
Seize the great thought, ere yet its power be past,
And bind, in words, the fleet emotion fast.

Then, should thy verse appear
    Halting and harsh, and all unaptly wrought,
Touch the crude line with fear,
    Save in the moment of impassioned thought;
Then summon back the original glow, and mend
The strain with rapture that with fire was penned.

Yet let no empty gust
    Of passion find an utterance in thy lay,
A blast that whirls the dust
    Along the howling street and dies away;
But feelings of calm power and mighty sweep,
Like currents journeying through the windless deep.

Seek'st thou, in living lays,
  To limn the beauty of the earth and sky?
Before thine inner gaze
  Let all that beauty in clear vision lie;
Look on it with exceeding love, and write
The words inspired by wonder and delight.

Of tempests wouldst thou sing,
  Or tell of battles—make thyself a part
Of the great tumult; cling
  To the tossed wreck with terror in thy heart;
Scale, with the assaulting host, the rampart's height,
And strike and struggle in the thickest fight.

So shalt thou frame a lay
  That haply may endure from age to age,
And they who read shall say:
  "What witchery hangs upon this poet's page!
What art is his the written spells to find
That sway from mood to mood the willing mind!"

Ralph Waldo Emerson

1 8 0 3 – 1 8 8 2

TWO EARLY POEMS

THOUGHT

I am not poor, but I am proud,
  Of one inalienable right,
Above the envy of the crowd,—
  Thought's holy light.

Better it is than gems or gold,
  And oh! it cannot die,
But thought will glow when the sun grows cold,
  And mix with Deity.

TO–DAY

I rake no coffined clay, nor publish wide
The resurrection of departed pride.
Safe in their ancient crannies, dark and deep,
Let kings and conquerors, saints and sinners sleep—
Late in the world,—too late perchance for fame,
Just late enough to reap abundant blame,—
I choose a novel theme, a bold abuse
Of critic charters, an unlaurelled Muse.

Old mouldy men and books and names and lands
Disgust my reason and defile my hands.
I had as lief respect an ancient shoe,
As love old things *for age*, and hate the new.

I spurn the Past, my mind disdains its nod,
Nor kneels in homage to so mean a God.
I laugh at those who, while they gape and gaze,
The bald antiquity of China praise.
Youth is (whatever cynic tubs pretend)
The fault that boys and nations soonest mend.

THE APOLOGY

Think me not unkind and rude
  That I walk alone in grove and glen;
I go to the god of the wood
  To fetch his word to men.

Tax not my sloth that I
  Fold my arms beside the brook;
Each cloud that floated in the sky
  Writes a letter in my book.

Chide me not, laborious band,
  For the idle flowers I brought;
Every aster in my hand
  Goes home loaded with a thought.

There was never mystery
  But 'tis figured in the flowers;
Was never secret history
  But birds tell it in the bowers.

One harvest from thy field
  Homeward brought the oxen strong;
A second crop thine acres yield
  Which I gather in a song.

THE RHODORA

On Being Asked, Whence Is the Flower?

In May, when sea-winds pierced our solitudes,
I found the fresh Rhodora in the woods,
Spreading its leafless blooms in a damp nook,
To please the desert and the sluggish brook.
The purple petals, fallen in the pool,
Made the black water with their beauty gay;
Here might the red-bird come his plumes to cool,
And court the flower that cheapens his array.
Rhodora! if the sages ask thee why
This charm is wasted on the earth and sky,
Tell them, dear, that if eyes were made for seeing,
Then Beauty is its own excuse for being:
Why thou wert there, O rival of the rose!
I never thought to ask, I never knew:
But, in my simple ignorance, suppose
The self-same Power that brought me there brought
    you.

EACH AND ALL

Little thinks, in the field, yon red-cloaked clown
Of thee from the hill-top looking down;
The heifer that lows in the upland farm,
Far-heard, lows not thine ear to charm;
The sexton, tolling his bell at noon,
Deems not that great Napoleon
Stops his horse, and lists with delight,
Whilst his files sweep round yon Alpine height;
Nor knowest thou what argument

Thy life to thy neighbor's creed has lent.
All are needed by each one;
Nothing is fair or good alone.
I thought the sparrow's note from heaven,
Singing at dawn on the alder bough;
I brought him home, in his nest, at even;
He sings the song, but it pleases not now,
For I did not bring home the river and sky;—
He sang to my ear,—they sang to my eye.
The delicate shells lay on the shore;
The bubbles of the latest wave
Fresh pearls to their enamel gave;
And the bellowing of the savage sea
Greeted their safe escape to me.
I wiped away the weeds and foam,
I fetch my sea-born treasures home;
But the poor, unsightly, noisome things
Had left their beauty on the shore
With the sun and the sand and the wild uproar.
The lover watched his graceful maid,
As 'mid the virgin train she strayed,
Nor knew her beauty's best attire
Was woven by the snow-white choir.
At last she came to his hermitage,
Like the bird from the woodlands to the cage;—
The gay enchantment was undone,
A gentle wife, but fairy none.
Then I said, "I covet truth;
Beauty is unripe childhood's cheat;
I leave it behind with the games of youth:"—
As I spoke, beneath my feet
The ground-pine curled its pretty wreath,
Running over the club-moss burrs;
I inhaled the violet's breath;
Around me stood the oaks and firs;

Pine-cones and acorns lay on the ground;
Over me soared the eternal sky,
Full of light and of deity;
Again I saw, again I heard,
The rolling river, the morning bird;—
Beauty through my senses stole;
I yielded myself to the perfect whole.

CONCORD HYMN

Sung at the Completion of the Battle Monument, July 4, 1837

By the rude bridge that arched the flood,
　　Their flag to April's breeze unfurled,
Here once the embattled farmers stood
　　And fired the shot heard round the world.

The foe long since in silence slept;
　　Alike the conqueror silent sleeps;
And Time the ruined bridge has swept
　　Down the dark stream which seaward creeps.

On this green bank, by this soft stream,
　　We set to-day a votive stone;
That memory may their deed redeem,
　　When, like our sires, our sons are gone.

Spirit, that made those heroes dare
　　To die, and leave their children free,
Bid Time and Nature gently spare
　　The shaft we raise to them and thee.

THE PROBLEM

I like a church; I like a cowl;
I love a prophet of the soul;
And on my heart monastic aisles
Fall like sweet strains, or pensive smiles;
Yet not for all his faith can see
Would I that cowlèd churchman be.

Why should the vest on him allure,
Which I could not on me endure?

Not from a vain or shallow thought
His awful Jove young Phidias brought;
Never from lips of cunning fell
The thrilling Delphic oracle;
Out from the heart of nature rolled
The burdens of the Bible old;
The litanies of nations came,
Like the volcano's tongue of flame,
Up from the burning core below,—
The canticles of love and woe:
The hand that rounded Peter's dome
And groined the aisles of Christian Rome
Wrought in a sad sincerity:
Himself from God he could not free;
He builded better than he knew;—
The conscious stone to beauty grew.

Know'st thou what wove yon woodbird's nest
Of leaves, and feathers from her breast?
Or how the fish outbuilt her shell,
Painting with morn her annual cell?
Or how the sacred pine-tree adds

To her old leaves new myriads?
Such and so grew these holy piles,
Whilst love and terror laid the tiles.
Earth proudly wears the Parthenon,
As the best gem upon her zone,
And Morning opes with haste her lids
To gaze upon the Pyramids;
O'er England's abbeys bends the sky,
As on its friends, with kindred eye;
For out of Thought's interior sphere
These wonders rose to upper air;
And Nature gladly gave them place,
Adopted them into her race,
And granted them an equal date
With Andes and with Ararat.

These temples grew as grows the grass;
Art might obey, but not surpass.
The passive Master lent his hand
To the vast soul that o'er him planned;
And the same power that reared the shrine
Bestrode the tribes that knelt within.
Ever the fiery Pentecost
Girds with one flame the countless host,
Trances the heart through chanting choirs,
And through the priest the mind inspires.
The word unto the prophet spoken
Was writ on tables yet unbroken;
The word by seers or sibyls told,
In groves of oak, or fanes of gold,
Still floats upon the morning wind,
Still whispers to the willing mind.
One accent of the Holy Ghost
The heedless world hath never lost.
I know what say the fathers wise,—

The Book itself before me lies,
Old *Chrysostom*, best Augustine,
And he who blent both in his line,
The younger *Golden Lips* or mines,
Taylor, the Shakespeare of divines.
His words are music in my ear,
I see his cowlèd portrait dear;
And yet, for all his faith could see,
I would not the good bishop be.

From WOODNOTES, I

[A FOREST SEER]

And such I knew, a forest seer,
A minstrel of the natural year,
Foreteller of the vernal ides,
Wise harbinger of spheres and tides,
A lover true, who knew by heart
Each joy the mountain dales impart;
It seemed that Nature could not raise
A plant in any secret place,
In quaking bog, on snowy hill,
Beneath the grass that shades the rill,
Under the snow, between the rocks,
In damp fields known to bird and fox,
But he would come in the very hour
It opened in its virgin bower,
As if a sunbeam showed the place,
And tell its long-descended race.
It seemed as if the breezes brought him;
It seemed as if the sparrows taught him;
As if by secret sight he knew

Where, in far fields, the orchis grew.
Many haps fall in the field
Seldom seen by wishful eyes;
But all her shows did Nature yield,
To please and win this pilgrim wise.
He saw the partridge drum in the woods;
He heard the woodcock's evening hymn;
He found the tawny thrushes' broods;
And the shy hawk did wait for him;
What others did at distance hear,
And guessed within the thicket's gloom,
Was shown to this philosopher,
And at his bidding seemed to come.

[A CHARMÉD DAY]

'Twas one of the charméd days
When the genius of God doth flow,
The wind may alter twenty ways,
A tempest cannot blow;
It may blow north, it still is warm;
Or south, it still is clear;
Or east, it smells like a clover-farm;
Or west, no thunder fear.
The musing peasant lowly great
Beside the forest water sate;
The rope-like pine roots crosswise grown
Composed the network of his throne;
The wide lake, edged with sand and grass,
Was burnished to a floor of glass,
Painted with shadows green and proud
Of the tree and of the cloud.
He was the heart of all the scene;
On him the sun looked more serene;

To hill and cloud his face was known,—
It seemed the likeness of their own;
They knew by secret sympathy
The public child of earth and sky.
"You ask," he said, "what guide
Me through trackless thickets led,
Through thick-stemmed woodlands rough and
      wide.
I found the water's bed.
The watercourses were my guide;
I travelled grateful by their side,
Or through their channel dry;
They led me through the thicket damp,
Through brake and fern, the beavers' camp,
Through beds of granite cut my road,
And their resistless friendship showed:
The falling waters led me,
The foodful waters fed me,
And brought me to the lowest land,
Unerring to the ocean sand.
The moss upon the forest bark
Was pole-star when the night was dark;
The purple berries in the wood
Supplied me necessary food;
For Nature ever faithful is
To such as trust her faithfulness.
When the forest shall mislead me,
When the night and morning lie,
When sea and land refuse to feed me,
'Twill be time enough to die;
Then will yet my mother yield
A pillow in her greenest field,
Nor the June flowers scorn to cover
The clay of their departed lover."

THE HUMBLE–BEE

Burly, dozing humble-bee,
Where thou art is clime for me.
Let them sail for Porto Rique,
Far-off heats through seas to seek;
I will follow thee alone,
Thou animated torrid-zone!
Zigzag steerer, desert cheerer,
Let me chase thy waving lines;
Keep me nearer, me thy hearer,
Singing over shrubs and vines.

Insect lover of the sun,
Joy of thy dominion!
Sailor of the atmosphere;
Swimmer through the waves of air;
Voyager of light and noon;
Epicurean of June;
Wait, I prithee, till I come
Within earshot of thy hum,—
All without is martyrdom.

When the south wind, in May days,
With a net of shining haze
Silvers the horizon wall,
And with softness touching all,
Tints the human countenance
With a color of romance,
And infusing subtle heats,
Turns the sod to violets,
Thou, in sunny solitudes,
Rover of the underwoods,
The green silence dost displace
With thy mellow, breezy bass.

Hot midsummer's petted crone,
Sweet to me thy drowsy tone
Tells of countless sunny hours,
Long days, and solid banks of flowers;
Of gulfs of sweetness without bound
In Indian wildernesses found;
Of Syrian peace, immortal leisure,
Firmest cheer, and bird-like pleasure.

Aught unsavory or unclean
Hath my insect never seen;
But violets and bilberry bells,
Maple-sap and daffodels,
Grass with green flag half-mast high,
Succory to match the sky,
Columbine with horn of honey,
Scented fern, and agrimony,
Clover, catchfly, adder's-tongue
And brier-roses, dwelt among;
All beside was unknown waste,
All was picture as he passed.

Wiser far than human seer,
Yellow-breeched philosopher!
Seeing only what is fair,
Sipping only what is sweet,
Thou dost mock at fate and care,
Leave the chaff, and take the wheat.
When the fierce northwestern blast
Cools sea and land so far and fast,
Thou already slumberest deep;
Woe and want thou canst outsleep;
Want and woe, which torture us,
Thy sleep makes ridiculous.

THE SNOW-STORM

Announced by all the trumpets of the sky,
Arrives the snow, and, driving o'er the fields,
Seems nowhere to alight: the whited air
Hides hills and woods, the river, and the heaven,
And veils the farm-house at the garden's end.
The sled and traveller stopped, the courier's feet
Delayed, all friends shut out, the housemates sit
Around the radiant fireplace, enclosed
In a tumultuous privacy of storm.

Come see the north-wind's masonry.
Out of an unseen quarry evermore
Furnished with tile, the fierce artificer
Curves his white bastions with projected roof
Round every windward stake, or tree, or door.
Speeding, the myriad-handed, his wild work
So fanciful, so savage, nought cares he
For number or proportion. Mockingly,
On coop or kennel he hangs Parian wreaths;
A swan-like form invests the hidden thorn;
Fills up the farmer's lane from wall to wall,
Maugre the farmer's sighs; and at the gate
A tapering turret overtops the work.
And when his hours are numbered, and the world
Is all his own, retiring, as he were not,
Leaves, when the sun appears, astonished Art
To mimic in slow structures, stone by stone,
Built in an age, the mad wind's night-work,
The frolic architecture of the snow.

THE BOHEMIAN HYMN

In many forms we try
To utter God's infinity,
But the boundless hath no form,
And the Universal Friend
Doth as far transcend
An angel as a worm.

The great Idea baffles wit,
Language falters under it,
It leaves the learned in the lurch;
Nor art, nor power, nor toil can find
The measure of the eternal Mind,
Nor hymn, nor prayer, nor church.

GRACE

How much, preventing God, how much I owe
To the defences thou hast round me set;
Example, custom, fear, occasion slow,—
These scornéd bondmen were my parapet.
I dare not peep over this parapet
To gauge with glance the roaring gulf below,
The depths of sin to which I had descended,
Had not these me against myself defended.

THE INFORMING SPIRIT

I

There is no great and no small
To the Soul that maketh all:
And where it cometh, all things are;
And it cometh everywhere.

II

I am the owner of the sphere,
And the seven stars and the solar year,
Of Caesar's hand, and Plato's brain,
Of Lord Christ's heart, and Shakspeare's
        strain.

COMPENSATION

The wings of Time are black and white,
Pied with morning and with night.
Mountain tall and ocean deep
Trembling balance duly keep.
In changing moon and tidal wave
Glows the feud of Want and Have.
Gauge of more and less through space,
Electric star or pencil plays,
The lonely Earth amid the balls
That hurry through the eternal halls,
A makeweight flying to the void,
Supplemental asteroid,
Or compensatory spark,
Shoots across the neutral Dark.

Man's the elm, and Wealth the vine;
Stanch and strong the tendrils twine:
Though the frail ringlets thee deceive,
None from its stock that vine can reave.
Fear not, then, thou child infirm,
There's no god dare wrong a worm;
Laurel crowns cleave to deserts,
And power to him who power exerts.
Hast not thy share? On wingéd feet,
Lo! it rushes thee to meet;
And all that Nature made thy own,
Floating in air or pent in stone,
Will rive the hills and swim the sea,
And, like thy shadow, follow thee.

EXPERIENCE

The lords of life, the lords of life,—
I saw them pass
In their own guise,
Like and unlike,
Portly and grim,—
Use and Surprise,
Surface and Dream,
Succession swift and spectral Wrong,
Temperament without a tongue,
And the inventor of the game
Omnipresent without name;—
Some to see, some to be guessed,
They marched from east to west:
Little man, least of all,
Among the legs of his guardians tall,
Walked about with puzzled look.

Him by the hand dear Nature took,
Dearest Nature, strong and kind,
Whispered, "Darling, never mind!
To-morrow they will wear another face,
The founder thou; these are thy race!"

MOTTOES FOR NATURE

I

A subtle chain of countless rings
The next unto the farthest brings;
The eye reads omens where it goes,
And speaks all languages the rose;
And, striving to be man, the worm
Mounts through all the spires of form.

II

The rounded world is fair to see,
Nine times folded in mystery:
Though baffled seers cannot impart
The secrets of its laboring heart,
Throb thine with Nature's throbbing
        breast,
And all is clear from east to west.
Spirit that lurks each form within
Beckons to spirit of its kin;
Self-kindled every atom glows
And hints the future which it owes.

MUSIC

Let me go where'er I will,
I hear a sky-born music still:
It sounds from all things old,
It sounds from all things young,
From all that's fair, from all that's foul,
Peals out a cheerful song.

It is not only in the rose,
It is not only in the bird,
Not only where the rainbow glows,
Nor in the song of woman heard,
But in the darkest, meanest things
There alway, alway something sings.

'Tis not in the high stars alone,
Nor in the cup of budding flowers,
Nor in the redbreast's mellow tone,
Nor in the bow that smiles in showers,
But in the mud and scum of things
There alway, alway something sings.

FORBEARANCE

Hast thou named all the birds without a gun?
Loved the wood-rose, and left it on its stalk?
At rich men's tables eaten bread and pulse?
Unarmed, faced danger with a heart of trust?
And loved so well a high behavior,
In man or maid, that thou from speech refrained,
Nobility more nobly to repay?
O, be my friend, and teach me to be thine!

THE VISIT

Askest, "How long thou shalt stay?"
Devastator of the day!
Know, each substance and relation,
Thorough nature's operation,
Hath its unit, bound and metre;
And every new compound
Is some product and repeater,—
Product of the earlier found.
But the unit of the visit,
The encounter of the wise,—
Say, what other metre is it
Than the meeting of the eyes?
Nature poureth into nature
Through the channels of that feature,
Riding on the ray of sight,
Fleeter far than whirlwinds go,
Or for service, or delight,
Hearts to hearts their meaning show,
Sum their long experience,
And import intelligence.
Single look has drained the breast;
Single moment years confessed.
The duration of a glance
Is the term of convenance,
And, though thy rede be church or state,
Frugal multiples of that.
Speeding Saturn cannot halt;
Linger,—thou shalt rue the fault:
If Love his moment overstay,
Hatred's swift repulsions play.

ODE TO BEAUTY

Who gave thee, O Beauty,
The keys of this breast,—
Too credulous lover
Of blest and unblest?
Say, when in lapsed ages
Thee knew I of old?
Or what was the service
For which I was sold?
When first my eyes saw thee,
I found me thy thrall,
By magical drawings,
Sweet tyrant of all!
I drank at thy fountain
False waters of thirst;
Thou intimate stranger,
Thou latest and first!
Thy dangerous glances
Make women of men;
New-born, we are melting
Into nature again.

Lavish, lavish promiser,
Nigh persuading gods to err!
Guest of million painted forms,
Which in turn thy glory warms!
The frailest leaf, the mossy bark,
The acorn's cup, the raindrop's arc,
The swinging spider's silver line,
The ruby of the drop of wine,
The shining pebble of the pond,
Thou inscribest with a bond,
In thy momentary play,
Would bankrupt nature to repay.

Ah, what avails it
To hide or to shun
Whom the Infinite One
Hath granted his throne?
The heaven high over
Is the deep's lover;
The sun and sea,
Informed by thee,
Before me run
And draw me on,
Yet fly me still,
As fate refuses
To me the heart Fate for me chooses.
Is it that my opulent soul
Was mingled from the generous whole;
Sea-valleys and the deep of skies
Furnished several supplies;
And the sands whereof I'm made
Draw me to them, self-betrayed?
I turn the proud portfolio
Which holds the grand designs
Of Salvator, of Guercino,
And Piranesi's lines.
I hear the lofty pæans
Of the masters of the shell,
Who hear the starry music
And recount the numbers well;
Olympian bards who sung
Divine Ideas below,
Which always find us young
And always keep us so.
Oft, in streets or humblest places,
I detect far-wandered graces,
Which, from Eden wide astray,
In lowly homes have lost their way.

Thee gliding through the sea of form,
Like the lightning through the storm,
Somewhat not to be possessed,
Somewhat not to be caressed,
No feet so fleet could ever find,
No perfect form could ever bind.
Thou eternal fugitive,
Hovering over all that live,
Quick and skilful to inspire
Sweet, extravagant desire,
Starry space and lily-bell
Filling with thy roseate smell,
Wilt not give the lips to taste
Of the nectar which thou hast.

All that's good and great with thee
Works in close conspiracy;
Thou hast bribed the dark and lonely
To report thy features only,
And the cold and purple morning
Itself with thoughts of thee adorning;
The leafy dell, the city mart,
Equal trophies of thine art;
E'en the flowing azure air
Thou hast touched for my despair;
And, if I languish into dreams,
Again I meet the ardent beams.
Queen of things! I dare not die
In Being's deeps past ear and eye;
Lest there I find the same deceiver,
And be the sport of Fate forever.
Dread Power, but dear! if God thou be,
Unmake me quite, or give thyself to me!

URIEL*

It fell in the ancient periods
   Which the brooding soul surveys,
Or ever the wild Time coined itself
   Into calendar months and days.

This was the lapse of Uriel,
Which in Paradise befell.
Once, among the Pleiads walking,
Seyd overheard the young gods talking;
And the treason, too long pent,
To his ears was evident.
The young deities discussed
Laws of form, and metre just,
Orb, quintessence, and sunbeams,
What subsisteth, and what seems.
One, with low tones that decide,
And doubt and reverend use defied,
With a look that solved the sphere,
And stirred the devils everywhere,
Gave his sentiment divine
Against the being of a line.
"Line in nature is not found;
Unit and universe are round;
In vain produced, all rays return;
Evil will bless, and ice will burn."
As Uriel spoke with piercing eye,
A shudder ran around the sky;
The stern old war-gods shook their heads,
The seraphs frowned from myrtle-beds;

* Uriel, the Archangel in charge of the heavenly bodies in Milton's
Paradise Lost, here becomes a symbol for the advanced thinker surrounded
by conventional minds. Emerson is picturing in parable the hostile recep-
tion of his own "Divinity School Address." *Seyd* is an Arabic word meaning "the Lord."

Seemed to the holy festival
The rash word boded ill to all;
The balance-beam of Fate was bent;
The bounds of good and ill were rent;
Strong Hades could not keep his own,
But all slid to confusion.

A sad self-knowledge, withering, fell
On the beauty of Uriel;
In heaven once eminent, the god
Withdrew, that hour, into his cloud;
Whether doomed to long gyration
In the sea of generation,
Or by knowledge grown too bright
To hit the nerve of feebler sight.
Straightway, a forgetting wind
Stole over the celestial kind,
And their lips the secret kept,
If in ashes the fire-seed slept.
But now and then, truth-speaking things
Shamed the angels' veiling wings;
And, shrilling from the solar course,
Or from fruit of chemic force,
Procession of a soul in matter,
Or the speeding change of water,
Or out of the good of evil born,
Came Uriel's voice of cherub scorn,
And a blush tinged the upper sky,
And the gods shook, they knew not why.

MITHRIDATES

I cannot spare water or wine,
    Tobacco-leaf, or poppy, or rose;
From the earth-poles to the line,
    All between that works or grows,
Everything is kin of mine.

Give me agates for my meat;
Give me cantharids to eat;
From air and ocean bring me foods,
From all zones and altitudes;—

From all natures, sharp and slimy,
    Salt and basalt, wild and tame:
Tree and lichen, ape, sea-lion,
    Bird, and reptile, be my game.

Ivy for my fillet band;
Blinding dog-wood in my hand;
Hemlock for my sherbet cull me,
And the prussic juice to lull me;
Swing me in the upas boughs,
Vampyre-fanned, when I carouse.

Too long shut in strait and few,
Thinly dieted on dew,
I will use the world, and sift it,
To a thousand humors shift it,
As you spin a cherry.
O doleful ghosts, and goblins merry!
O all you virtues, methods, mights,
Means, appliances, delights,
Reputed wrongs and braggart rights,
Smug routine, and things allowed,

Minorities, things under cloud!
Hither! take me, use me, fill me,
Vein and artery, though ye kill me!

TO J. W.

Set not thy foot on graves;
Hear what wine and roses say;
The mountain chase, the summer waves,
The crowded town, thy feet may well delay.

Set not thy foot on graves;
Nor seek to unwind the shroud
Which charitable Time
And Nature have allowed
To wrap the errors of a sage sublime.

Set not thy foot on graves;
Care not to strip the dead
Of his sad ornament,
His myrrh, and wine, and rings,

His sheet of lead,
And trophies buriëd:
Go, get them where he earned them when alive;
As resolutely dig or dive.

Life is too short to waste
In critic peep or cynic bark,
Quarrel or reprimand:
'Twill soon be dark;
Up! mind thine own aim, and
God speed the mark!

HAMATREYA*

Bulkeley, Hunt, Willard, Hosmer, Meriam, Flint,
Possessed the land which rendered to their toil
Hay, corn, roots, hemp, flax, apples, wool and wood.
Each of these landlords walked amidst his farm,
Saying, " 'Tis mine, my children's and my name's.
How sweet the west wind sounds in my own trees!
How graceful climb those shadows on my hill!
I fancy these pure waters and the flags
Know me, as does my dog: we sympathize;
And, I affirm, my actions smack of the soil."

Where are these men? Asleep beneath their grounds:
And strangers, fond as they, their furrows plough.
Earth laughs in flowers, to see her boastful boys
Earth-proud, proud of the earth which is not theirs;
Who steer the plough, but cannot steer their feet
Clear of the grave.
They added ridge to valley, brook to pond,
And sighed for all that bounded their domain;
"This suits me for a pasture; that's my park;
We must have clay, lime, gravel, granite-ledge,
And misty lowland, where to go for peat.
The land is well,—lies fairly to the south.
'Tis good, when you have crossed the sea and back,
To find the sitfast acres where you left them."
Ah! the hot owner sees not Death, who adds
Him to his land, a lump of mould the more.
Hear what the Earth says:

* Hamatreya or Maitreya, a Hindoo proper name. "These were the verses,
Maitreya, which Earth recited and by listening to which ambition fades
away like snow before the sun." *Vishnu Purana*, Book IV.

EARTH-SONG

"Mine and yours;
Mine, not yours.
Earth endures;
Stars abide—
Shine down in the old sea;
Old are the shores;
But where are old men?
I who have seen much,
Such have I never seen.

"The lawyer's deed
Ran sure,
In tail,
To them, and to their heirs
Who shall succeed,
Without fail,
Forevermore.

"Here is the land,
Shaggy with wood,
With its old valley,
Mound and flood.
But the heritors?—
Fled like the flood's foam.
The lawyer, and the laws,
And the kingdom,
Clean swept herefrom.

"They called me theirs,
Who so controlled me;
Yet every one
Wished to stay, and is gone,
How am I theirs,

> If they cannot hold me,
> But I hold them?"

When I heard the Earth-song
I was no longer brave;
My avarice cooled
Like lust in the chill of the grave.

SUUM CUIQUE *

The rain has spoiled the farmer's day;
Shall sorrow put my books away?
   Thereby two days are lost:
Nature shall mind her own affairs;
I will attend my proper cares,
   In rain, or sun, or frost.

ODE

Inscribed to W. H. Channing†

Though loath to grieve
The evil time's sole patriot,
I cannot leave
My honied thought
For the priest's cant,
Or statesman's rant.

* From *Poems* (1847). Never reprinted.
† W. H. Channing, a nephew of the Rev. William Ellery Channing, was active in the antislavery crusade.

If I refuse
My study for their politique,
Which at the best is trick,
The angry Muse
Puts confusion in my brain.

But who is he that prates
Of the culture of mankind,
Of better arts and life?
Go, blindworm, go,
Behold the famous States
Harrying Mexico
With rifle and with knife!

Or who, with accent bolder,
Dare praise the freedom-loving mountaineer?
I found by thee, O rushing Contoocook!
And in thy valleys, Agiochook!
The jackals of the negro-holder.

The God who made New Hampshire
Taunted the lofty land
With little men;—
Small bat and wren
House in the oak:—
If earth-fire cleave
The upheaved land, and bury the folk,
The southern crocodile would grieve.
Virtue palters; Right is hence;
Freedom praised, but hid;
Funeral eloquence
Rattles the coffin-lid.

What boots thy zeal,
O glowing friend,

That would indignant rend
The northland from the south?
Wherefore? to what good end?
Boston Bay and Bunker Hill
Would serve things still;—
Things are of the snake.

The horseman serves the horse,
The neatherd serves the neat,
The merchant serves the purse,
The eater serves his meat;
'Tis the day of the chattel,
Web to weave, and corn to grind;
Things are in the saddle,
And ride mankind.

There are two laws discrete,
Not reconciled,—
Law for man, and law for thing;
The last builds town and fleet,
But it runs wild,
And doth the man unking.

'Tis fit the forest fall,
The steep be graded,
The mountain tunnelled,
The sand shaded,
The orchard planted,
The glebe tilled,
The prairie granted,
The steamer built.

Let man serve law for man;
Live for friendship, live for love,
For truth's and harmony's behoof;

The state may follow how it can,
As Olympus follows Jove.

   Yet do not I implore
The wrinkled shopman to my sounding woods,
Nor bid the unwilling senator
Ask votes of thrushes in the solitudes.
Every one to his chosen work;—
Foolish hands may mix and mar;
Wise and sure the issues are.
Round they roll till dark is light,
Sex to sex, and even to odd;—
The over-god
Who marries Right to Might,
Who peoples, unpeoples,—
He who exterminates
Races by stronger races,
Black by white faces,—
Knows to bring honey
Out of the lion;
Grafts gentlest scion
On pirate and Turk.

The Cossack eats Poland,
Like stolen fruit;
Her last noble is ruined,
Her last poet mute:
Straight, into double band
The victors divide;
Half for freedom strike and stand;—
The astonished Muse finds thousands at her side.

GIVE ALL TO LOVE

Give all to love;
Obey thy heart;
Friends, kindred, days,
Estate, good-fame,
Plans, credit and the Muse,—
Nothing refuse.

'Tis a brave master;
Let it have scope:
Follow it utterly,
Hope beyond hope:
High and more high
It dives into noon,
With wing unspent,
Untold intent;
But it is a god,
Knows its own path
And the outlets of the sky.

It was never for the mean;
It requireth courage stout.
Souls above doubt,
Valor unbending,
It will reward,—
They shall return
More than they were,
And ever ascending.

Leave all for love;
Yet, hear me, yet,
One word more thy heart behoved,
One pulse more of firm endeavor,—
Keep thee to-day,

To-morrow, forever,
Free as an Arab
Of thy beloved.

Cling with life to the maid;
But when the surprise,
First vague shadow of surmise
Flits across her bosom young,
Of a joy apart from thee,
Free be she, fancy-free;
Nor thou detain her vesture's hem,
Nor the palest rose she flung
From her summer diadem.

Though thou loved her as thyself,
As a self of purer clay,
Though her parting dims the day,
Stealing grace from all alive;
Heartily know,
When half-gods go,
The gods arrive.

MERLIN

I

Thy trivial harp will never please
Or fill my craving ear;
Its chords should ring as blows the breeze,
Free, peremptory, clear.
No jingling serenader's art,
Nor tinkle of piano strings,
Can make the wild blood start

In its mystic springs.
The kingly bard
Must smite the chords rudely and hard,
As with hammer or with mace;
That they may render back
Artful thunder, which conveys
Secrets of the solar track,
Sparks of the supersolar blaze.
Merlin's blows are strokes of fate,
Chiming with the forest tone,
When boughs buffet boughs in the wood;
Chiming with the gasp and moan
Of the ice-imprisoned flood;
With the pulse of manly hearts;
With the voice of orators;
With the din of city arts;
With the cannonade of wars;
With the marches of the brave;
And prayers of might from martyrs' cave.

Great is the art,
Great be the manners, of the bard.
He shall not his brain encumber
With the coil of rhythm and number;
But, leaving rule and pale forethought,
He shall aye climb
For his rhyme.
"Pass in, pass in," the angels say,
"In to the upper doors,
Nor count compartments of the floors,
But mount to paradise
By the stairway of surprise."

Blameless master of the games,
King of sport that never shames,

He shall daily joy dispense
Hid in song's sweet influence.
Forms more cheerly live and go,
What time the subtle mind
Sings aloud the tune whereto
Their pulses beat,
And march their feet,
And their members are combined.

By Sybarites beguiled,
He shall no task decline;
Merlin's mighty line
Extremes of nature reconciled,—
Bereaved a tyrant of his will,
And made the lion mild.
Songs can the tempest still,
Scattered on the stormy air,
Mould the year to fair increase,
And bring in poetic peace.

He shall not seek to weave,
In weak, unhappy times,
Efficacious rhymes;
Wait his returning strength.
Bird that from the nadir's floor
To the zenith's top can soar,—
The soaring orbit of the muse exceeds that journey's length.
Nor profane affect to hit
Or compass that, by meddling wit,
Which only the propitious mind
Publishes when 'tis inclined.
There are open hours
When the God's will sallies free,
And the dull idiot might see
The flowing fortunes of a thousand years;—

Sudden, at unawares,
Self-moved, fly-to the doors,
Nor sword of angels could reveal
What they conceal.

MERLIN

II

The rhyme of the poet
Modulates the king's affairs;
Balance-loving Nature
Made all things in pairs.
To every foot its antipode;
Each color with its counter glowed;
To every tone beat answering tones,
Higher or graver;
Flavor gladly blends with flavor;
Leaf answers leaf upon the bough;
And match the paired cotyledons.
Hands to hands, and feet to feet,
In one body grooms and brides;
Eldest rite, two married sides
In every mortal meet.
Light's far furnace shines,
Smelting balls and bars,
Forging double stars,
Glittering twins and trines.
The animals are sick with love,
Lovesick with rhyme;
Each with all propitious Time
Into chorus wove.
Like the dancers' ordered band,

Thoughts come also hand in hand;
In equal couples mated,
Or else alternated;
Adding by their mutual gage,
One to other, health and age.
Solitary fancies go
Short-lived wandering to and fro,
Most like to bachelors,
Or an ungiven maid,
Not ancestors,
With no posterity to make the lie afraid,
Or keep truth undecayed.
Perfect-paired as eagle's wings,
Justice is the rhyme of things;
Trade and counting use
The self-same tuneful muse;
And Nemesis,
Who with even matches odd,
Who athwart space redresses
The partial wrong,
Fills the just period,
And finishes the song.

Subtle rhymes, with ruin rife,
Murmur in the house of life,
Sung by the Sisters as they spin;
In perfect time and measure they
Build and unbuild our echoing clay.
As the two twilights of the day
Fold us music-drunken in.

BACCHUS

Bring me wine, but wine which never grew
In the belly of the grape,
Or grew on vine whose tap-roots, reaching through
Under the Andes to the Cape,
Suffered no savor of the earth to scape.

Let its grapes the morn salute
From a nocturnal root,
Which feels the acrid juice
Of Styx and Erebus;
And turns the woe of Night,
By its own craft, to a more rich delight.

We buy ashes for bread;
We buy diluted wine;
Give me of the true,—
Whose ample leaves and tendrils curled
Among the silver hills of heaven,
Draw everlasting dew;
Wine of wine,
Blood of the world,
Form of forms, and mould of statures,
That I intoxicated,
And by the draught assimilated,
May float at pleasure through all natures;
The bird-language rightly spell,
And that which roses say so well.

Wine that is shed
Like the torrents of the sun
Up the horizon walls,
Or like the Atlantic streams, which run
When the South Sea calls.

Water and bread,
Food which needs no transmuting,
Rainbow-flowering, wisdom-fruiting,
Wine which is already man,
Food which teach and reason can.

Wine which Music is,—
Music and wine are one,—
That I, drinking this,
Shall hear far Chaos talk with me;
Kings unborn shall walk with me;
And the poor grass shall plot and plan
What it will do when it is man.
Quickened so, will I unlock
Every crypt of every rock.

I thank the joyful juice
For all I know;—
Winds of remembering
Of the ancient being blow,
And seeming-solid walls of use
Open and flow.

Pour, Bacchus! the remembering wine;
Retrieve the loss of me and mine!
Vine for vine be antidote,
And the grape requite the lote!
Haste to cure the old despair,—
Reason in Nature's lotus drenched,
The memory of ages quenched;
Give them again to shine;
Let wine repair what this undid;
And where the infection slid,
A dazzling memory revive;
Refresh the faded tints,

Recut the aged prints,
And write my old adventures with the pen
Which on the first day drew,
Upon the tablets blue,
The dancing Pleiads and eternal men.

THRENODY

The South-wind brings
Life, sunshine and desire,
And on every mount and meadow
Breathes aromatic fire;
But over the dead he has no power,
The lost, the lost, he cannot restore;
And, looking over the hills, I mourn
The darling who shall not return.

I see my empty house,
I see my trees repair their boughs;
And he, the wondrous child,*
Whose silver warble wild
Outvalued every pulsing sound
Within the air's cerulean round,—
The hyacinthine boy, for whom
Morn well might break and April bloom,—
The gracious boy, who did adorn
The world whereinto he was born,
And by his countenance repay
The favor of the loving Day,—
Has disappeared from the Day's eye;
Far and wide she cannot find him;
My hopes pursue, they cannot bind him.

* Emerson's six-year-old son, Waldo.

Returned this day, the south wind searches,
And finds young pines and budding birches;
But finds not the budding man;
Nature, who lost, cannot remake him;
Fate let him fall, Fate can't retake him;
Nature, Fate, men, him seek in vain.
And whither now, my truant wise and sweet,
O, whither tend thy feet?
I had the right, few days ago,
Thy steps to watch, thy place to know:
How have I forfeited the right?
Hast thou forgot me in a new delight?
I hearken for thy household cheer,
O eloquent child!
Whose voice, an equal messenger,
Conveyed thy meaning mild.
What though the pains and joys
Whereof it spoke were toys
Fitting his age and ken,
Yet fairest dames and bearded men,
Who heard the sweet request,
So gentle, wise and grave,
Bended with joy to his behest
And let the world's affairs go by,
A while to share his cordial game,
Or mend his wicker wagon-frame,
Still plotting how their hungry ear
That winsome voice again might hear;
For his lips could well pronounce
Words that were persuasions.

Gentlest guardians marked serene
His early hope, his liberal mien;
Took counsel from his guiding eyes
To make this wisdom earthly wise.

Ah, vainly do these eyes recall
The school-march, each day's festival,
When every morn my bosom glowed
To watch the convoy on the road;
The babe in willow wagon closed,
With rolling eyes and face composed;
With children forward and behind,
Like Cupids studiously inclined;
And he the chieftain paced beside,
The centre of the troop allied,
With sunny face of sweet repose,
To guard the babe from fancied foes.
The little captain innocent
Took the eye with him as he went;
Each village senior paused to scan
And speak the lovely caravan.
From the window I look out
To mark thy beautiful parade,
Stately marching in cap and coat
To some tune by fairies played;—
A music heard by thee alone
To works as noble led thee on.

Now Love and Pride, alas! in vain,
Up and down their glances strain.
The painted sled stands where it stood;
The kennel by the corded wood;
His gathered sticks to stanch the wall
Of the snow-tower, when snow should fall;
The ominous hole he dug in the sand,
And childhood's castles built or planned:
His daily haunts I well discern,—
The poultry-yard, the shed, the barn,—
And every inch of garden ground
Paced by the blessed feet around,

From the roadside to the brook
Whereinto he loved to look.
Step the meek fowls where erst they ranged;
The wintry garden lies unchanged;
The brook into the stream runs on;
But the deep-eyed boy is gone.

On that shaded day,
Dark with more clouds than tempests are,
When thou didst yield thy innocent breath
In birdlike heavings unto death,
Night came, and Nature had not thee;
I said, "We are mates in misery."
The morrow dawned with needless glow;
Each snowbird chirped, each fowl must crow;
Each tramper started; but the feet
Of the most beautiful and sweet
Of human youth had left the hill
And garden,—they were bound and still.
There's not a sparrow or a wren,
There's not a blade of autumn grain,
Which the four seasons do not tend
And tides of life and increase lend;
And every chick of every bird,
And weed and rock-moss is preferred.
O ostrich-like forgetfulness!
O loss of larger in the less!
Was there no star that could be sent,
No watcher in the firmament,
No angel from the countless host
That loiters round the crystal coast,
Could stoop to heal that only child,
Nature's sweet marvel undefiled,
And keep the blossom of the earth,
Which all her harvests were not worth?

Not mine,—I never called thee mine,
But Nature's heir,—if I repine,
And seeing rashly torn and moved
Not what I made, but what I loved,
Grow early old with grief that thou
Must to the wastes of Nature go,—
'Tis because a general hope
Was quenched, and all must doubt and grope.
For flattering planets seemed to say
This child should ills of ages stay,
By wondrous tongue, and guided pen,
Bring the flown Muses back to men.
Perchance not he but Nature ailed,
The world and not the infant failed.
It was not ripe yet to sustain
A genius of so fine a strain,
Who gazed upon the sun and moon
As if he came unto his own,
And, pregnant with his grander thought,
Brought the old order into doubt.
His beauty once their beauty tried;
They could not feed him, and he died,
And wandered backward as in scorn,
To wait an æon to be born.
Ill day which made this beauty waste,
Plight broken, this high face defaced!
Some went and came about the dead;
And some in books of solace read;
Some to their friends the tidings say;
Some went to write, some went to pray;
One tarried here, there hurried one;
But their heart abode with none.
Covetous death bereaved us all,
To aggrandize one funeral.
The eager fate which carried thee

Took the largest part of me:
For this losing is true dying;
This is lordly man's down-lying,
This his slow but sure reclining,
Star by star his world resigning.

O child of paradise,
Boy who made dear his father's home,
In whose deep eyes
Men read the welfare of the times to come,
I am too much bereft.
The world dishonored thou hast left.
O truth's and nature's costly lie!
O trusted broken prophecy!
O richest fortune sourly crossed!
Born for the future, to the future lost!

The deep Heart answered, "Weepest thou?
Worthier cause for passion wild
If I had not taken the child.
And deemest thou as those who pore,
With aged eyes, short way before,—
Think'st Beauty vanished from the coast
Of matter, and thy darling lost?
Taught he not thee—the man of eld,
Whose eyes within his eyes beheld
Heaven's numerous hierarchy span
The mystic gulf from God to man?
To be alone wilt thou begin
When worlds of lovers hem thee in?
To-morrow, when the masks shall fall
That dizen Nature's carnival,
The pure shall see by their own will,
Which overflowing Love shall fill,
'Tis not within the force of fate

The fate-conjoined to separate.
But thou, my votary, weepest thou?
I gave thee sight—where is it now?
I taught thy heart beyond the reach
Of ritual, bible, or of speech;
Wrote in thy mind's transparent table,
As far as the incommunicable;
Taught thee each private sign to raise
Lit by the supersolar blaze.
Past utterance, and past belief,
And past the blasphemy of grief,
The mysteries of Nature's heart;
And though no Muse can these impart,
Throb thine with Nature's throbbing breast,
And all is clear from east to west.

'I came to thee as to a friend;
Dearest, to thee I did not send
Tutors, but a joyful eye,
Innocence that matched the sky,
Lovely locks, a form of wonder,
Laughter rich as woodland thunder,
That thou might'st entertain apart
The richest flowering of all art:
And, as the great all-loving Day
Through smallest chambers takes its way,
That thou might'st break thy daily bread
With prophet, savior and head;
That thou might'st cherish for thine own
The riches of sweet Mary's Son,
Boy-Rabbi, Israel's paragon.
And thoughtest thou such guest
Would in thy hall take up his rest?
Would rushing life forget her laws,
Fate's glowing revolution pause?

High omens ask diviner guess;
Not to be conned to tediousness.
And know my higher gifts unbind
The zone that girds the incarnate mind.
When the scanty shores are full
With Thought's perilous, whirling pool;
When frail Nature can no more,
Then the Spirit strikes the hour:
My servant Death, with solving rite,
Pours finite into infinite.
Wilt thou freeze love's tidal flow,
Whose streams through nature circling go?
Nail the wild star to its track
On the half-climbed zodiac?
Light is light which radiates,
Blood is blood which circulates,
Life is life which generates,
And many-seeming life is one,—
Wilt thou transfix and make it none?
Its onward force too starkly pent
In figure, bone, and lineament?
Wilt thou, uncalled, interrogate,
Talker! the unreplying Fate?
Nor see the genius of the whole
Ascendant in the private soul,
Beckon it when to go and come,
Self-announced its hour of doom?
Fair the soul's recess and shrine,
Magic-built to last a season;
Masterpiece of love benign,
Fairer that expansive reason
Whose omen 'tis, and sign.
Wilt thou not ope thy heart to know
What rainbows teach, and sunsets show?
Verdict which accumulates

From lengthening scroll of human fates,
Voice of earth to earth returned,
Prayers of saints that inly burned,—
Saying, *What is excellent,*
As God lives, is permanent;
Hearts are dust, hearts' loves remain;
Heart's love will meet thee again.
Revere the Maker; fetch thine eye
Up to his style, and manners of the sky.
Not of adamant and gold
Built he heaven stark and cold;
No, but a nest of bending reeds,
Flowering grass and scented weeds;
Or like a traveller's fleeing tent,
Or bow above the tempest bent;
Built of tears and sacred flames,
And virtue reaching to its aims;
Built of furtherance and pursuing,
Not of spent deeds, but of doing.
Silent rushes the swift Lord
Through ruined systems still restored,
Broadsowing, bleak and void to bless,
Plants with worlds the wilderness;
Waters with tears of ancient sorrow
Apples of Eden ripe to-morrow.
House and tenant go to ground,
Lost in God, in Godhead found."

DAYS

Daughters of Time, the hypocritic Days,
Muffled and dumb like barefoot dervishes,
And marching single in an endless file,

Bring diadems and fagots in their hands.
To each they offer gifts after his will,
Bread, kingdoms, stars, and sky that holds them all.
I, in my pleachèd garden, watched the pomp,
Forgot my morning wishes, hastily
Took a few herbs and apples, and the Day
Turned and departed silent. I, too late,
Under her solemn fillet saw the scorn.

WALDEINSAMKEIT*

I do not count the hours I spend
In wandering by the sea;
The forest is my loyal friend,
Like God it useth me.

In plains that room for shadows make
Of skirting hills to lie,
Bound in by streams which give and take
Their colors from the sky;

Or on the mountain-crest sublime,
Or down the oaken glade,
O what have I to do with time?
For this the day was made.

Cities of mortals woe-begone
Fantastic care derides,
But in the serious landscape lone
Stern benefit abides.

* "World-loneliness." The German word reminded Emerson of Walden
Pond, where he would often walk to commune with nature.

Sheen will tarnish, honey cloy,
And merry is only a mask of sad,
But, sober on a fund of joy,
The woods at heart are glad.

There the great Planter plants
Of fruitful worlds the grain,
And with a million spells enchants
The souls that walk in pain.

Still on the seeds of all he made
The rose of beauty burns;
Through times that wear and forms that fade,
Immortal youth returns.

The black ducks mounting from the lake,
The pigeon in the pines,
The bittern's boom, a desert make
Which no false art refines.

Down in yon watery nook,
Where bearded mists divide,
The gray old gods whom Chaos knew,
The sires of Nature, hide.

Aloft, in secret veins of air,
Blows the sweet breath of song,
O, few to scale those uplands dare,
Though they to all belong!

See thou bring not to field or stone
The fancies found in books;
Leave authors' eyes, and fetch your own,
To brave the landscape's looks.

Oblivion here thy wisdom is,
Thy thrift, the sleep of cares;
For a proud idleness like this
Crowns all thy mean affairs.

BRAHMA

If the red slayer think he slays,
  Or if the slain think he is slain,
They know not well the subtle ways
  I keep, and pass, and turn again.

Far or forgot to me is near;
  Shadow and sunlight are the same;
The vanished gods to me appear;
  And one to me are shame and fame.

They reckon ill who leave me out;
  When me they fly, I am the wings;
I am the doubter and the doubt,
  And I the hymn the Brahmin sings.

The strong gods pine for my abode,
  And pine in vain the sacred Seven;
But thou, meek lover of the good!
  Find me, and turn thy back on heaven.

TWO RIVERS

Thy summer voice, Musketaquit,*
Repeats the music of the rain;
But sweeter rivers pulsing flit
Through thee, as thou through Concord Plain.

Thou in thy narrow banks art pent:
The stream I love unbounded goes
Through flood and sea and firmament;
Through light, through life, it forward flows.

I see the inundation sweet,
I hear the spending of the stream
Through years, through men, through Nature fleet,
Through love and thought, through power and dream.

Musketaquit, a goblin strong,
Of shard and flint makes jewels gay;
They lose their grief who hear his song,
And where he winds is the day of day.

So forth and brighter fares my stream,—
Who drink it shall not thirst again;
No darkness stains its equal gleam,
And ages drop in it like rain.

From VOLUNTARIES

In an age of fops and toys,
Wanting wisdom, void of right,
Who shall nerve heroic boys

* The Indian name for Concord River.

To hazard all in Freedom's fight,—
Break sharply off their jolly games,
Forsake their comrades gay
And quit proud homes and youthful dames
For famine, toil and fray?
Yet on the nimble air benign
Speed nimbler messages,
That waft the breath of grace divine
To hearts in sloth and ease.
So nigh is grandeur to our dust,
So near is God to man,
When Duty whispers low, *Thou must*,
The youth replies, *I can*.

CONSIDERATIONS BY THE WAY

Hear what British Merlin sung,
Of keenest eye and truest tongue.
Say not, the chiefs who first arrive
Usurp the seats for which all strive;
The forefathers this land who found
Failed to plant the vantage-ground;
Ever from one who comes to-morrow
Men wait their good and truth to borrow.
But wilt thou measure all thy road,
See thou lift the lightest load.
Who has little, to him who has less, can spare.
And thou, Cyndyllan's son! beware
Ponderous gold and stuffs to bear,
To falter ere thou thy task fulfil,—
Only the light-armed climb the hill.
The richest of all lords is Use,
And ruddy Health the loftiest Muse.

Live in the sunshine, swim the sea,
Drink the wild air's salubrity:
Where the star Canope shines in May,
Shepherds are thankful, and nations gay.
The music that can deepest reach,
And cure all ill, is cordial speech:
Mask thy wisdom with delight,
Toy with the bow, yet hit the white.
Of all wit's uses, the main one
Is to live well with who has none.
Cleave to thine acre; the round year
Will fetch all fruits and virtues here:
Fool and foe may harmless roam,
Loved and lovers bide at home.
A day for toil, an hour for sport,
But for a friend is life too short.

TERMINUS

It is time to be old,
To take in sail:—
The god of bounds,
Who sets to seas a shore,
Came to me in his fatal rounds,
And said: "No more!
No farther shoot
Thy broad ambitious branches, and thy root.
Fancy departs: no more invent;
Contract thy firmament
To compass of a tent.
There's not enough for this and that,
Make thy option which of two;
Economize the failing river,

Not the less revere the Giver,
Leave the many and hold the few.
Timely wise accept the terms,
Soften the fall with wary foot;
A little while
Still plan and smile,
And,—fault of novel germs,—
Mature the unfallen fruit.
Curse, if thou wilt, thy sires,
Bad husbands of their fires,
Who, when they gave thee breath,
Failed to bequeath
The needful sinew stark as once,
The Baresark marrow to thy bones,
But left a legacy of ebbing veins,
Inconstant heat and nerveless reins,—
Amid the Muses, left thee deaf and dumb,
Amid the gladiators, halt and numb."

As the bird trims her to the gale,
I trim myself to the storm of time,
I man the rudder, reef the sail,
Obey the voice at eve obeyed at prime:
"Lowly faithful, banish fear,
Right onward drive unharmed;
The port, well worth the cruise, is near,
And every wave is charmed."

Henry Wadsworth Longfellow

1807–1882

THE SKELETON IN ARMOR *

"Speak! speak! thou fearful guest!
Who, with thy hollow breast
Still in rude armor drest,
  Comest to daunt me!
Wrapt not in Eastern balms,
But with thy fleshless palms
Stretched, as if asking alms,
  Why dost thou haunt me?"

Then, from those cavernous eyes
Pale flashes seemed to rise,
As when the Northern skies
  Gleam in December;
And, like the water's flow
Under December's snow,
Came a dull voice of woe
  From the heart's chamber.

"I was a Viking old!
My deeds, though manifold,
No Skald in song has told,
  No Saga taught thee!
Take heed that in thy verse
Thou dost the tale rehearse,
Else dread a dead man's curse;
  For this I sought thee.

* Suggested by the mysterious Round Tower at Newport and by a skeleton clad in full armor lately dug up at Fall River.

94

"Far in the Northern Land,
By the wild Baltic's strand,
I, with my childish hand,
    Tamed the gerfalcon;
And, with my skates fast-bound,
Skimmed the half-frozen Sound,
That the poor whimpering hound
    Trembled to walk on.

"Oft to his frozen lair
Tracked I the grisly bear,
While from my path the hare
    Fled like a shadow;
Oft through the forest dark
Followed the were-wolf's bark,
Until the soaring lark
    Sang from the meadow.

"But when I older grew,
Joining a corsair's crew,
O'er the dark sea I flew
    With the marauders.
Wild was the life we led;
Many the souls that sped,
Many the hearts that bled,
    By our stern orders.

"Many a wassail-bout
Wore the long winter out;
Often our midnight shout
    Set the cocks crowing,
As we the Berserk's tale
Measured in cups of ale,
Draining the oaken pail,
    Filled to o'erflowing.

"Once as I told in glee
Tales of the stormy sea,
Soft eyes did gaze on me,
    Burning yet tender;
And as the white stars shine
On the dark Norway pine,
On that dark heart of mine
    Fell their soft splendor.

"I wooed the blue-eyed maid,
Yielding, yet half afraid,
And in the forest's shade
    Our vows were plighted.
Under its loosened vest
Fluttered her little breast,
Like birds within their nest
    By the hawk frighted.

"Bright in her father's hall
Shields gleamed upon the wall,
Loud sang the minstrels all,
    Chanting his glory;
When of old Hildebrand
I asked his daughter's hand,
Mute did the minstrels stand
    To hear my story.

"While the brown ale he quaffed,
Loud then the champion laughed,
And as the wind-gusts waft
    The sea-foam brightly,
So the loud laugh of scorn
Out of those lips unshorn,
From the deep drinking-horn
    Blew the foam lightly.

"She was a Prince's child,
I but a Viking wild,
And though she blushed and smiled,
    I was discarded!
Should not the dove so white
Follow the sea-mew's flight,
Why did they leave that night
    Her nest unguarded?

"Scarce had I put to sea,
Bearing the maid with me,
Fairest of all was she
    Among the Norsemen!
When on the white sea-strand,
Waving his armèd hand,
Saw we old Hildebrand,
    With twenty horsemen.

"Then launched they to the blast,
Bent like a reed each mast,
Yet we were gaining fast,
    When the wind failed us;
And with a sudden flaw
Came round the gusty Skaw,
So that our foe we saw
    Laugh as he hailed us.

"And as to catch the gale
Round veered the flapping sail,
'Death!' was the helmsman's hail,
    'Death without quarter!'
Midships with iron keel
Struck we her ribs of steel;
Down her black hulk did reel
    Through the black water!

"As with his wings aslant,
Sails the fierce cormorant,
Seeking some rocky haunt,
    With his prey laden,—
So toward the open main,
Beating to sea again,
Through the wild hurricane,
    Bore I the maiden.

"Three weeks we westward bore,
And when the storm was o'er,
Cloud-like we saw the shore
    Stretching to leeward;
There for my lady's bower
Built I the lofty tower,
Which, to this very hour,
    Stands looking seaward.

"There lived we many years;
Time dried the maiden's tears;
She had forgot her fears,
    She was a mother;
Death closed her mild blue eyes,
Under that tower she lies;
Ne'er shall the sun arise
    On such another!

"Still grew my bosom then,
Still as a stagnant fen!
Hateful to me were men,
    The sunlight hateful!
In the vast forest here,
Clad in my warlike gear,
Fell I upon my spear,
    Oh, death was grateful!

"Thus, seamed with many scars,
Bursting these prison bars
Up to its native stars
  My soul ascended!
There from the flowing bowl
Deep drinks the warrior's soul,
Skoal! to the Northland! *skoal!*"
  Thus the tale ended.

MEZZO CAMMIN*

Half of my life is gone, and I have let
  The years slip from me and have not fulfilled
  The aspiration of my youth, to build
  Some tower of song with lofty parapet.
Not indolence, nor pleasure, nor the fret
  Of restless passions that would not be stilled,
  But sorrow, and a care that almost killed,
  Kept me from what I may accomplish yet;
Though, half-way up the hill, I see the Past
  Lying beneath me with its sounds and sights,—
  A city in the twilight dim and vast,
With smoking roofs, soft bells, and gleaming lights,—
  And hear above me on the autumnal blast
  The cataract of Death far thundering from the heights.

* "Mid-way along the road" of life. From the first line of Dante's *Commedia*.

SEAWEED

When descends on the Atlantic
    The gigantic
Storm-wind of the equinox,
Landward in his wrath he scourges
    The toiling surges,
Laden with seaweed from the rocks:

From Bermuda's reefs; from edges
    Of sunken ledges,
In some far-off, bright Azore;
From Bahama, and the dashing,
    Silver-flashing
Surges of San Salvador;

From the tumbling surf, that buries
    The Orkneyan skerries,
Answering the hoarse Hebrides;
And from wrecks of ships, and drifting
    Spars, uplifting
On the desolate, rainy seas;—

Ever drifting, drifting, drifting
    On the shifting
Currents of the restless main;
Till in sheltered coves, and reaches
    Of sandy beaches,
All have found repose again.

So when storms of wild emotion
    Strike the ocean
Of the poet's soul, erelong

From each cave and rocky fastness,
  In its vastness,
Floats some fragment of a song:

From the far-off isles enchanted,
  Heaven has planted
With the golden fruit of Truth;
From the flashing surf, whose vision
  Gleams Elysian
In the tropic clime of Youth;

From the strong Will, and the Endeavor
  That forever
Wrestle with the tides of Fate;
From the wreck of Hopes far-scattered,
  Tempest-shattered,
Floating waste and desolate;—

Ever drifting, drifting, drifting
  On the shifting
Currents of the restless heart;
Till at length in books recorded,
  They, like hoarded
Household words, no more depart.

TO THE DRIVING CLOUD

Gloomy and dark art thou, O chief of the mighty Omahas;
Gloomy and dark as the driving cloud, whose name thou hast
  taken!
Wrapped in thy scarlet blanket, I see thee stalk through the
  city's
Narrow and populous streets, as once by the margin of rivers

Stalked those birds unknown, that have left us only their footprints.
What, in a few short years, will remain of thy race but the footprints?

How canst thou walk these streets, who hast trod the green turf
of the prairies?
How canst thou breathe this air, who hast breathed the sweet
air of the mountains?
Ah! 'tis in vain that with lordly looks of disdain thou dost
challenge
Looks of disdain in return, and question these walls and these
pavements,
Claiming the soil for thy hunting-grounds, while down-trodden
millions
Starve in the garrets of Europe, and cry from its caverns that
they, too,
Have been created heirs of the earth, and claim its division!

Back, then, back to thy woods in the regions west of the
Wabash!
There as a monarch thou reignest. In autumn the leaves of the
maple
Pave the floors of thy palace-halls with gold, and in summer
Pine-trees waft through its chambers the odorous breath of their
branches.
There thou art strong and great, a hero, a tamer of horses!
There thou chasest the stately stag on the banks of the Elkhorn,
Or by the roar of the Running-Water, or where the Omaha
Calls thee, and leaps through the wild ravine like a brave of the
Blackfeet!

Hark! what murmurs arise from the heart of those mountainous
deserts?
Is it the cry of the Foxes and Crows, or the mighty Behemoth.

Who, unharmed, on his tusks once caught the bolts of the
    thunder,
And now lurks in his lair to destroy the race of the red man?
Far more fatal to thee and thy race than the Crows and the
    Foxes,
Far more fatal to thee and thy race than the tread of Behemoth,
Lo! the big thunder-canoe, that steadily breasts the Missouri's
Merciless current! and yonder, afar on the prairies, the camp-fires
Gleam through the night; and the cloud of dust in the gray of
    the daybreak
Marks not the buffalo's track, nor the Mandan's dexterous
    horse-race;
It is a caravan, whitening the desert where dwell the Camanches!
Ha! how the breath of these Saxons and Celts, like the blast of
    the east-wind,
Drifts evermore to the west the scanty smokes of thy wigwams!

From EVANGELINE

THE FOREST PRIMEVAL

This is the forest primeval. The murmuring pines and the
    hemlocks,
Bearded with moss, and in garments green, indistinct in the
    twilight,
Stand like Druids of eld, with voices sad and prophetic,
Stand like harpers hoar, with beards that rest on their bosoms.
Loud from its rocky caverns, the deep-voiced neighboring ocean
Speaks, and in accents disconsolate answers the wail of the
    forest.

This is the forest primeval; but where are the hearts that be-
    neath it

Leaped like the roe, when he hears in the woodland the voice
of the huntsman?

Where is the thatch-roofed village, the home of Acadian
farmers,—

Men whose lives glided on like rivers that water the woodlands,

Darkened by shadows of earth, but reflecting an image of
heaven?

Waste are those pleasant farms, and the farmers forever departed!

Scattered like dust and leaves, when the mighty blasts of
October

Seize them, and whirl them aloft, and sprinkle them far o'er the
ocean.

Naught but tradition remains of the beautiful village of Grand-
Pré.

IN THE CHURCHYARD AT CAMBRIDGE

In the village churchyard she lies,
Dust is in her beautiful eyes,
    No more she breathes, nor feels, nor stirs;
At her feet and at her head
Lies a slave to attend the dead,
    But their dust is white as hers.

Was she, a lady of high degree,
So much in love with the vanity
    And foolish pomp of this world of ours?
Or was it Christian charity,
And lowliness and humility,
    The richest and rarest of all dowers?

Who shall tell us? No one speaks;
No color shoots into those cheeks,
    Either of anger or of pride,

At the rude question we have asked;
Nor will the mystery be unmasked
  By those who are sleeping at her side.

Hereafter?—And do you think to look
On the terrible pages of that Book
  To find her failings, faults, and errors?
Ah, you will then have other cares,
In your own shortcomings and despairs,
  In your own secret sins and terrors!

THE WARDEN OF THE CINQUE PORTS*

A mist was driving down the British Channel,
  The day was just begun,
And through the window-panes, on floor and panel,
  Streamed the red autumn sun.

It glanced on flowing flag and rippling pennon,
  And the white sails of ships;
And, from the frowning rampart, the black cannon
  Hailed it with feverish lips.

Sandwich and Romney, Hastings, Hithe, and Dover
  Were all alert that day,
To see the French war-steamers speeding over,
  When the fog cleared away.

Sullen and silent, and like couchant lions,
  Their cannon, through the night,
Holding their breath, had watched, in grim defiance,
  The sea-coast opposite.

* On the death of the Duke of Wellington.

And now they roared at drum-beat from their stations
  On every citadel;
Each answering each, with morning salutations,
  That all was well.

And down the coast, all taking up the burden,
  Replied the distant forts,
As if to summon from his sleep the Warden
  And Lord of the Cinque Ports.

Him shall no sunshine from the fields of azure,
  No drum-beat from the wall,
No morning gun from the black fort's embrasure,
  Awaken with its call!

No more, surveying with an eye impartial
  The long line of the coast,
Shall the gaunt figure of the old Field Marshal
  Be seen upon his post!

For in the night, unseen, a single warrior,
  In sombre harness mailed,
Dreaded of man, and surnamed the Destroyer,
  The rampart wall had scaled.

He passed into the chamber of the sleeper,
  The dark and silent room,
And as he entered, darker grew, and deeper,
  The silence and the gloom.

He did not pause to parley or dissemble,
  But smote the Warden hoar;
Ah! what a blow! that made all England tremble
  And groan from shore to shore.

Meanwhile, without, the surly cannon waited,
  The sun rose bright o'erhead;
Nothing in Nature's aspect intimated
  That a great man was dead.

THE JEWISH CEMETERY AT NEWPORT

How strange it seems! These Hebrews in their graves,
  Close by the street of this fair seaport town,
Silent beside the never-silent waves,
  At rest in all this moving up and down!

The trees are white with dust, that o'er their sleep
  Wave their broad curtains in the south-wind's breath,
While underneath these leafy tents they keep
  The long, mysterious Exodus of Death.

And these sepulchral stones, so old and brown,
  That pave with level flags their burial-place,
Seem like the tablets of the Law, thrown down
  And broken by Moses at the mountain's base.

The very names recorded here are strange,
  Of foreign accent, and of different climes;
Alvares and Rivera interchange
  With Abraham and Jacob of old times.

"Blessed be God, for he created Death!"
  The mourners said, "and Death is rest and peace";
Then added, in the certainty of faith,
  "And giveth Life that nevermore shall cease."

Closed are the portals of their Synagogue,
    No Psalms of David now the silence break,
No Rabbi reads the ancient Decalogue
    In the grand dialect the Prophets spake.

Gone are the living, but the dead remain,
    And not neglected; for a hand unseen,
Scattering its bounty, like a summer rain,
    Still keeps their graves and their remembrance green.

How came they here? What burst of Christian hate,
    What persecution, merciless and blind,
Drove o'er the sea—that desert desolate—
    These Ishmaels and Hagars of mankind?

They lived in narrow streets and lanes obscure,
    Ghetto and Judenstrass, in mirk and mire;
Taught in the school of patience to endure
    The life of anguish and the death of fire.

All their lives long, with the unleavened bread
    And bitter herbs of exile and its fears,
The wasting famine of the heart they fed,
    And slaked its thirst with marah of their tears.

Anathema maranatha! was the cry
    That rang from town to town, from street to street;
At every gate the accursed Mordecai
    Was mocked and jeered, and spurned by Christian feet.

Pride and humiliation hand in hand
    Walked with them through the world where'er they went;
Trampled and beaten were they as the sand,
    And yet unshaken as the continent.

For in the background figures vague and vast
  Of patriarchs and of prophets rose sublime,
And all the great traditions of the Past
  They saw reflected in the coming time.

And thus forever with reverted look
  The mystic volume of the world they read,
Spelling it backward, like a Hebrew book,
  Till life became a Legend of the Dead.

But ah! what once has been shall be no more!
  The groaning earth in travail and in pain
Brings forth its races, but does not restore,
  And the dead nations never rise again.

THE GOLDEN MILE-STONE

  Leafless are the trees; their purple branches
  Spread themselves abroad, like reefs of coral,
      Rising silent
  In the Red Sea of the winter sunset.

  From the hundred chimneys of the village,
  Like the Afreet in the Arabian story,
      Smoky columns
  Tower aloft into the air of amber.

  At the window winks the flickering firelight;
  Here and there the lamps of evening glimmer,
      Social watch-fires
  Answering one another through the darkness.

On the hearth the lighted logs are glowing,
And like Ariel in the cloven pine-tree
    For its freedom
Groans and sighs the air imprisoned in them.

By the fireside there are old men seated,
Seeing ruined cities in the ashes,
    Asking sadly
Of the Past what it can ne'er restore them.

By the fireside there are youthful dreamers,
Building castles fair, with stately stairways,
    Asking blindly
Of the Future what it cannot give them.

By the fireside tragedies are acted
In whose scenes appear two actors only,
    Wife and husband,
And above them God the sole spectator.

By the fireside there are peace and comfort,
Wives and children, with fair, thoughtful faces,
    Waiting, watching
For a well-known footstep in the passage.

Each man's chimney is his Golden Mile-stone;
Is the central point, from which he measures
    Every distance
Through the gateways of the world around him.

In his farthest wanderings still he sees it;
Hears the talking flame, the answering night-wind,
    As he heard them
When he sat with those who were, but are not.

Happy he whom neither wealth nor fashion,
Nor the march of the encroaching city,
      Drives an exile
From the hearth of his ancestral homestead.

We may build more splendid habitations,
Fill our rooms with paintings and with sculptures,
      But we cannot
Buy with gold the old associations!

· MY LOST YOUTH

Often I think of the beautiful town
   That is seated by the sea;
Often in thought go up and down
The pleasant streets of that dear old town,
   And my youth comes back to me.
     And a verse of a Lapland song
     Is haunting my memory still:
     "A boy's will is the wind's will,
And the thoughts of youth are long, long thoughts."

I can see the shadowy lines of its trees,
   And catch, in sudden gleams,
The sheen of the far-surrounding seas,
And islands that were the Hesperides
   Of all my boyish dreams.
     And the burden of that old song,
     It murmurs and whispers still:
     "A boy's will is the wind's will,
And the thoughts of youth are long, long thoughts."

I remember the black wharves and the slips,
   And the sea-tides tossing free;
And Spanish sailors with bearded lips,
And the beauty and mystery of the ships,
   And the magic of the sea.
      And the voice of that wayward song
      Is singing and saying still:
      "A boy's will is the wind's will,
And the thoughts of youth are long, long thoughts."

I remember the bulwarks by the shore,
   And the fort upon the hill;
The sunrise gun, with its hollow roar,
The drum-beat repeated o'er and o'er,
   And the bugle wild and shrill.
      And the music of that old song
      Throbs in my memory still:
      "A boy's will is the wind's will,
And the thoughts of youth are long, long thoughts."

I remember the sea-fight far away,
   How it thundered o'er the tide!
And the dead captains, as they lay
In their graves, o'erlooking the tranquil bay
   Where they in battle died.
      And the sound of that mournful song
      Goes through me with a thrill:
      "A boy's will is the wind's will,
And the thoughts of youth are long, long thoughts."

I can see the breezy dome of groves,
   The shadows of Deering's Woods;
And the friendships old and the early loves
Come back with a Sabbath sound, as of doves
   In quiet neighborhoods.

And the verse of that sweet old song,
  It flutters and murmurs still:
  "A boy's will is the wind's will,
And the thoughts of youth are long, long thoughts."

I remember the gleams and glooms that dart
  Across the school-boy's brain;
The song and the silence in the heart,
That in part are prophecies, and in part
  Are longings wild and vain.
    And the voice of that fitful song
    Sings on, and is never still:
    "A boy's will is the wind's will,
And the thoughts of youth are long, long thoughts."

There are things of which I may not speak;
  There are dreams that cannot die;
There are thoughts that make the strong heart weak,
And bring a pallor into the cheek,
  And a mist before the eye.
    And the words of that fatal song
    Come over me like a chill:
    "A boy's will is the wind's will,
And the thoughts of youth are long, long thoughts."

Strange to me now are the forms I meet
  When I visit the dear old town;
But the native air is pure and sweet,
And the trees that o'ershadow each well-known street,
  As they balance up and down,
    Are singing the beautiful song,
    Are sighing and whispering still:
    "A boy's will is the wind's will,
And the thoughts of youth are long, long thoughts."

And Deering's Woods are fresh and fair,
    And with joy that is almost pain
My heart goes back to wander there,
And among the dreams of the days that were,
    I find my lost youth again.
        And the strange and beautiful song,
        The groves are repeating it still:
        "A boy's will is the wind's will,
And the thoughts of youth are long, long thoughts."

THE CHILDREN'S HOUR

Between the dark and the daylight,
    When the night is beginning to lower,
Comes a pause in the day's occupations,
    That is known as the Children's Hour.

I hear in the chamber above me
    The patter of little feet,
The sound of a door that is opened,
    And voices soft and sweet.

From my study I see in the lamplight,
    Descending the broad hall stair,
Grave Alice, and laughing Allegra,
    And Edith with golden hair.

A whisper, and then a silence:
    Yet I know by their merry eyes
They are plotting and planning together
    To take me by surprise.

A sudden rush from the stairway,
　A sudden raid from the hall!
By three doors left unguarded
　They enter my castle wall!

They climb up into my turret
　O'er the arms and back of my chair;
If I try to escape, they surround me;
　They seem to be everywhere.

They almost devour me with kisses,
　Their arms about me entwine,
Till I think of the Bishop of Bingen
　In his Mouse-Tower on the Rhine!

Do you think, O blue-eyed banditti,
　Because you have scaled the wall,
Such an old mustache as I am
　Is not a match for you all!

I have you fast in my fortress,
　And will not let you depart,
But put you down into the dungeon
　In the round-tower of my heart.

And there will I keep you forever,
　Yes, forever and a day,
Till the walls shall crumble to ruin,
　And moulder in dust away!

SNOW–FLAKES

Out of the bosom of the Air,
  Out of the cloud-folds of her garments shaken,
Over the woodlands brown and bare,
  Over the harvest-fields forsaken,
    Silent, and soft, and slow
    Descends the snow.

Even as our cloudy fancies take
  Suddenly shape in some divine expression,
Even as the troubled heart doth make
  In the white countenance confession,
    The troubled sky reveals
    The grief it feels.

This is the poem of the air,
  Slowly in silent syllables recorded;
This is the secret of despair,
  Long in its cloudy bosom hoarded,
    Now whispered and revealed
    To wood and field.

From TALES OF A WAYSIDE INN

THE LANDLORD'S TALE

PAUL REVERE'S RIDE

Listen, my children, and you shall hear
Of the midnight ride of Paul Revere,
On the eighteenth of April, in Seventy-five;
Hardly a man is now alive
Who remembers that famous day and year.

He said to his friend, "If the British march
By land or sea from the town to-night,
Hang a lantern aloft in the belfry arch
Of the North Church tower as a signal light,—
One, if by land, and two, if by sea;
And I on the opposite shore will be,
Ready to ride and spread the alarm
Through every Middlesex village and farm,
For the country folk to be up and to arm."

Then he said, "Good night!" and with muffled oar
Silently rowed to the Charlestown shore,
Just as the moon rose over the bay,
Where swinging wide at her moorings lay
The Somerset, British man-of-war;
A phantom ship, with each mast and spar
Across the moon like a prison bar,
And a huge black hulk, that was magnified
By its own reflection in the tide.

Meanwhile, his friend, through alley and street,
Wanders and watches with eager ears,
Till in the silence around him he hears
The muster of men at the barrack door,
The sound of arms, and the tramp of feet,
And the measured tread of the grenadiers,
Marching down to their boats on the shore.

Then he climbed the tower of the Old North Church,
By the wooden stairs, with stealthy tread,
To the belfry-chamber overhead,
And startled the pigeons from their perch
On the sombre rafters, that round him made
Masses and moving shapes of shade,—
By the trembling ladder, steep and tall,

To the highest window in the wall,
Where he paused to listen and look down
A moment on the roofs of the town,
And the moonlight flowing over all.

Beneath, in the churchyard, lay the dead,
In their night-encampment on the hill,
Wrapped in silence so deep and still
That he could hear, like a sentinel's tread,
The watchful night-wind, as it went
Creeping along from tent to tent,
And seeming to whisper, "All is well!"
A moment only he feels the spell
Of the place and the hour, and the secret dread
Of the lonely belfry and the dead;
For suddenly all his thoughts are bent
On a shadowy something far away,
Where the river widens to meet the bay,—
A line of black that bends and floats
On the rising tide, like a bridge of boats.

Meanwhile, impatient to mount and ride,
Booted and spurred, with a heavy stride
On the opposite shore walked Paul Revere.
Now he patted his horse's side,
Now gazed at the landscape far and near,
Then, impetuous, stamped the earth,
And turned and tightened his saddle-girth;
But mostly he watched with eager search
The belfry-tower of the Old North Church,
As it rose above the graves on the hill,
Lonely and spectral and sombre and still.
And lo! as he looks, on the belfry's height
A glimmer, and then a gleam of light!
He springs to the saddle, the bridle he turns,

But lingers and gazes, till full on his sight
A second lamp in the belfry burns!

A hurry of hoofs in a village street,
A shape in the moonlight, a bulk in the dark,
And beneath, from the pebbles, in passing, a spark
Struck out by a steed flying fearless and fleet:
That was all! And yet, through the gloom and the light,
The fate of a nation was riding that night;
And the spark struck out by that steed, in his flight,
Kindled the land into flame with its heat.

He has left the village and mounted the steep,
And beneath him, tranquil and broad and deep,
Is the Mystic, meeting the ocean tides;
And under the alders that skirt its edge,
Now soft on the sand, now loud on the ledge,
Is heard the tramp of his steed as he rides.

It was twelve by the village clock,
When he crossed the bridge into Medford town.
He heard the crowing of the cock,
And the barking of the farmer's dog,
And felt the damp of the river fog,
That rises after the sun goes down.

It was one by the village clock,
When he galloped into Lexington.
He saw the gilded weathercock
Swim in the moonlight as he passed,
And the meeting-house windows, blank and bare,
Gaze at him with a spectral glare,
As if they already stood aghast
At the bloody work they would look upon.

It was two by the village clock,
When he came to the bridge in Concord town.
He heard the bleating of the flock,
And the twitter of birds among the trees,
And felt the breath of the morning breeze
Blowing over the meadows brown.
And one was safe and asleep in his bed
Who at the bridge would be first to fall,
Who that day would be lying dead,
Pierced by a British musket-ball.

You know the rest. In the books you have read,
How the British Regulars fired and fled,—
How the farmers gave them ball for ball,
From behind each fence and farm-yard wall,
Chasing the red-coats down the lane,
Then crossing the fields to emerge again
Under the trees at the turn of the road,
And only pausng to fire and load.

So through the night rode Paul Revere;
And so through the night went his cry of alarm
To every Middlesex village and farm,—
A cry of defiance and not of fear,
A voice in the darkness, a knock at the door,
And a word that shall echo forevermore!
For, borne on the night-wind of the Past,
Through all our history, to the last,
In the hour of darkness and peril and need,
The people will waken and listen to hear
The hurrying hoof-beats of that steed,
And the midnight message of Paul Revere.

INTERLUDE

And then the blue-eyed Norseman told
A Saga of the days of old.
"There is," said he, "a wondrous book
Of Legends in the old Norse tongue,
Of the dead kings of Norroway,—
Legends that once were told or sung
In many a smoky fireside nook
Of Iceland, in the ancient day,
By wandering Saga-man or Scald;
'Heimskringla' is the volume called;
And he who looks may find therein
The story that I now begin."

And in each pause the story made
Upon his violin he played,
As an appropriate interlude,
Fragments of old Norwegian tunes
That bound in one the separate runes,
And held the mind in perfect mood,
Entwining and encircling all
The strange and antiquated rhymes
With melodies of olden times;
As over some half-ruined wall,
Disjointed and about to fall,
Fresh woodbines climb and interlace,
And keep the loosened stones in place.

THE MUSICIAN'S TALE

THE SAGA OF KING OLAF

I

THE CHALLENGE OF THOR

I am the God Thor,
I am the War God,
I am the Thunderer!
Here in my Northland,
My fastness and fortress,
Reign I forever!

Here amid icebergs
Rule I the nations;
This is my hammer,
Miölner the mighty;
Giants and sorcerers
Cannot withstand it!

These are the gauntlets
Wherewith I wield it,
And hurl it afar off;
This is my girdle;
Whenever I brace it,
Strength is redoubled!

The light thou beholdest
Stream through the heavens,
In flashes of crimson,
Is but my red beard
Blown by the night-wind,
Affrighting the nations!

Jove is my brother;
Mine eyes are the lightning;
The wheels of my chariot
Roll in the thunder,
The blows of my hammer
Ring in the earthquake!

Force rules the world still,
Has ruled it, shall rule it;
Meekness is weakness,
Strength is triumphant,
Over the whole earth
Still is it Thor's-Day!

Thou art a God too,
O Galilean!
And thus single-handed
Unto the combat,
Gauntlet or Gospel,
Here I defy thee!

II

KING OLAF'S RETURN

And King Olaf heard the cry,
Saw the red light in the sky,
    Laid his hand upon his sword,
As he leaned upon the railing,
And his ships went sailing, sailing
    Northward into Drontheim fiord.

There he stood as one who dreamed;
And the red light glanced and gleamed
    On the armor that he wore;

And he shouted, as the rifted
Streamers o'er him shook and shifted,
  "I accept thy challenge, Thor!"

To avenge his father slain,
And reconquer realm and reign,
  Came the youthful Olaf home,
Through the midnight sailing, sailing,
Listening to the wild wind's wailing,
  And the dashing of the foam.

To his thoughts the sacred name
Of his mother Astrid came,
  And the tale she oft had told
Of her flight by secret passes
Through the mountains and morasses,
  To the home of Hakon old.

Then strange memories crowded back
Of Queen Gunhild's wrath and wrack,
  And a hurried flight by sea;
Of grim Vikings, and the rapture
Of the sea-fight, and the capture,
  And the life of slavery.

How a stranger watched his face
In the Esthonian market-place,
  Scanned his features one by one,
Saying, "We should know each other;
I am Sigurd, Astrid's brother,
  Thou art Olaf, Astrid's son!"

Then as Queen Allogia's page,
Old in honors, young in age,
  Chief of all her men-at-arms;

Till vague whispers, and mysterious,
Reached King Valdemar, the imperious,
  Filling him with strange alarms.

Then his cruisings o'er the seas,
Westward to the Hebrides
  And to Scilly's rocky shore;
And the hermit's cavern dismal,
Christ's great name and rites baptismal
  In the ocean's rush and roar.

All these thoughts of love and strife
Glimmered through his lurid life,
  As the stars' intenser light
Through the red flames o'er him trailing,
As his ships went sailing, sailing
  Northward in the summer night.

Trained for either camp or court,
Skilful in each manly sport,
  Young and beautiful and tall;
Art of warfare, craft of chases,
Swimming, skating, snow-shoe races,
  Excellent alike in all.

When at sea, with all his rowers,
He along the bending oars
  Outside of his ship could run.
He the Smalsor Horn ascended,
And his shining shield suspended
  On its summit, like a sun.

On the ship-rails he could stand,
Wield his sword with either hand,
  And at once two javelins throw;

At all feasts where ale was strongest
Sat the merry monarch longest,
  First to come and last to go.

Norway never yet had seen
One so beautiful of mien,
  One so royal in attire,
When in arms completely furnished,
Harness gold-inlaid and burnished,
  Mantle like a flame of fire.

Thus came Olaf to his own,
When upon the night-wind blown
  Passed that cry along the shore;
And he answered, while the rifted
Streamers o'er him shook and shifted,
  "I accept thy challenge, Thor!"

III

THORA OF RIMOL

"Thora of Rimol! hide me! hide me!
Danger and shame and death betide me!
For Olaf the King is hunting me down
Through field and forest, through thorp and town!"
  Thus cried Jarl Hakon
  To Thora, the fairest of women.

"Hakon Jarl! for the love I bear thee
Neither shall shame nor death come near thee!
But the hiding-place wherein thou must lie
Is the cave underneath the swine in the sty."
  Thus to Jarl Hakon
  Said Thora, the fariest of women.

So Hakon Jarl and his base thrall Karker
Crouched in the cave, than a dungeon darker,
As Olaf came riding, with men in mail,
Through the forest roads into Orkadale,
  Demanding Jarl Hakon
  Of Thora, the fairest of women.

"Rich and honored shall be whoever
The head of Hakon Jarl shall dissever!"
Hakon heard him, and Karker the slave,
Through the breathing-holes of the darksome cave.
  Alone in her chamber
  Wept Thora, the fairest of women.

Said Karker, the crafty, "I will not slay thee!
For all the king's gold I will never betray thee!"
"Then why dost thou turn so pale, O churl,
And then again black as the earth?" said the Earl.
  More pale and more faithful
  Was Thora, the fairest of women.

From a dream in the night the thrall started, saying,
"Round my neck a gold ring King Olaf was laying!"
And Hakon answered, "Beware of the king!
He will lay round thy neck a blood-red ring."
  At the ring on her finger
  Gazed Thora, the fairest of women.

At daybreak slept Hakon, with sorrows encumbered,
But screamed and drew up his feet as he slumbered;
The thrall in the darkness plunged with his knife,
And the Earl awakened no more in this life.
  But wakeful and weeping
  Sat Thora, the fairest of women.

At Nidarholm the priests are all singing,
Two ghastly heads on the gibbet are swinging;
One is Jarl Hakon's and one is his thrall's,
And the people are shouting from windows and walls;
    While alone in her chamber
    Swoons Thora, the fairest of women.

IV

QUEEN SIGRID THE HAUGHTY

Queen Sigrid the Haughty sat proud and aloft
In her chamber, that looked over meadow and croft.
    Heart's dearest,
    Why dost thou sorrow so?

The floor with tassels of fir was besprent,
Filling the room with their fragrant scent.

She heard the birds sing, she saw the sun shine,
The air of summer was sweeter than wine.

Like a sword without scabbard the bright river lay
Between her own kingdom and Norroway.

But Olaf the King had sued for her hand,
The sword would be sheathed, the river be spanned.

Her maidens were seated around her knee,
Working bright figures in tapestry.

And one was singing the ancient rune
Of Brynhilda's love and the wrath of Gudrun.

And through it, and round it, and over it all
Sounded incessant the waterfall.

The Queen in her hand held a ring of gold,
From the door of Ladé's Temple old.

King Olaf had sent her this wedding gift,
But her thoughts as arrows were keen and swift.

She had given the ring to her goldsmiths twain,
Who smiled, as they handed it back again.

And Sigrid the Queen, in her haughty way,
Said, "Why do you smile, my goldsmiths, say?"

And they answered: "O Queen! if the truth must be told,
The ring is of copper, and not of gold!"

The lightning flashed o'er her forehead and cheek,
She only murmured, she did not speak:

"If in his gifts he can faithless be,
There will be no gold in his love to me."

A footstep was heard on the outer stair,
And in strode King Olaf with royal air.

He kissed the Queen's hand, and he whispered of love,
And swore to be true as the stars are above.

But she smiled with contempt as she answered: "O King,
Will you swear it, as Odin once swore, on the ring?"

And the King: "Oh speak not of Odin to me,
The wife of King Olaf a Christian must be."

Looking straight at the King, with her level brows,
She said, "I keep true to my faith and my vows."

Then the face of King Olaf was darkened with gloom,
He rose in his anger and strode through the room.

"Why, then, should I care to have thee?" he said,—
"A faded old woman, a heathenish jade!"

His zeal was stronger than fear or love,
And he struck the Queen in the face with his glove.

Then forth from the chamber in anger he fled,
And the wooden stairway shook with his tread.

Queen Sigrid the Haughty said under her breath,
"This insult, King Olaf, shall be thy death!"
  Heart's dearest,
  Why dost thou sorrow so?

V

THE SKERRY OF SHRIEKS

Now from all King Olaf's farms
  His men-at-arms
Gathered on the Eve of Easter;
To his house at Angvalds-ness
  Fast they press,
Drinking with the royal feaster.

Loudly through the wide-flung door
  Came the roar
Of the sea upon the Skerry;
And its thunder loud and near
  Reached the ear,
Mingling with their voices merry.

"Hark!" said Olaf to his Scald,
  Halfred the Bald,
"Listen to that song, and learn it!
Half my kingdom would I give,
  As I live,
If by such songs you would earn it!

"For of all the runes and rhymes
  Of all times,
Best I like the ocean's dirges,
When the old harper heaves and rocks,
  His hoary locks
Flowing and flashing in the surges!"

Halfred answered: "I am called
  The Unappalled!
Nothing hinders me or daunts me.
Hearken to me, then, O King,
  While I sing
The great Ocean Song that haunts me."

"I will hear your song sublime
  Some other time,"
Says the drowsy monarch, yawning,
And retires; each laughing guest
  Applauds the jest;
Then they sleep till day is dawning.

Pacing up and down the yard,
  King Olaf's guard
Saw the sea-mist slowly creeping
O'er the sands, and up the hill,
  Gathering still
Round the house where they were sleeping.

It was not the fog he saw,
  Nor misty flaw,
That above the landscape brooded;
It was Eyvind Kallda's crew
  Of warlocks blue
With their caps of darkness hooded!

Round and round the house they go,
  Weaving slow
Magic circles to encumber
And imprison in their ring
  Olaf the King,
As he helpless lies in slumber.

Then athwart the vapors dun
  The Easter sun
Streamed with one broad track of splendor!
In their real forms appeared
  The warlocks weird,
Awful as the Witch of Endor.

Blinded by the light that glared,
  They groped and stared,
Round about with steps unsteady;
From his window Olaf gazed,
  And, amazed,
"Who are these strange people?" said he.

"Eyvind Kallda and his men!"
  Answered then
From the yard a sturdy farmer;
While the men-at-arms apace
  Filled the place,
Busily buckling on their armor.

From the gates they sallied forth,
　South and north,
Scoured the island coast around them,
Seizing all the warlock band,
　Foot and hand
On the Skerry's rocks they bound them.

And at eve the king again
　Called his train,
And, with all the candles burning,
Silent sat and heard once more
　The sullen roar
Of the ocean tides returning.

Shrieks and cries of wild despair
　Filled the air,
Growing fainter as they listened;
Then the bursting surge alone
　Sounded on;—
Thus the sorcerers were christened!

"Sing O Scald, your song sublime,
　Your ocean-rhyme,"
Cried King Olaf: "it will cheer me!"
Said the Scald, with pallid cheeks,
　"The Skerry of Shrieks
Sings too loud for you to hear me!"

VI

THE WRATH OF ODIN

The guests were loud, the ale was strong,
King Olaf feasted late and long;
The hoary Scalds together sang;

O'erhead the smoky rafters rang.
    Dead rides Sir Morten of Fogelsang.

The door swung wide, with creak and din;
A blast of cold night-air came in,
And on the threshold shivering stood
A one-eyed guest, with cloak and hood.
    Dead rides Sir Morten of Fogelsang.

The King exclaimed, "O graybeard pale!
Come warm thee with this cup of ale."
The foaming draught the old man quaffed,
The noisy guests looked on and laughed.
    Dead rides Sir Morten of Fogelsang.

Then spake the King: "Be not afraid:
Sit here by me." The guest obeyed,
And, seated at the table, told
Tales of the sea, and Sagas old.
    Dead rides Sir Morten of Fogelsang.

And ever, when the tale was o'er,
The King demanded yet one more;
Till Sigurd the Bishop smiling said,
" 'Tis late, O King, and time for bed."
    Dead rides Sir Morten of Fogelsang.

The King retired; the stranger guest
Followed and entered with the rest;
The lights were out, the pages gone,
But still the garrulous guest spake on.
    Dead rides Sir Morten of Fogelsang.

As one who from a volume reads,
He spake of heroes and their deeds,

Of lands and cities he had seen,
And stormy gulfs that tossed between.
  Dead rides Sir Morten of Fogelsang.

Then from his lips in music rolled
The Havamal of Odin old,
With sounds mysterious as the roar
Of billows on a distant shore.
  Dead rides Sir Morten of Fogelsang.

"Do we not learn from runes and rhymes
Made by the gods in elder times,
And do not still the great Scalds teach
That silence better is than speech?"
  Dead rides Sir Morten of Fogelsang.

Smiling at this, the King replied,
"Thy lore is by thy tongue belied;
For never was I so enthralled
Either by Saga-man or Scald."
  Dead rides Sir Morten of Fogelsang.

The Bishop said, "Late hours we keep!
Night wanes, O King! 'tis time for sleep!"
Then slept the King, and when he woke
The guest was gone, the morning broke.
  Dead rides Sir Morten of Fogelsang.

They found the doors securely barred,
They found the watch-dog in the yard,
There was no footprint in the grass,
And none had seen the stranger pass.
  Dead rides Sir Morten of Fogelsang.

King Olaf crossed himself and said:
"I know that Odin the Great is dead;
Sure is the triumph of our Faith,
The one-eyed stranger was his wraith."
  Dead rides Sir Morten of Fogelsang.

VII

IRON-BEARD

Olaf the King, one summer morn,
  Blew a blast on his bugle-horn,
Sending his signal through the land of Drontheim.

And to the Hus-Ting held at Mere
  Gathered the farmers far and near,
With their war weapons ready to confront him.

Ploughing under the morning star,
  Old Iron-Beard in Yriar
Heard the summons, chuckling with a low laugh.

He wiped the sweat-drops from his brow,
  Unharnessed his horses from the plough,
And clattering came on horseback to King Olaf.

He was the churliest of the churls;
  Little he cared for king or earls;
Bitter as home-brewed ale were his foaming passions.

Hodden-gray was the garb he wore,
  And by the Hammer of Thor he swore;
He hated the narrow town, and all its fashions.

But he loved the freedom of his farm,
His ale at night, by the fireside warm,
Gudrun his daughter, with her flaxen tresses.

He loved his horses and his herds,
The smell of the earth, and the song of birds,
His well-filled barns, his brook with its watercresses.

Huge and cumbersome was his frame;
His beard, from which he took his name,
Frosty and fierce, like that of Hymer the Giant.

So at the Hus-Ting he appeared,
The farmer of Yriar, Iron-Beard,
On horseback, in an attitude defiant.

And to King Olaf he cried aloud,
Out of the middle of the crowd,
That tossed about him like a stormy ocean:

"Such sacrifices shalt thou bring
To Odin and to Thor, O King,
As other kings have done in their devotion!"

King Olaf answered: "I command
This land to be a Christian land;
Here is my Bishop who the folk baptizes!

"But if you ask me to restore
Your sacrifices, stained with gore,
Then will I offer human sacrifices!

"Not slaves and peasants shall they be,
But men of note and high degree,
Such men as Orm of Lyra and Kar of Gryting!"

Then to their Temple strode he in,
And loud behind him heard the din
Of his men-at-arms and the peasants fiercely fighting.

There in the Temple, carved in wood,
The image of great Odin stood,
And other gods, with Thor supreme among them.

King Olaf smote them with the blade
Of his huge war-axe, gold inlaid,
And downward shattered to the pavement flung them.

At the same moment rose without,
From the contending crowd, a shout,
A mingled sound of triumph and of wailing.

And there upon the trampled plain
The farmer Iron-Beard lay slain,
Midway between the assailed and the assailing.

King Olaf from the doorway spoke:
"Choose ye between two things, my folk,
To be baptized or given up to slaughter!"

And seeing their leader stark and dead,
The people with a murmur said,
"O King, baptize use with thy holy water."

So all the Drontheim land became
A Christian land in name and fame,
In the old gods no more believing and trusting.

And as a blood-atonement, soon
King Olaf wed the fair Gudrun;
And thus in peace ended the Drontheim Hus-Ting!

VIII

GUDRUN

On King Olaf's bridal night
Shines the moon with tender light,
And across the chamber streams
   Its tide of dreams.

At the fatal midnight hour,
When all evil things have power,
In the glimmer of the moon
   Stands Gudrun.

Close against her heaving breast
Something in her hand is pressed;
Like an icicle, its sheen
   Is cold and keen.

On the cairn are fixed her eyes
Where her murdered father lies,
And a voice remote and drear
   She seems to hear.

What a bridal night is this!
Cold will be the dagger's kiss;
Laden with the chill of death
   Is its breath.

Like the drifting snow she sweeps
To the couch where Olaf sleeps;
Suddenly he wakes and stirs,
   His eyes meet hers.

"What is that," King Olaf said,
"Gleams so bright above my head?

Wherefore standest thou so white
  In pale moonlight?"

" 'Tis the bodkin that I wear
When at night I bind my hair;
It woke me falling on the floor;
  'Tis nothing more."

"Forests have ears, and fields have eyes;
Often treachery lurking lies
Underneath the fairest hair!
  Gudrun beware!"

Ere the earliest peep of morn
Blew King Olaf's bugle-horn;
And forever sundered ride
  Bridegroom and bride!

IX

THANGBRAND THE PRIEST

Short of stature, large of limb,
  Burly face and russet beard,
All the women stared at him,
  When in Iceland he appeared.
    "Look!" they said,
    With nodding head,
"There goes Thangbrand, Olaf's Priest."

All the prayers he knew by rote,
  He could preach like Chrysostome,
From the Fathers he could quote,
  He had even been at Rome.
    A learned clerk,

A man of mark,
Was this Thangbrand, Olaf's Priest.

He was quarrelsome and loud,
  And impatient of control,
Boisterous in the market crowd,
  Boisterous at the wassail-bowl,
    Everywhere
    Would drink and swear,
Swaggering Thangbrand, Olaf's Priest.

In his house this malcontent
  Could the King no longer bear,
So to Iceland he was sent
  To convert the heathen there,
    And away
    One summer day
Sailed this Thangbrand, Olaf's Priest.

There in Iceland, o'er their books
  Pored the people day and night,
But he did not like their looks,
  Nor the songs they used to write.
    "All this rhyme
    Is waste of time!"
Grumbled Thangbrand, Olaf's Priest.

To the alehouse, where he sat,
  Came the Scalds and Saga-men;
Is it to be wondered at
  That they quarrelled now and then,
    When o'er his beer
    Began to leer
Drunken Thangbrand, Olaf's Priest?

All the folk in Altafiord
   Boasted of their island grand;
Saying in a single word,
   "Iceland is the finest land
      That the sun
      Doth shine upon!"
Loud laughed Thangbrand, Olaf's Priest.

And he answered: "What's the use
   Of this bragging up and down,
When three women and one goose
   Make a market in your town!"
      Every Scald
      Satires drawled
On poor Thangbrand, Olaf's Priest.

Something worse they did than that;
   And what vexed him most of all
Was a figure in shovel hat,
   Drawn in charcoal on the wall;
      With words that go
      Sprawling below,
"This is Thangbrand, Olaf's Priest."

Hardly knowing what he did,
   Then he smote them might and main,
Thorvald Veile and Veterlid
   Lay there in the alehouse slain.
      "To-day we are gold,
      To-morrow mould!"
Muttered Thangbrand, Olaf's Priest.

Much in fear of axe and rope,
   Back to Norway sailed he then.
"O King Olaf! little hope

Is there of these Iceland men!"
   Meekly said,
    With bending head,
Pious Thangbrand, Olaf's Priest.

X

RAUD THE STRONG

"All the old gods are dead,
All the wild warlocks fled;
But the White Christ lives and reigns,
And throughout my wide domains
His Gospel shall be spread!"
   On the Evangelists
   Thus swore King Olaf.

But still in dreams of the night
Beheld he the crimson light,
And heard the voice that defied
Him who was crucified,
And challenged him to the fight.
   To Sigurd the Bishop
   King Olaf confessed it.

And Sigurd the Bishop said,
"The old gods are not dead,
For the great Thor still reigns,
And among the Jarls and Thanes
The old witchcraft still is spread."
   Thus to King Olaf
   Said Sigurd the Bishop.

"Far north in the Salten Fiord,
By rapine, fire, and sword,

Lives the Viking, Raud the Strong;
All the Godoe Isles belong
To him and his heathen horde."
   Thus went on speaking
   Sigurd the Bishop.

"A warlock, a wizard is he,
And the lord of the wind and the sea;
And whichever way he sails,
He has ever favoring gales,
By his craft in sorcery."
   Here the sign of the cross
   Made devoutly King Olaf.

"With rites that we both abhor,
He worships Odin and Thor;
So it cannot yet be said,
That all the old gods are dead,
And the warlocks are no more,"
   Flushing with anger
   Said Sigurd the Bishop.

Then King Olaf cried aloud:
"I will talk with this mighty Raud,
And along the Salten Fiord
Preach the Gospel with my sword,
Or be brought back in my shroud!"
   So northward from Drontheim
   Sailed King Olaf!

XI

BISHOP SIGURD OF SALTEN FIORD

Loud the angry wind was wailing
As King Olaf's ships came sailing

Northward out of Drontheim haven
  To the mouth of Salten Fiord.

Though the flying sea-spray drenches
Fore and aft the rowers' benches,
Not a single heart is craven
  Of the champions there on board.

All without the Fiord was quiet,
But within it storm and riot,
Such as on his Viking cruises
  Raud the Strong was wont to ride.

And the sea through all its tide-ways
Swept the reeling vessels sideways,
As the leaves are swept through sluices,
  When the flood-gates open wide.

" 'Tis the warlock! 'tis the demon
Raud!" cried Sigurd to the seamen;
"But the Lord is not affrighted
  By the witchcraft of his foes."

To the ship's bow he ascended,
By his choristers attended,
Round him were the tapers lighted,
  And the sacred incense rose.

On the bow stood Bishop Sigurd,
In his robes, as one transfigured,
And the Crucifix he planted
  High amid the rain and mist.

Then with holy water sprinkled
All the ship; the mass-bells tinkled:

Loud the monks around him chanted,
   Loud he read the Evangelist.

As into the Fiord they darted,
On each side the water parted;
Down a path like silver molten
   Steadily rowed King Olaf's ships;

Steadily burned all night the tapers,
And the White Christ through the vapors
Gleamed across the Fiord of Salten,
   As through John's Apocalypse,—

Till at last they reached Raud's dwelling
On the little isle of Gelling;
Not a guard was at the doorway,
   Not a glimmer of light was seen.

But at anchor, carved and gilded,
Lay the dragon-ship he builded;
'Twas the grandest ship in Norway,
   With its crest and scales of green.

Up the stairway, softly creeping,
To the loft where Raud was sleeping,
With their fists they burst asunder
   Bolt and bar that held the door.

Drunken with sleep and ale they found him,
Dragged him from his bed and bound him,
While he stared with stupid wonder
   At the look and garb they wore.

Then King Olaf said: "O Sea-King!
Little time have we for speaking,

Choose between the good and evil;
   Be baptized! or thou shalt die!"

But in scorn the heathen scoffer
Answered: "I disdain thine offer;
Neither fear I God nor Devil;
   Thee and thy Gospel I defy!"

Then between his jaws distended,
When his frantic struggles ended,
Through King Olaf's horn an adder,
   Touched by fire, they forced to glide.

Sharp his tooth was as an arrow,
As he gnawed through bone and marrow;
But without a groan or shudder,
   Raud the Strong blaspheming died.

Then baptized they all that region,
Swarthy Lap and fair Norwegian,
Far as swims the salmon, leaping,
   Up the streams of Salten Fiord.

In their temples Thor and Odin
Lay in dust and ashes trodden,
As King Olaf, onward sweeping,
   Preached the Gospel with his sword.

Then he took the carved and gilded
Dragon-ship that Raud had builded,
And the tiller single-handed
   Grasping, steered into the main.

Southward sailed the sea-gulls o'er him,
Southward sailed the ship that bore him,

Till at Drontheim haven landed
  Olaf and his crew again.

XII

KING OLAF'S CHRISTMAS

At Drontheim, Olaf the King
Heard the bells of Yule-tide ring,
  As he sat in his banquet-hall,
Drinking the nut-brown ale,
With his bearded Berserks hale
  And tall.

Three days his Yule-tide feasts
He held with Bishops and Priests,
  And his horn filled up to the brim;
But the ale was never too strong,
Nor the Saga-man's tale too long,
  For him.

O'er his drinking-horn, the sign
He made of the cross divine,
  As he drank, and muttered his prayers;
But the Berserks evermore
Made the sign of the Hammer of Thor
  Over theirs.

The gleams of the fire-light dance
Upon helmet and hauberk and lance,
  And laugh in the eyes of the King;
And he cries to Halfred the Scald,
Gray-bearded, wrinkled, and bald,
  "Sing!"

"Sing me a song divine,
With a sword in every line,
  And this shall be thy reward."
And he loosened the belt at his waist,
And in front of the singer placed
  His sword.

"Quern-biter of Hakon the Good,
Wherewith at a stroke he hewed
  The millstone through and through,
And Foot-breadth of Thoralf the Strong,
Were neither so broad nor so long,
  Nor so true."

Then the Scald took his harp and sang,
And loud through the music rang
  The sound of that shining word;
And the harp-strings a clangor made,
As if they were struck with the blade
  Of a sword.

And the Berserks round about
Broke forth into a shout
  That made the rafters ring:
They smote with their fists on the board,
And shouted, "Long live the Sword,
  And the King!"

But the King said, "O my son,
I miss the bright word in one
  Of thy measures and thy rhymes."
And Halfred the Scald replied,
"In another 'twas multiplied
  Three times."

Then King Olaf raised the hilt
Of iron, cross-shaped and gilt,
   And said, "Do not refuse;
Count well the gain and the loss,
Thor's hammer or Christ's cross:
   Choose!"

And Halfred the Scald said, "This
In the name of the Lord I kiss,
   Who on it was crucified!"
And a shout went round the board,
"In the name of Christ the Lord,
   Who died!"

Then over the waste of snows
The noonday sun uprose,
   Through the driving mists revealed,
Like the lifting of the Host,
By incense-clouds almost
   Concealed.

On the shining wall a vast
And shadowy cross was cast
   From the hilt of the lifted sword,
And in foaming cups of ale
The Berserks drank "Was-hael!
   To the Lord!"

XIII

THE BUILDING OF THE LONG SERPENT

Thorberg Skafting, master-builder,
   In his ship-yard by the sea,
Whistling, said, "It would bewilder

Any man but Thorberg Skafting,
  Any man but me!"

Near him lay the Dragon stranded,
  Built of old by Raud the Strong,
And King Olaf had commanded
He should build another Dragon,
  Twice as large and long.

Therefore whistled Thorberg Skafting,
  As he sat with half-closed eyes,
And his head turned sideways, drafting
That new vessel for King Olaf
  Twice the Dragon's size.

Round him busily hewed and hammered
  Mallet huge and heavy axe;
Workmen laughed and sang and clamored;
Whirred the wheels, that into rigging
  Spun the shining flax!

All this tumult heard the master,—
  It was music to his ear;
Fancy whispered all the faster,
"Men shall hear of Thorberg Skafting
  For a hundred year!"

Workmen sweating at the forges
  Fashioned iron bolt and bar,
Like a warlock's midnight orgies
Smoked and bubbled the black caldron
  With the boiling tar.

Did the warlocks mingle in it,
  Thorberg Skafting, any curse?

Could you not be gone a minute
But some mischief must be doing,
   Turning bad to worse?

'Twas an ill wind that came wafting
   From his homestead words of woe;
To his farm went Thorberg Skafting,
Oft repeating to his workmen,
   Build ye thus and so.

After long delays returning
   Came the master back by night;
To his ship-yard longing, yearning,
Hurried he, and did not leave it
   Till the morning's light.

"Come and see my ship, my darling!"
   On the morrow said the King;
"Finished now from keel to carling;
Never yet was seen in Norway
   Such a wondrous thing!"

In the ship-yard, idly talking,
   At the ship the workmen stared:
Some one, all their labor balking,
Down her sides had cut deep gashes,
   Not a plank was spared!

"Death be to the evil-doer!"
   With an oath King Olaf spoke;
"But rewards to his pursuer!"
And with wrath his face grew redder
   Than his scarlet cloak.

Straight the master-builder, smiling,
　Answered thus the angry King:
"Cease blaspheming and reviling,
Olaf, it was Thorberg Skafting
　Who has done this thing!"

Then he chipped and smoothed the planking,
　Till the King, delighted, swore,
With much lauding and much thanking,
"Handsomer is now my Dragon
　Than she was before!"

Seventy ells and four extended
　On the grass the vessel's keel;
High above it, gilt and splendid,
Rose the figure-head ferocious
　With its crest of steel.

Then they launched her from the tressels,
　In the ship-yard by the sea;
She was the grandest of all vessels,
Never ship was built in Norway
　Half so fine as she!

The Long Serpent was she christened,
　'Mid the roar of cheer on cheer!
They who to the Saga listened
Heard the name of Thorberg Skafting
　For a hundred year!

XIV

THE CREW OF THE LONG SERPENT

Safe at anchor in Drontheim bay
King Olaf's fleet assembled lay,
　　And, striped with white and blue,
Downward fluttered sail and banner,
As alights the screaming lanner;
Lustily cheered, in their wild manner,
　　The Long Serpent's crew.

Her forecastle man was Ulf the Red;
Like a wolf's was his shaggy head,
　　His teeth as large and white;
His beard, of gray and russet blended,
Round as a swallow's nest descended;
As standard-bearer he defended
　　Olaf's flag in the fight.

Near him Kolbiorn had his place,
Like the King in garb and face,
　　So gallant and so hale;
Every cabin-boy and varlet
Wondered at his cloak of scarlet;
Like a river, frozen and star-lit,
　　Gleamed his coat of mail.

By the bulkhead, tall and dark,
Stood Thrand Rame of Thelemark,
　　A figure gaunt and grand;
On his hairy arm imprinted
Was an anchor, azure-tinted;
Like Thor's hammer, huge and dinted
　　Was his brawny hand.

Einar Tamberskelver, bare
To the winds his golden hair,
   By the mainmast stood;
Graceful was his form, and slender,
And his eyes were deep and tender
As a woman's, in the splendor
   Of her maidenhood.

In the fore-hold Biorn and Bork
Watched the sailors at their work:
   Heavens! how they swore!
Thirty men they each commanded,
Iron-sinewed, horny-handed,
Shoulders broad, and chests expanded,
   Tugging at the oar.

These, and many more like these,
With King Olaf sailed the seas,
   Till the waters vast
Filled them with a vague devotion,
With the freedom and the motion,
With the roll and roar of ocean
   And the sounding blast.

When they landed from the fleet,
How they roared through Drontheim's street,
   Boisterous as the gale!
How they laughed and stamped and pounded,
Till the tavern roof resounded
And the host looked on astounded
   As they drank the ale!

Never saw the wild North Sea
Such a gallant company
   Sail its billows blue!

Never, while they cruised and quarrelled,
Old King Gorm, or Blue-Tooth Harald,
Owned a ship so well apparelled,
    Boasted such a crew!

XV

A LITTLE BIRD IN THE AIR

A little bird in the air
Is singing of Thyri the fair,
    The sister of Svend the Dane;
And the song of the garrulous bird
In the streets of the town is heard,
    And repeated again and again.
        Hoist up your sails of silk,
        And flee away from each other.

To King Burislaf, it is said,
Was the beautiful Thyri wed,
    And a sorrowful bride went she;
And after a week and a day
She has fled away and away
    From his town by the stormy sea.
        Hoist up your sails of silk,
        And flee away from each other.

They say, that through heat and through cold,
Through weald, they say, and through wold,
    By day and by night, they say,
She has fled; and the gossips report
She has come to King Olaf's court,
    And the town is all in dismay.
        Hoist up your sails of silk,
        And flee away from each other.

It is whispered King Olaf has seen,
Has talked with the beautiful Queen;
  And they wonder how it will end;
For surely, if here she remain,
It is war with King Svend the Dane,
  And King Burislaf the Vend!
    Hoist up your sails of silk,
    And flee away from each other.

Oh, greatest wonder of all!
It is published in hamlet and hall,
  It roars like a flame that is fanned!
The King—yes, Olaf the King—
Has wedded her with his ring,
  And Thyri is Queen in the land!
    Hoist up your sails of silk,
    And flee away from each other.

XVI

QUEEN THYRI AND THE ANGELICA STALKS

Northward over Drontheim,
Flew the clamorous sea-gulls,
Sang the lark and linnet
  From the meadows green;

Weeping in her chamber,
Lonely and unhappy,
Sat the Drottning Thyri,
  Sat King Olaf's Queen.

In at all the windows
Streamed the pleasant sunshine,
On the roof above her
  Softly cooed the dove;

But the sound she heard not,
Nor the sunshine heeded,
For the thoughts of Thyri
  Were not thoughts of love.

Then King Olaf entered,
Beautiful as morning,
Like the sun at Easter
  Shone his happy face;

In his hand he carried
Angelicas uprooted,
With delicious fragrance
  Filling all the place.

Like a rainy midnight
Sat the Drottning Thyri,
Even the smile of Olaf
  Could not cheer her gloom;

Nor the stalks he gave her
With a gracious gesture,
And with words as pleasant
  As their own perfume.

In her hands he placed them,
And her jewelled fingers
Through the green leaves glistened
  Like the dews of morn;

But she cast them from her,
Haughty and indignant,
On the floor she threw them
  With a look of scorn.

"Richer presents," said she,
"Gave King Harald Gormson
To the Queen, my mother,
    Than such worthless weeds;

"When he ravaged Norway,
Laying waste the kingdom,
Seizing scatt and treasure
    For her royal needs.

"But thou darest not venture
Through the Sound to Vendland,
My domains to rescue
    From King Burislaf;

"Lest King Svend of Denmark,
Forked Beard, my brother,
Scatter all thy vessels
    As the wind the chaff."

Then up sprang King Olaf,
Like a reindeer bounding,
With an oath he answered
    Thus the luckless Queen:

"Never yet did Olaf
Fear King Svend of Denmark;
This right hand shall hale him
    By his forked chin!"

Then he left the chamber,
Thundering through the doorway,
Loud his steps resounded
    Down the outer stair.

Smarting with the insult,
Through the streets of Drontheim
Strode he red and wrathful,
    With his stately air.

All his ships he gathered,
Summoned all his forces,
Making his war levy
    In the region round.

Down the coast of Norway,
Like a flock of sea-gulls,
Sailed the fleet of Olaf
    Through the Danish Sound.

With his own hand fearless
Steered he the Long Serpent,
Strained the creaking cordage,
    Bent each boom and gaff;

Till in Vendland landing,
The domains of Thyri
He redeemed and rescued
    From King Burislaf.

Then said Olaf, laughing,
"Not ten yoke of oxen
Have the power to draw us
    Like a woman's hair!

"Now will I confess it,
Better things are jewels
Than angelica stalks are
    For a queen to wear."

XVII

KING SVEND OF THE FORKÉD BEARD

Loudly the sailors cheered
Svend of the Forkéd Beard,
As with his fleet he steered
    Southward to Vendland;
Where with their courses hauled
All were together called,
Under the Isle of Svald
    Near to the mainland.

After Queen Gunhild's death,
So the old Saga saith,
Plighted King Svend his faith
    To Sigrid the Haughty;
And to avenge his bride,
Soothing her wounded pride,
Over the waters wide
    King Olaf sought he.

Still on her scornful face,
Blushing with deep disgrace,
Bore she the crimson trace
    Of Olaf's gauntlet;
Like a malignant star,
Blazing in heaven afar,
Red shone the angry scar
    Under her frontlet.

Oft to King Svend she spake,
"For thine own honor's sake
Shalt thou swift vengeance take
    On the vile coward!"

Until the King at last,
Gusty and overcast,
Like a tempestuous blast
   Threatened and lowered.

Soon as the Spring appeared,
Svend of the Forkéd Beard
High his red standard reared,
   Eager for battle;
While every warlike Dane,
Seizing his arms again,
Left all unsown the grain,
   Unhoused the cattle.

Likewise the Swedish King
Summoned in haste a Thing,
Weapons and men to bring
   In aid of Denmark;
Eric the Norseman, too,
As the war-tidings flew,
Sailed with a chosen crew
   From Lapland and Finmark.

So upon Easter day
Sailed the three kings away,
Out of the sheltered bay,
   In the bright season;
With them Earl Sigvald came,
Eager for spoil and fame;
Pity that such a name
   Stooped to such treason!

Safe under Svald at last,
Now were their anchors cast,
Safe from the sea and blast,
   Plotted the three kings;

While, with a base intent,
Southward Earl Sigvald went,
On a foul errand bent,
  Unto the Sea-kings.

Thence to hold on his course
Unto King Olaf's force,
Lying within the hoarse
  Mouths of Stet-haven;
Him to ensnare and bring
Unto the Danish king,
Who his dead corse would fling
  Forth to the raven!

XVIII

KING OLAF AND EARL SIGVALD

On the gray sea-sands
King Olaf stands,
Northward and seaward
He points with his hands.

With eddy and whirl
The sea-tides curl,
Washing the sandals
Of Sigvald the Earl.

The mariners shout,
The ships swing about,
The yards are all hoisted,
The sails flutter out.

The war-horns are played,
The anchors are weighed,

Like moths in the distance
The sails flit and fade.

The sea is like lead,
The harbor lies dead,
As a corse on the sea-shore,
Whose spirit has fled!

On that fatal day,
The histories say,
Seventy vessels
Sailed out of the bay.

But soon scattered wide
O'er the billows they ride,
While Sigvald and Olaf
Sail side by side.

Cried the Earl: "Follow me!
I your pilot will be,
For I know all the channels
Where flows the deep sea!"

So into the strait
Where his foes lie in wait,
Gallant King Olaf
Sails to his fate!

Then the sea-fog veils
The ships and their sails;
Queen Sigrid the Haughty,
Thy vengeance prevails!

XIX

KING OLAF'S WAR-HORNS

"Strike the sails!" King Olaf said;
"Never shall men of mine take flight;
Never away from battle I fled,
Never away from my foes!
  Let God dispose
Of my life in the fight!"

"Sound the horns!" said Olaf the King;
And suddenly through the drifting brume
The blare of the horns began to ring,
Like the terrible trumpet shock
  Of Regnarock,
On the Day of Doom!

Louder and louder the war-horns sang
Over the level floor of the flood;
All the sails came down with a clang,
And there in the midst overheard
  The sun hung red
As a drop of blood.

Drifting down on the Danish fleet
Three together the ships were lashed,
So that neither should turn and retreat;
In the midst, but in front of the rest,
  The burnished crest
Of the Serpent flashed.

King Olaf stood on the quarter-deck,
With bow of ash and arrows of oak,
His gilded shield was without a fleck,

His helmet inlaid with gold,
 And in many a fold
Hung his crimson cloak.

On the forecastle Ulf the Red
Watched the lashing of the ships;
"If the Serpent lie so far ahead,
We shall have hard work of it here,"
 Said he with a sneer
On his bearded lips.

King Olaf laid an arrow on string,
"Have I a coward on board?" said he.
"Shoot it another way, O King!"
Sullenly answered Ulf,
 The old sea-wolf;
"You have need of me!"

In front came Svend, the King of the Danes,
Sweeping down with his fifty rowers;
To the right, the Swedish king with his thanes;
And on board of the Iron Beard
 Earl Eric steered
To the left with his oars.

"These soft Danes and Swedes," said the King,
"At home with their wives had better stay,
Than come within reach of my Serpent's sting:
But where Eric the Norseman leads
 Heroic deeds
Will be done to-day!"

Then as together the vessels crashed,
Eric severed the cables of hide,
With which King Olaf's ships were lashed,

And left them to drive and drift
   With the currents swift
Of the outward tide.

Louder the war-horns growl and snarl,
Sharper the dragons bite and sting!
Eric the son of Hakon Jarl
A death-drink salt as the sea
   Pledges to thee,
Olaf the King!

XX

EINAR TAMBERSKELVER

It was Einar Tamberskelver
   Stood beside the mast;
From his yew-bow, tipped with silver,
   Flew the arrows fast;
Aimed at Eric unavailing,
   As he sat concealed,
Half behind the quarter-railing,
   Half behind his shield.

First an arrow struck the tiller,
   Just above his head;
"Sing, O Eyvind Skaldaspiller,"
   Then Earl Eric said.
"Sing the song of Hakon dying,
   Sing his funeral wail!"
And another arrow flying
   Grazed his coat of mail.

Turning to a Lapland yeoman,
   As the arrow passed,
Said Earl Eric, "Shoot that bowman

Standing by the mast."
Sooner than the word was spoken
    Flew the yeoman's shaft;
Einar's bow in twain was broken,
    Einar only laughed.

"What was that?" said Olaf, standing
    On the quarter-deck.
"Something heard I like the stranding
    Of a shattered wreck."
Einar then, the arrow taking
    From the loosened string,
Answered, "That was Norway breaking
    From thy hand, O King!"

"Thou art but a poor diviner,"
    Straightway Olaf said;
"Take my bow, and swifter, Einar,
    Let thy shafts be sped."
Of his bows the fairest choosing,
    Reached he from above;
Einar saw the blood-drops oozing
    Through his iron glove.

But the bow was thin and narrow;
    At the first assay,
O'er its head he drew the arrow,
    Flung the bow away;
Said, with hot and angry temper
    Flushing in his cheek,
"Olaf! for so great a Kämper
    Are thy bows too weak!"

Then, with smile of joy defiant
    On his beardless lip,

Scaled he, light and self-reliant,
  Eric's dragon-ship.
Loose his golden locks were flowing,
  Bright his armor gleamed;
Like Saint Michael overthrowing
  Lucifer he seemed.

XXI

KING OLAF'S DEATH-DRINK

All day has the battle raged,
All day have the ships engaged,
But not yet is assuaged
  The vengeance of Eric the Earl.

The decks with blood are red,
The arrows of death are sped,
The ships are filled with the dead,
  And the spears the champions hurl.

They drift as wrecks on the tide,
The grappling-irons are plied,
The boarders climb up the side,
  The shouts are feeble and few.

Ah! never shall Norway again
See her sailors come back o'er the main;
They all lie wounded or slain,
  Or asleep in the billows blue!

On the deck stands Olaf the King,
Around him whistle and sing
The spears that the foemen fling,
  And the stones they hurl with their hands.

In the midst of the stones and the spears,
Kolbiorn, the marshal, appears,
His shield in the air he uprears,
    By the side of King Olaf he stands.

Over the slippery wreck
Of the Long Serpent's deck
Sweeps Eric with hardly a check,
    His lips with anger are pale;

He hews with his axe at the mast,
Till it falls, with the sails overcast,
Like a snow-covered pine in the vast
    Dim forests of Orkadale.

Seeking King Olaf then,
He rushes aft with his men,
As a hunter into the den
    Of the bear, when he stands at bay.

"Remember Jarl Hakon!" he cries;
When lo! on his wondering eyes,
Two kingly figures arise,
    Two Olafs in warlike array!

Then Kolbiorn speaks in the ear
Of King Olaf a word of cheer,
In a whisper that none may hear,
    With a smile on his tremulous lip;

Two shields raised high in the air,
Two flashes of golden hair,
Two scarlet meteors' glare,
    And both have leaped from the ship.

Earl Eric's men in the boats
Seize Kolbiorn's shield as it floats,
And cry, from their hairy throats,
   "See! it is Olaf the King!"

While far on the opposite side
Floats another shield on the tide,
Like a jewel set in the wide
   Sea-current's eddying ring.

There is told a wonderful tale,
How the King stripped off his mail,
Like leaves of the brown sea-kale,
   As he swam beneath the main;

But the young grew old and gray,
And never, by night or by day,
In his kingdom of Norroway
   Was King Olaf seen again!

XXII

THE NUN OF NIDAROS

In the convent of Drontheim,
Alone in her chamber
Knelt Astrid the Abbess,
At midnight, adoring,
Beseeching, entreating
The Virgin and Mother.

She heard in the silence
The voice of one speaking,
Without in the darkness,

In gusts of the night-wind,
Now louder, now nearer,
Now lost in the distance.

The voice of a stranger
It seemed as she listened,
Of some one who answered
Beseeching, imploring,
A cry from afar off
She could not distinguish.

The voice of Saint John,
The beloved disciple,
Who wandered and waited
The Master's appearance,
Alone in the darkness,
Unsheltered and friendless.

"It is accepted,
The angry defiance,
The challenge of battle!
It is accepted,
But not with the weapons
Of war that thou wieldest!

"Cross against corselet,
Love against hatred,
Peace-cry for war-cry!
Patience is powerful;
He that o'ercometh
Hath power o'er the nations!

"As torrents in summer,
Half dried in their channels,
Suddenly rise, though the

Sky is still cloudless,
For rain has been falling
Far off at their fountains;

"So hearts that are fainting
Grow full to o'erflowing,
And they that behold it
Marvel, and know not
That God at their fountains
Far off has been raining!

"Stronger than steel
Is the sword of the Spirit;
Swifter than arrows
The light of the truth is,
Greater than anger
Is love, and subdueth!

"Thou art a phantom,
A shape of the sea-mist,
A shape of the brumal
Rain, and the darkness
Fearful and formless;
Day dawns and thou art not!

"The dawn is not distant,
Nor is the night starless;
Love is eternal!
God is still God, and
His faith shall not fail us;
Christ is eternal!"

THE CUMBERLAND

At anchor in Hampton Roads we lay,
  On board of the Cumberland, sloop-of-war;
And at times from the fortress across the bay
    The alarum of drums swept past,
    Or a bugle blast
  From the camp on the shore.

Then far away to the south uprose
  A little feather of snow-white smoke,
And we knew that the iron ship of our foes
    Was steadily steering its course
    To try the force
  Of our ribs of oak.

Down upon us heavily runs,
  Silent and sullen, the floating fort;
Then comes a puff of smoke from her guns,
    And leaps the terrible death,
    With fiery breath,
  From each open port.

We are not idle, but send her straight
  Defiance back in a full broadside!
As hail rebounds from a roof of slate,
    Rebounds our heavier hail
    From each iron scale
  Of the monster's hide.

"Strike your flag!" the rebel cries,
  In his arrogant old plantation strain.
"Never!" our gallant Morris replies;
    "It is better to sink than to yield!"

And the whole air pealed
With the cheers of our men.

Then, like a kraken huge and black,
   She crushed our ribs in her iron grasp!
Down went the Cumberland all a wrack,
     With a sudden shudder of death,
     And the cannon's breath
   For her dying gasp.

Next morn, as the sun rose over the bay,
   Still floated our flag at the mainmast head.
Lord, how beautiful was Thy day!
     Every waft of the air
     Was a whisper of prayer,
   Or a dirge for the dead.

Ho! brave hearts that went down in the seas!
   Ye are at peace in the troubled stream;
Ho! brave land! with hearts like these,
     Thy flag, that is rent in twain,
     Shall be one again,
   And without a seam!

DIVINA COMMEDIA*

I

Oft have I seen at some cathedral door
A laborer, pausing in the dust and heat,
Lay down his burden, and with reverent feet
Enter, and cross himself, and on the floor

* Published with Longfellow's translation of Dante's *Commedia*.

Kneel to repeat his paternoster o'er;
Far off the noises of the world retreat;
The loud vociferations of the street
Become an undistinguishable roar.
So, as I enter here from day to day,
And leave my burden at this minster gate,
Kneeling in prayer, and not ashamed to pray,
The tumult of the time disconsolate
To inarticulate murmurs dies away,
While the eternal ages watch and wait.

II

How strange the sculptures that adorn these towers!
This crowd of statues, in whose folded sleeves
Birds build their nests; while canopied with leaves
Parvis and portal bloom like trellised bowers,
And the vast minster seems a cross of flowers!
But fiends and dragons on the gargoyled eaves
Watch the dead Christ between the living thieves,
And, underneath, the traitor Judas lowers!
Ah! from what agonies of heart and brain,
What exultations trampling on despair,
What tenderness, what tears, what hate of wrong,
What passionate outcry of a soul in pain,
Uprose this poem of the earth and air,
This mediæval miracle of song!

III

I enter, and I see thee in the gloom
Of the long aisles, O poet saturnine!
And strive to make my steps keep pace with thine.
The air is filled with some unknown perfume;
The congregation of the dead make room

For thee to pass; the votive tapers shine;
Like rooks that haunt Ravenna's groves of pine
The hovering echoes fly from tomb to tomb.
From the confessionals I hear arise
Rehearsals of forgotten tragedies,
And lamentations from the crypts below;
And then a voice celestial that begins
With the pathetic words, "Although your sins
As scarlet be," and ends with "as the snow."

IV

With snow-white veil and garments as of flame,
She stands before thee, who so long ago
Filled thy young heart with passion and the woe
From which thy song and all its splendors came;
And while with stern rebuke she speaks thy name,
The ice about thy heart melts as the snow
On mountain heights, and in swift overflow
Comes gushing from thy lips in sobs of shame.
Thou makest full confession; and a gleam,
As of the dawn on some dark forest cast,
Seems on thy lifted forehead to increase;
Lethe and Eunoë—the remembered dream
And the forgotten sorrow—bring at last
That perfect pardon which is perfect peace.

V

I lift mine eyes, and all the windows blaze
With forms of Saints and holy men who died,
Here martyred and hereafter glorified;
And the great Rose upon its leaves displays
Christ's Triumph, and the angelic roundelays,
With splendor upon splendor multiplied;

And Beatrice again at Dante's side
No more rebukes, but smiles her words of praise.
And then the organ sounds, and unseen choirs
Sing the old Latin hymns of peace and love
And benedictions of the Holy Ghost;
And the melodious bells among the spires
O'er all the house-tops and through heaven above
Proclaim the elevation of the Host!

VI

O star of morning and of liberty!
O bringer of the light, whose splendor shines
Above the darkness of the Apennines,
Forerunner of the day that is to be!
The voices of the city and the sea,
The voices of the mountains and the pines,
Repeat thy song, till the familiar lines
Are footpaths for the thought of Italy!
Thy flame is blown abroad from all the heights,
Through all the nations, and a sound is heard,
As of a mighty wind, and men devout,
Strangers of Rome, and the new proselytes,
In their own language hear the wondrous word,
And many are amazed and many doubt.

From THE GOLDEN LEGEND

THE FLIGHT INTO EGYPT *

Here JOSEPH *shall come in, leading an ass,
on which are seated* MARY *and the* CHILD.

MARY

Here will we rest us, under these
O'erhanging branches of the trees,
Where robins chant their Litanies
   And canticles of joy.

JOSEPH

My saddle-girths have given way
With trudging through the heat to-day;
To you I think it is but play
   To ride and hold the boy.

MARY

Hark! how the robins shout and sing,
As if to hail their infant King!
I will alight at yonder spring
   To wash his little coat.

JOSEPH

And I will hobble well the ass,
Lest, being loose upon the grass,
He should escape; for, by the mass,
   He's nimble as a goat.

Here MARY *shall alight and go to the spring.*

* The fifth scene from "The Nativity: A Miracle-Play," which is included
in the second part of *Christus: A Mystery.*

MARY

O Joseph! I am much afraid,
For men are sleeping in the shade;
I fear that we shall be waylaid,
    And robbed and beaten sore!

*Here a band of robbers shall be seen sleeping,
two of whom shall rise and come forward.*

DUMACHUS

Cock's soul! deliver up your gold!

JOSEPH

I pray you, Sirs, let go your hold!
You see that I am weak and old,
    Of wealth I have no store.

DUMACHUS

Give up your money!

TITUS

                        Prithee cease.
Let these people go in peace.

DUMACHUS

First let them pay for their release,
    And then go on their way.

TITUS

These forty groats I give in fee,
If thou wilt only silent be.

MARY

May God be merciful to thee
Upon the Judgment Day!

JESUS

When thirty years shall have gone by,
I at Jerusalem shall die,
By Jewish hands exalted high
  On the accursed tree,
Then on my right and my left side,
These thieves shall both be crucified,
And Titus thenceforth shall abide
  In paradise with me.

Here a great rumor of trumpets and horses, like the noise of a king with his army, and the robbers shall take flight.

CHAUCER

An old man in a lodge within a park;
  The chamber walls depicted all around
  With portraitures of huntsman, hawk, and hound,
  And the hurt deer. He listeneth to the lark,
Whose song comes with the sunshine through the dark
  Of painted glass in leaden lattice bound;
  He listeneth and he laugheth at the sound,
  Then writeth in a book like any clerk.
He is the poet of the dawn, who wrote
  The Canterbury Tales, and his old age
  Made beautiful with song; and as I read
I hear the crowing cock, I hear the note
  Of lark and linnet, and from every page
  Rise odors of ploughed field or flowery mead.

THE SOUND OF THE SEA

The sea awoke at midnight from its sleep,
    And round the pebbly beaches far and wide
    I heard the first wave of the rising tide
    Rush onward with uninterrupted sweep;
A voice out of the silence of the deep,
    A sound mysteriously multiplied
    As of a cataract from the mountain's side,
    Or roar of winds upon a wooded steep.
So comes to us at times, from the unknown
    And inaccessible solitudes of being,
    The rushing of the sea-tides of the soul;
And inspirations, that we deem our own,
    Are some divine foreshadowing and foreseeing
    Of things beyond our reason or control.

BOSTON

St. Botolph's Town! Hither across the plains
    And fens of Lincolnshire, in garb austere,
    There came a Saxon monk, and founded here
    A Priory, pillaged by marauding Danes,
So that thereof no vestige now remains;
    Only a name, that, spoken loud and clear,
    And echoed in another hemisphere,
    Survives the sculptured walls and painted panes.
St. Botolph's Town! Far over leagues of land
    And leagues of sea looks forth its noble tower,
    And far around the chiming bells are heard;
So may that sacred name forever stand
    A landmark, and a symbol of the power,
    That lies concentred in a single word.

A DUTCH PICTURE

Simon Danz has come home again,
  From cruising about with his buccaneers;
He has singed the beard of the King of Spain,
And carried away the Dean of Jaen
  And sold him in Algiers.

In his house by the Maese, with its roof of tiles,
  And weathercocks flying aloft in air,
There are silver tankards of antique styles,
Plunder of convent and castle, and piles
  Of carpets rich and rare.

In his tulip-garden there by the town,
  Overlooking the sluggish stream,
With his Moorish cap and dressing-gown,
The old sea-captain, hale and brown,
  Walks in a waking dream.

A smile in his gray mustachio lurks
  Whenever he thinks of the King of Spain,
And the listed tulips look like Turks,
And the silent gardener as he works
  Is changed to the Dean of Jaen.

The windmills on the outermost
  Verge of the landscape in the haze,
To him are towers on the Spanish coast,
With whiskered sentinels at their post,
  Though this is the river Maese.

But when the winter rains begin,
  He sits and smokes by the blazing brands,

And old seafaring men come in,
Goat-bearded, gray, and with double chin,
    And rings upon their hands.

They sit there in the shadow and shine
    Of the flickering fire of the winter night;
Figures in color and design
Like those by Rembrandt of the Rhine,
    Half darkness and half light.

And they talk of ventures lost or won,
    And their talk is ever and ever the same,
While they drink the red wine of Tarragon,
From the cellars of some Spanish Don,
    Or convent set on flame.

Restless at times with heavy strides
    He paces his parlor to and fro;
He is like a ship that at anchor rides,
And swings with the rising and falling tides,
    And tugs at her anchor-tow.

Voices mysterious far and near,
    Sound of the wind and sound of the sea,
Are calling and whispering in his ear,
"Simon Danz! Why stayest thou here?
    Come forth and follow me!"

So he thinks he shall take to the sea again
    For one more cruise with his buccaneers,
To singe the beard of the King of Spain,
And capture another Dean of Jaen
    And sell him in Algiers.

THE LEAP OF ROUSHAN BEG

Mounted on Kyrat strong and fleet,
His chestnut steed with four white feet,
  Roushan Beg, called Kurroglou,
Son of the road and bandit chief,
Seeking refuge and relief,
  Up the mountain pathway flew.

Such was Kyrat's wondrous speed,
Never yet could any steed
  Reach the dust-cloud in his course.
More than maiden, more than wife,
More than gold and next to life
  Roushan the Robber loved his horse.

In the land that lies beyond
Erzeroum and Trebizond,
  Garden-girt his fortress stood;
Plundered khan, or caravan
Journeying north from Koordistan,
  Gave him wealth and wine and food.

Seven hundred and fourscore
Men at arms his livery wore,
  Did his bidding night and day;
Now, through regions all unknown,
He was wandering, lost, alone,
  Seeking without guide his way.

Suddenly the pathway ends,
Sheer the precipice descends,
  Loud the torrent roars unseen;
Thirty feet from side to side

Yawns the chasm; on air must ride
He who crosses this ravine.

Following close in his pursuit,
At the precipice's foot
    Reyhan the Arab of Orfah
Halted with his hundred men,
Shouting upward from the glen,
    "La Illáh illa Alláh!"

Gently Roushan Beg caressed
Kyrat's forehead, neck, and breast;
    Kissed him upon both his eyes,
Sang to him in his wild way,
As upon the topmost spray
    Sings a bird before it flies.

"O my Kyrat, O my steed,
Round and slender as a reed,
    Carry me this peril through!
Satin housings shall be thine,
Shoes of gold, O Kyrat mine,
    O thou soul of Kurroglou!

"Soft thy skin as silken skein,
Soft as woman's hair thy mane,
    Tender are thine eyes and true;
All thy hoofs like ivory shine,
Polished bright; O life of mine,
    Leap, and rescue Kurroglou!"

Kyrat, then, the strong and fleet,
Drew together his four white feet,
    Paused a moment on the verge,
Measured with his eye the space,

And into the air's embrace
  Leaped as leaps the ocean surge.

As the ocean surge o'er sand
Bears a swimmer safe to land,
  Kyrat safe his rider bore;
Rattling down the deep abyss
Fragments of the precipice
  Rolled like pebbles on a shore.

Roushan's tasselled cap of red
Trembled not upon his head,
  Careless sat he and upright;
Neither hand nor bridle shook,
Nor his head he turned to look,
  As he galloped out of sight.

Flash of harness in the air,
Seen a moment like the glare
  Of a sword drawn from its sheath;
Thus the phantom horseman passed,
And the shadow that he cast
  Leaped the cataract underneath.

Reyhan the Arab held his breath
While this vision of life and death
  Passed above him. "Allahu!"
Cried he. "In all Koordistan
Lives there not so brave a man
  As this Robber Kurroglou!"

KÉRAMOS

Turn, turn, my wheel! Turn round and round
Without a pause, without a sound:
  So spins the flying world away!
This clay, well mixed with marl and sand,
Follows the motion of my hand;
For some must follow, and some command,
  Though all are made of clay!

Thus sang the Potter at his task
Beneath the blossoming hawthorn-tree,
While o'er his features, like a mask,
The quilted sunshine and leaf-shade
Moved, as the boughs above him swayed,
And clothed him, till he seemed to be
A figure woven in tapestry,
So sumptuously was he arrayed
In that magnificent attire
Of sable tissue flaked with fire.
Like a magician he appeared,
A conjurer without book or beard;
And while he plied his magic art—
For it was magical to me—
I stood in silence and apart,
And wondered more and more to see
That shapeless, lifeless mass of clay
Rise up to meet the master's hand,
And now contract and now expand,
And even his slightest touch obey;
While ever in a thoughtful mood
He sang his ditty, and at times
Whistled a tune between the rhymes,
As a melodious interlude.

Turn, turn, my wheel! All things must change
To something new, to something strange;
  Nothing that is can pause or stay;
The moon will wax, the moon will wane,
The mist and cloud will turn to rain,
The rain to mist and cloud again,
  To-morrow be to-day.

Thus still the Potter sang, and still,
By some unconscious act of will,
The melody and even the words
Were intermingled with my thought,
As bits of colored thread are caught
And woven into nests of birds.
And thus to regions far remote,
Beyond the ocean's vast expanse,
This wizard in the motley coat
Transported me on wings of song,
And by the northern shores of France
Bore me with restless speed along.

What land is this that seems to be
A mingling of the land and sea?
This land of sluices, dikes, and dunes?
This water-net, that tessellates
The landscape? this unending maze
Of gardens, through whose latticed gates
The imprisoned pinks and tulips gaze;
Where in long summer afternoons
The sunshine, softened by the haze,
Comes streaming down as through a screen;
Where over fields and pastures green
The painted ships float high in air,
And over all and everywhere

The sails of windmills sink and soar
Like wings of sea-gulls on the shore?

What land is this? Yon pretty town
Is Delft, with all its wares displayed;
The pride, the market-place, the crown
And centre of the Potter's trade.
See! every house and room is bright
With glimmers of reflected light
From plates that on the dresser shine;
Flagons to foam with Flemish beer,
Or sparkle with the Rhenish wine,
And pilgrim flasks with fleurs-de-lis,
And ships upon a rolling sea,
And tankards pewter topped, and queer
With comic mask and musketeer!
Each hospitable chimney smiles
A welcome from its painted tiles;
The parlor walls, the chamber floors,
The stairways and the corridors,
The borders of the garden walks,
Are beautiful with fadeless flowers,
That never droop in winds or showers,
And never wither on their stalks.

Turn, turn, my wheel! All life is brief;
What now is bud will soon be leaf,
   What now is leaf will soon decay;
The wind blows east, the wind blows west;
The blue eggs in the robin's nest
Will soon have wings and beak and breast,
   And flutter and fly away.

Now southward through the air I glide,
The song my only pursuivant,

And see across the landscape wide
The blue Charente, upon whose tide
The belfries and the spires of Saintes
Ripple and rock from side to side,
As, when an earthquake rends its walls,
A crumbling city reels and falls.

Who is it in the suburbs here,
This Potter, working with such cheer,
In this mean house, this mean attire,
His manly features bronzed with fire,
Whose figulines and rustic wares
Scarce find him bread from day to day?
This madman, as the people say,
Who breaks his tables and his chairs
To feed his furnace fires, nor cares
Who goes unfed if they are fed,
Nor who may live if they are dead?
This alchemist with hollow cheeks
And sunken, searching eyes, who seeks,
By mingled earths and ores combined
With potency of fire, to find
Some new enamel, hard and bright,
His dream, his passion, his delight?

O Palissy! within thy breast
Burned the hot fever of unrest;
Thine was the prophet's vision, thine
The exultation, the divine
Insanity of noble minds,
That never falters nor abates,
But labors and endures and waits,
Till all that it foresees it finds,
Or what it cannot find creates!

Turn, turn, my wheel! This earthen jar
A touch can make, a touch can mar;
  And shall it to the Potter say,
What makest thou? Thou hast no hand?
As men who think to understand
A world by their Creator planned,
  Who wiser is than they.

Still guided by the dreamy song,
As in a trance I float along
Above the Pyrenean chain,
Above the fields and farms of Spain,
Above the bright Majorcan isle
That lends its softened name to art,—
A spot, a dot upon the chart,
Whose little towns, red-roofed with tile,
Are ruby-lustred with the light
Of blazing furnaces by night,
And crowned by day with wreaths of smoke
Then eastward, wafted in my flight
On my enchanter's magic cloak,
I sail across the Tyrrhene Sea
Into the land of Italy,
And o'er the windy Apennines,
Mantled and musical with pines.

The palaces, the princely halls,
The doors of houses and the walls
Of churches and of belfry towers,
Cloister and castle, street and mart,
Are garlanded and gay with flowers
That blossom in the fields of art.
Here Gubbio's workshops gleam and glow
With brilliant, iridescent dyes,
The dazzling whiteness of the snow,

The cobalt blue of summer skies;
And vase and scutcheon, cup and plate,
In perfect finish emulate
Faenza, Florence, Pesaro.

Forth from Urbino's gate there came
A youth with the angelic name
Of Raphael, in form and face
Himself angelic, and divine
In arts of color and design.
From him Francesco Xanto caught
Something of his transcendent grace,
And into fictile fabrics wrought
Suggestions of the master's thought.
Nor less Maestro Giorgio shines
With madre-perl and golden lines
Of arabesques, and interweaves
His birds and fruits and flowers and leaves
About some landscape, shaded brown,
With olive tints on rock and town.

Behold this cup within whose bowl,
Upon a ground of deepest blue
With yellow-lustred stars o'erlaid,
Colors of every tint and hue
Mingle in one harmonious whole!
With large blue eyes and steadfast gaze,
Her yellow hair in net and braid,
Necklace and ear-rings all ablaze
With golden lustre o'er the glaze,
A woman's portrait; on the scroll,
Cana, the Beautiful! A name
Forgotten save for such brief fame
As this memorial can bestow,—

A gift some lover long ago
Gave with his heart to this fair dame.

A nobler title to renown
Is thine, O pleasant Tuscan town,
Seated beside the Arno's stream;
For Luca della Robbia there
Created forms so wondrous fair,
They made thy sovereignty supreme.
These choristers with lips of stone,
Whose music is not heard, but seen,
Still chant, as from their organ-screen,
Their Maker's praise; nor these alone,
But the more fragile forms of clay,
Hardly less beautiful than they,
These saints and angels that adorn
The walls of hospitals, and tell
The story of good deeds so well
That poverty seems less forlorn,
And life more like a holiday.

Here in this old neglected church,
That long eludes the traveller's search,
Lies the dead bishop on his tomb;
Earth upon earth he slumbering lies,
Life-like and death-like in the gloom;
Garlands of fruit and flowers in bloom
And foliage deck his resting-place;
A shadow in the sightless eyes,
A pallor on the patient face,
Made perfect by the furnace heat;
All earthly passions and desires
Burnt out by purgatorial fires;
Seeming to say, "Our years are fleet,
And to the weary death is sweet."

But the most wonderful of all
The ornaments on tomb or wall
That grace the fair Ausonian shores
Are those the faithful earth restores,
Near some Apulian town concealed,
In vineyard or in harvest field,—
Vases and urns and bas-reliefs,
Memorials of forgotten griefs,
Or records of heroic deeds
Of demigods and mighty chiefs:
Figures that almost move and speak,
And, buried amid mould and weeds,
Still in their attitudes attest
The presence of the graceful Greek,—
Achilles in his armor dressed,
Alcides with the Cretan bull,
And Aphrodite with her boy,
Or lovely Helena of Troy,
Still living and still beautiful.

Turn, turn, my wheel! 'Tis nature's plan
The child should grow into the man,
The man grow wrinkled, old, and gray;
In youth the heart exults and sings,
The pulses leap, the feet have wings;
In age the cricket chirps, and brings
The harvest-home of day.

And now the winds that southward blow,
And cool the hot Sicilian isle,
Bear me away. I see below
The long line of the Libyan Nile,
Flooding and feeding the parched lands
With annual ebb and overflow,
A fallen palm whose branches lie

Beneath the Abyssinian sky,
Whose roots are in Egyptian sands.
On either bank huge water-wheels,
Belted with jars and dripping weeds,
Send forth their melancholy moans,
As if, in their gray mantles hid,
Dead anchorites of the Thebaid
Knelt on the shore and told their beads,
Beating their breasts with loud appeals
And penitential tears and groans.

This city, walled and thickly set
With glittering mosque and minaret,
Is Cairo, in whose gay bazaars
The dreaming traveller first inhales
The perfume of Arabian gales,
And sees the fabulous earthen jars,
Huge as were those wherein the maid
Morgiana found the Forty Thieves
Concealed in midnight ambuscade;
And seeing, more than half believes
The fascinating tales that run
Through all the Thousand Nights and One,
Told by the fair Scheherezade.

More strange and wonderful than these
Are the Egyptian deities,
Ammon, and Emeth, and the grand
Osiris, holding in his hand
The lotus; Isis, crowned and veiled;
The sacred Ibis, and the Sphinx;
Bracelets with blue enamelled links;
The Scarabee in emerald mailed,
Or spreading wide his funeral wings;
Lamps that perchance their night-watch kept

And stamp with honor or with shame
  These vessels made of clay.

Cradled and rocked in Eastern seas,
The islands of the Japanese
Beneath me lie; o'er lake and plain
The stork, the heron, and the crane
Through the clear realms of azure drift,
And on the hillside I can see
The villages of Imari,
Whose thronged and flaming workshops lift
Their twisted columns of smoke on high,
Cloud cloisters that in ruins lie,
With sunshine streaming through each rift,
And broken arches of blue sky.

All the bright flowers that fill the land,
Ripple of waves on rock or sand,
The snow on Fusiyama's cone,
The midnight heaven so thickly sown
With constellations of bright stars,
The leaves that rustle, the reeds that make
A whisper by each stream and lake,
The saffron dawn, the sunset red,
Are painted on these lovely jars;
Again the skylark sings, again
The stork, the heron, and the crane
Float through the azure overhead,
The counterfeit and counterpart
Of Nature reproduced in Art.

Art is the child of Nature; yes,
Her darling child, in whom we trace
The features of the mother's face,
Her aspect and her attitude;

All her majestic loveliness
Chastened and softened and subdued
Into a more attractive grace,
And with a human sense imbued.
He is the greatest artist, then,
Whether of pencil or of pen,
Who follows Nature. Never man,
As artist or as artisan,
Pursuing his own fantasies,
Can touch the human heart, or please,
Or satisfy our nobler needs,
As he who sets his willing feet
In Nature's footprints, light and fleet,
And follows fearless where she leads.

Thus mused I on that morn in May,
Wrapped in my visions like the Seer,
Whose eyes behold not what is near,
But only what is far away,
When, suddenly sounding peal on peal,
The church-bell from the neighboring town
Proclaimed the welcome hour of noon.
The Potter heard, and stopped his wheel,
His apron on the grass threw down,
Whistled his quiet little tune,
Not overloud nor overlong,
And ended thus his simple song:

Stop, stop, my wheel! Too soon, too soon
The noon will be the afternoon,
   Too soon to-day be yesterday;
Behind us in our path we cast
The broken potsherds of the past,
And all are ground to dust at last,
   And trodden into clay!

THE THREE SILENCES OF MOLINOS *

Three Silences there are: the first of speech,
The second of desire, the third of thought;
This is the lore a Spanish monk, distraught
With dreams and visions, was the first to teach.
These Silences, commingling each with each,
Made up the perfect Silence that he sought
And prayed for, and wherein at times he caught
Mysterious sounds from realms beyond our reach.
O thou, whose daily life anticipates
The life to come, and in whose thought and word
The spiritual world preponderates,
Hermit of Amesbury! thou too hast heard
Voices and melodies from beyond the gates,
And speakest only when thy soul is stirred!

THE CROSS OF SNOW — about his wife

In the long, sleepless watches of the night,
  A gentle face—the face of one long dead—
  Looks at me from the wall, where round its head
  The night-lamp casts a halo of pale light.
Here in this room she died; and soul more white
  Never through martyrdom of fire was led
  To its repose; nor can in books be read
  The legend of a life more benedight.
There is a mountain in the distant West
  That, sun-defying, in its deep ravines
  Displays a cross of snow upon its side.

* To John Greenleaf Whittier on his seventieth birthday.

Such is the cross I wear upon my breast
    These eighteen years, through all the changing scenes
  And seasons, changeless since the day she died.

THE TIDE RISES, THE TIDE FALLS

The tide rises, the tide falls,
The twilight darkens, the curlew calls;
Along the sea-sands damp and brown
The traveller hastens toward the town,
   And the tide rises, the tide falls.

Darkness settles on roofs and walls,
But the sea, the sea in the darkness calls;
The little waves, with their soft, white hands,
Efface the footprints in the sands,
   And the tide rises, the tide falls.

The morning breaks; the steeds in their stalls
Stamp and neigh, as the hostler calls;
The day returns, but nevermore
Returns the traveller to the shore,
   And the tide rises, the tide falls.

John Greenleaf Whittier

1807 – 1892

PROEM

I love the old melodious lays
Which softly melt the ages through,
   The songs of Spenser's golden days,
   Arcadian Sidney's silvery phrase,
Sprinkling our noon of time with freshest morning dew.

Yet, vainly in my quiet hours
To breathe their marvellous notes I try;
   I feel them, as the leaves and flowers
   In silence feel the dewy showers,
And drink with glad, still lips the blessing of the sky.

The rigor of a frozen clime,
The harshness of an untaught ear,
   The jarring words of one whose rhyme
   Beat often Labor's hurried time,
Or Duty's rugged march through storm and strife, are here.

Of mystic beauty, dreamy grace,
No rounded art the lack supplies;
   Unskilled the subtle lines to trace,
   Or softer shades of Nature's face,
I view her common forms with unanointed eyes.

Nor mine the seer-like power to show
The secrets of the heart and mind;
   To drop the plummet-line below

Our common world of joy and woe,
A more intense despair or brighter hope to find.

Yet here at least an earnest sense
Of human right and weal is shown;
    A hate of tyranny intense,
    And hearty in its vehemence,
As if my brother's pain and sorrow were my own.

O Freedom! if to me belong
Nor mighty Milton's gift divine,
    Nor Marvell's wit and graceful song,
    Still with a love as deep and strong
As theirs, I lay, like them, my best gifts on thy shrine!

CASSANDRA SOUTHWICK
1658

To the God of all sure mercies let my blessing rise to-day,
From the scoffer and the cruel He hath plucked the spoil away,—
Yea, He who cooled the furnace around the faithful three,
And tamed the Chaldean lions, hath set his handmaid free!

Last night I saw the sunset melt through my prison bars,
Last night across my damp earth-floor fell the pale gleam of
        stars;
In the coldness and the darkness all through the long night-time,
My grated casement whitened with autumn's early rime.

Alone, in that dark sorrow, hour after hour crept by;
Star after star looked palely in and sank adown the sky;
No sound amid night's stillness, save that which seemed to be
The dull and heavy beating of the pulses of the sea;

All night I sat unsleeping, for I knew that on the morrow
The ruler and the cruel priest would mock me in my sorrow,
Dragged to their place of market, and bargained for and sold,
Like a lamb before the shambles, like a heifer from the fold!

Oh, the weakness of the flesh was there,—the shrinking and the
  shame;
And the low voice of the Tempter like whispers to me came:
"Why sit'st thou thus forlornly!" the wicked murmur said,
"Damp walls thy bower of beauty, cold earth thy maiden bed?

"Where be the smiling faces, and voices soft and sweet,
Seen in thy father's dwelling, heard in the pleasant street?
Where be the youths whose glances, the summer Sabbath
  through,
Turned tenderly and timidly unto thy father's pew?

"Why sit'st thou here, Cassandra?—Bethink thee with what
  mirth
Thy happy schoolmates gather around the warm bright hearth;
How the crimson shadows tremble on foreheads white and fair,
On eyes of merry girlhood, half hid in golden hair.

"Not for thee the hearth-fire brightens, not for thee kind words
  are spoken,
Not for thee the nuts of Wenham woods by laughing boys are
  broken,
No first-fruits of the orchard within thy lap are laid,
For thee no flowers of autumn the youthful hunters braid.

"O, weak, deluded maiden!—by crazy fancies led,
With wild and raving railers an evil path to tread;
To leave a wholesome worship, and teaching pure and sound;
And mate with maniac women, loose-haired and sackcloth
  bound.

"Mad scoffers of the priesthood, who mock at things divine,
Who rail against the pulpit, and holy bread and wine;
Sore from their cart-tail scourgings, and from the pillory lame,
Rejoicing in their wretchedness, and glorying in their shame.

"And what a fate awaits thee?—a sadly toiling slave,
Dragging the slowly lengthening chain of bondage to the grave!
Think of thy woman's nature, subdued in hopeless thrall,
The easy prey of any, the scoff and scorn of all!"

O, ever as the Tempter spoke, and feeble Nature's fears
Wrung drop by drop the scalding flow of unavailing tears,
I wrestled down the evil thoughts, and strove in silent prayer,
To feel, O Helper of the weak! that Thou indeed wert there!

I thought of Paul and Silas, within Philippi's cell,
And how from Peter's sleeping limbs the prison-shackles fell,
Till I seemed to hear the trailing of an angel's robe of white,
And to feel a blessed presence invisible to sight.

Bless the Lord for all his mercies!—for the peace and love I felt,
Like dew of Hermon's holy hill, upon my spirit melt;
When "Get behind me, Satan!" was the language of my heart,
And I felt the Evil Tempter with all his doubts depart.

Slow broke the gray cold morning; again the sunshine fell,
Flecked with the shade of bar and grate within my lonely cell;
The hoar-frost melted on the wall, and upward from the street
Came careless laugh and idle word, and tread of passing feet.

At length the heavy bolts fell back, my door was open cast,
And slowly at the sheriff's side, up the long street I passed;
I heard the murmur round me, and felt, but dared not see,
How, from every door and window, the people gazed on me.

And doubt and fear fell on me, shame burned upon my cheek,
Swam earth and sky around me, my trembling limbs grew weak:
"O Lord! support thy handmaid; and from her soul cast out
The fear of man, which brings a snare,—the weakness and the
     doubt."

Then the dreary shadows scattered, like a cloud in morning's
     breeze,
And a low deep voice within me seemed whispering words like
     these:
"Though thy earth be as the iron, and thy heaven a brazen wall,
Trust still His loving-kindness whose power is over all."

We paused at length, where at my feet the sunlit waters broke
On glaring reach of shining beach, and shingly wall of rock;
The merchant-ships lay idly there, in hard clear lines on high,
Tracing with rope and slender spar their network on the sky.

And there were ancient citizens, cloak-wrapped and grave and
     cold,
And grim and stout sea-captains with faces bronzed and old,
And on his horse, with Rawson, his cruel clerk at hand,
Sat dark and haughty Endicott, the ruler of the land.

And poisoning with his evil words the ruler's ready ear,
The priest leaned o'er his saddle, with laugh and scoff and jeer;
It stirred my soul, and from my lips the seal of silence broke,
As if through woman's weakness a warning spirit spoke.

I cried, "The Lord rebuke thee, thou smiter of the meek,
Thou robber of the righteous, thou trampler of the weak!
Go light the dark, cold hearth-stones,—go turn the prison lock
Of the poor hearts thou hast hunted, thou wolf amid the flock!"

Dark lowered the brows of Endicott, and with a deeper red
O'er Rawson's wine-empurpled cheek the flush of anger spread;
"Good people," quoth the white-lipped priest, "heed not her
    words so wild,
Her Master speaks within her,—the Devil owns his child!"

But gray heads shook, and young brows knit, the while the
    sheriff read
That law the wicked rulers against the poor have made,
Who to their house of Rimmon and idol priesthood bring
No bended knee of worship, nor gainful offering.

Then to the stout sea-captains the sheriff, turning, said,—
"Which of ye, worthy seamen, will take this Quaker maid?
In the Isle of fair Barbadoes, or on Virginia's shore,
You may hold her at a higher price than Indian girl or Moor."

Grim and silent stood the captains; and when again he cried,
"Speak out, my worthy seamen!"—no voice, no sign replied;
But I felt a hard hand press my own, and kind words met my
    ear,—
"God bless thee, and preserve thee, my gentle girl and dear!"

A weight seemed lifted from my heart,—a pitying friend was
    nigh,
I felt it in his hard, rough hand, and saw it in his eye;
And when again the sheriff spoke, that voice, so kind to me,
Growled back its stormy answer like the roaring of the sea,—

"Pile my ship with bars of silver,—pack with coins of Spanish
    gold,
From keel-piece up to deck-plank, the roomage of her hold,
By the living God who made me!—I would sooner in your bay
Sink ship and crew and cargo, than bear this child away!"

"Well answered, worthy captain, shame on their cruel laws!"
Ran through the crowd in murmurs loud the people's just
     applause.
"Like the herdsman of Tekoa, in Israel of old,
Shall we see the poor and righteous again for silver sold?"

I looked on haughty Endicott; with weapon half-way drawn,
Swept round the throng his lion glare of bitter hate and scorn;
Fiercely he drew his bridle-rein, and turned in silence back,
And sneering priest and baffled clerk rode murmuring in his
     track.

Hard after them the sheriff looked, in bitterness of soul;
Thrice smote his staff upon the ground, and crushed his parch-
     ment roll.
"Good friends," he said, "since both have fled, the ruler and the
     priest,
Judge ye, if from their further work I be not well released."

Loud was the cheer which, full and clear, swept round the silent
     bay,
As, with kind words and kinder looks, he bade me go my way;
For He who turns the courses of the streamlet of the glen,
And the river of great waters, had turned the hearts of men.

O, at that hour the very earth seemed changed beneath my eye,
A holier wonder round me rose the blue walls of the sky,
A lovelier light on rock and hill and stream and woodland lay,
And softer lapsed on sunnier sands the waters of the bay.

Thanksgiving to the Lord of life!—to Him all praises be,
Who from the hands of evil men hath set his handmaid free;
All praise to Him before whose power the mighty are afraid,
Who takes the crafty in the snare which for the poor is laid!

Sing, O my soul, rejoicingly, on evening's twilight calm
Uplift the loud thanksgiving,—pour forth the grateful psalm;
Let all dear hearts with me rejoice, as did the saints of old,
When of the Lord's good angel the rescued Peter told.

And weep and howl, ye evil priests and mighty men of wrong,
The Lord shall smite the proud, and lay his hand upon the
    strong.
Woe to the wicked rulers in his avenging hour!
Woe to the wolves who seek the flocks to raven and devour!

But let the humble ones arise,—the poor in heart be glad,
And let the mourning ones again with robes of praise be clad,
For He who cooled the furnace, and smoothed the stormy wave,
And tamed the Chaldean lions, is mighty still to save!

MASSACHUSETTS TO VIRGINIA *

The blast from Freedom's Northern hills, upon its Southern
    way,
Bears greeting to Virginia from Massachusetts Bay:
No word of haughty challenging, nor battle bugle's peal,
Nor steady tread of marching files, nor clang of horsemen's
    steel,

No trains of deep-mouthed cannon along our highways go;
Around our silent arsenals untrodden lies the snow;
And to the land-breeze of our ports, upon their errands far,
A thousand sails of commerce swell, but none are spread for
    war.

* Occasioned by the seizure in Boston of George Latimer, an alleged fugitive slave.

We hear thy threats, Virginia! thy stormy words and high
Swell harshly on the Southern winds which melt along our sky;
Yet, not one brown, hard hand foregoes its honest labor here,
No hewer of our mountain oaks suspends his axe in fear.

Wild are the waves which lash the reefs along St. George's
    bank;
Cold on the shores of Labrador the fog lies white and dank;
Through storm, and wave, and blinding mist, stout are the
    hearts which man
The fishing-smacks of Marblehead, the sea-boats of Cape Ann.

The cold north light and wintry sun glare on their icy forms,
Bent grimly o'er their straining lines or wrestling with the
    storms;
Free as the winds they drive before, rough as the waves they
    roam,
They laugh to scorn the slaver's threat against their rocky home.

What means the Old Dominion? Hath she forgot the day
When o'er her conquered valleys swept the Briton's steel array?
How, side by side with sons of hers, the Massachusetts men
Encountered Tarleton's charge of fire, and stout Cornwallis,
    then?

Forgets she how the Bay State, in answer to the call
Of her old House of Burgesses, spoke out from Faneuil Hall?
When, echoing back her Henry's cry, came pulsing on each
    breath
Of Northern winds, the thrilling sounds of "Liberty or Death!"

What asks the Old Dominion? If now her sons have proved
False to their fathers' memory, false to the faith they loved;
If she can scoff at Freedom, and its great charter spurn,
Must we of Massachusetts from truth and duty turn?

We hunt your bondmen, flying from Slavery's hateful hell;
Our voices, at your bidding, take up the bloodhound's yell;
We gather, at your summons, above our fathers' graves,
From Freedom's holy altar-horns to tear your wretched slaves!

Thank God! not yet so vilely can Massachusetts bow;
The spirit of her early time is with her even now;
Dream not because her Pilgrim blood moves slow and calm and
      cool,
She thus can stoop her chainless neck, a sister's slave and tool!

All that a *sister* State should do, all that a *free* State may,
Heart, hand, and purse we proffer, as in our early day;
But that one dark loathsome burden ye must stagger with alone,
And reap the bitter harvest which ye yourselves have sown!

Hold, while ye may, your struggling slaves, and burden God's
      free air
With woman's shriek beneath the lash, and manhood's wild
      despair;
Cling closer to the "cleaving curse" that writes upon your plains
The blasting of Almighty wrath against a land of chains.

Still shame your gallant ancestry, the cavaliers of old,
By watching round the shambles where human flesh is sold;
Gloat o'er the new-born child, and count his market value,
      when
The maddened mother's cry of woe shall pierce the slaver's den!

Lower than plummet soundeth, sink the Virginia name;
Plant, if ye will, your fathers' graves with rankest weeds of
      shame;
Be, if ye will, the scandal of God's fair universe;
We wash our hands forever, of your sin and shame and curse.

A voice from lips whereon the coal from Freedom's shrine hath
    been,
Thrilled, as but yesterday, the hearts of Berkshire's mountain
    men:
The echoes of that solemn voice are sadly lingering still
In all our sunny valleys, on every windswept hill.

And when the prowling man-thief came hunting for his prey
Beneath the very shadow of Bunker's shaft of gray,
How, through the free lips of the son, the father's warning
    spoke;
How, from its bonds of trade and sect, the pilgrim city broke!

A hundred thousand right arms were lifted up on high,
A hundred thousand voices sent back their loud reply;
Through the thronged towns of Essex the startling summons
    rang,
And up from bench and loom and wheel her young mechanics
    sprang!

The voice of free, broad Middlesex, of thousands as of one,
The shaft of Bunker calling to that of Lexington;
From Norfolk's ancient villages, from Plymouth's rocky bound
To where Nantucket feels the arms of ocean close her round;

From rich and rural Worcester, where through the calm repose
Of cultured vales and fringing woods the gentle Nashua flows,
To where Wachuset's wintry blasts the mountain larches stir,
Swelled up to Heaven the thrilling cry of "God save Latimer!"

And sandy Barnstable rose up, wet with the salt sea spray;
And Bristol sent her answering shout down Narragansett Bay!
Along the broad Connecticut old Hampden felt the thrill,
And the cheer of Hampshire's woodmen swept down from
    Holyoke Hill.

The voice of Massachusetts! Of her free sons and daughters,
Deep calling unto deep aloud, the sound of many waters!
Against the burden of that voice what tyrant power shall stand?
No fetters in the Bay State! No slave upon her land!

Look to it well, Virginians! In calmness we have borne,
In answer to our faith and trust, your insult and your scorn;
You've spurned our kindest counsels; you've hunted for our
      lives;
And shaken round our hearths and homes your manacles and
      gyves!

We wage no war, we lift no arm, we fling no torch within
The fire-damps of the quaking mine beneath your soil of sin;
We leave ye with your bondmen, to wrestle, while ye can,
With the strong upward tendencies and god-like soul of man!

But for us and for our children, the vow which we have given
For freedom and humanity, is registered in heaven;
No slave-hunt in our borders,—no pirate on our strand!
No fetters in the Bay State,—no slave upon our land!

ICHABOD*

So fallen! so lost! the light withdrawn
    Which once he wore!
The glory from his gray hairs gone
    Forevermore!

Revile him not, the Tempter hath
    A snare for all;

* A vote of no confidence in Daniel Webster after he had accepted the
notorious "Compromise" which included the Fugitive Slave Law.

And pitying tears, not scorn and wrath,
   Befit his fall!

Oh, dumb be passion's stormy rage,
   When he who might
Have lighted up and led his age,
   Falls back in night.

Scorn! would the angels laugh, to mark
   A bright soul driven,
Fiend-goaded, down the endless dark,
   From hope and heaven!

Let not the land once proud of him
   Insult him now,
Nor brand with deeper shame his dim,
   Dishonored brow.

But let its humbled sons, instead,
   From sea to lake,
A long lament, as for the dead,
   In sadness make.

Of all we loved and honored, naught
   Save power remains;
A fallen angel's pride of thought,
   Still strong in chains.

All else is gone; from those great eyes
   The soul has fled:
When faith is lost, when honor dies,
   The man is dead!

Then pay the reverence of old days
   To his dead fame;

Walk backward, with averted gaze,
And hide the shame!

FIRST–DAY THOUGHTS

In calm and cool and silence, once again
  I find my old accustomed place among
  My brethren, where, perchance, no human tongue
  Shall utter words; where never hymn is sung,
  Nor deep-toned organ blown, nor censer swung,
Nor dim light falling through the pictured pane!
There, syllabled by silence, let me hear
The still small voice which reached the prophet's ear;
Read in my heart a still diviner law
Than Israel's leader on his table saw!
There let me strive with each besetting sin
  Recall my wandering fancies, and restrain
  The sore disquiet of a restless brain;
  And, as the path of duty is made plain,
May grace be given that I may walk therein,
  Not like the hireling, for his selfish gain,
With backward glances and reluctant tread,
Making a merit of his coward dread,
  But, cheerful, in the light around me thrown,
  Walking as one to pleasant service led;
  Doing God's will as if it were my own,
Yet trusting not in mine, but in His strength alone!

MY NAMESAKE

You scarcely need my tardy thanks,
  Who, self-rewarded, nurse and tend—
A green leaf on your own Green Banks—
  The memory of your friend.

For me, no wreath, bloom-woven, hides
  The sobered brow and lessening hair:
For aught I know, the myrtled sides
  Of Helicon are bare.

Their scallop-shells so many bring
  The fabled founts of song to try,
They've drained, for aught I know, the spring
  Of Aganippe dry.

Ah well!—The wreath the Muses braid
  Proves often Folly's cap and bell;
Methinks, my ample beaver's shade
  May serve my turn as well.

Let Love's and Friendship's tender debt
  Be paid by those I love in life.
Why should the unborn critic whet
  For me his scalping-knife?

Why should the stranger peer and pry
  One's vacant house of life about,
And drag for curious ear and eye
  His faults and follies out?—

Why stuff, for fools to gaze upon,
  With chaff of words, the garb he wore,

As corn-husks when the ear is gone
   Are rustled all the more?

Let kindly Silence close again,
   The picture vanish from the eye,
And on the dim and misty main
   Let the small ripple die.

Yet not the less I own your claim
   To grateful thanks, dear friends of mine.
Hang, if it please you so, my name
   Upon your household line.

Let Fame from brazen lips blow wide
   Her chosen names, I envy none:
A mother's love, a father's pride,
   Shall keep alive my own!

Still shall that name as now recall
   The young leaf wet with morning dew,
The glory where the sunbeams fall
   The breezy woodlands through.

That name shall be a household word,
   A spell to waken smile or sigh;
In many an evening prayer be heard
   And cradle lullaby.

And thou, dear child, in riper days
   When asked the reason of thy name,
Shalt answer: "One 'twere vain to praise
   Or censure bore the same.

"Some blamed him, some believed him good,—
   The truth lay doubtless 'twixt the two,—

He reconciled as best he could
   Old faith and fancies new.

"In him the grave and playful mixed,
   And wisdom held with folly truce,
And Nature compromised betwixt
   Good fellow and recluse.

"He loved his friends, forgave his foes;
   And, if his words were harsh at times,
He spared his fellow-men,—his blows
   Fell only on their crimes.

"He loved the good and wise, but found
   His human heart to all akin
Who met him on the common ground
   Of suffering and of sin.

"Whate'er his neighbors might endure
   Of pain or grief his own became;
For all the ills he could not cure
   He held himself to blame.

"His good was mainly an intent,
   His evil not of forethought done;
The work he wrought was rarely meant
   Or finished as begun.

"Ill served his tides of feeling strong
   To turn the common mills of use;
And, over restless wings of song,
   His birthright garb hung loose!

"His eye was beauty's powerless slave,
   And his the ear which discord pains;

Few guessed beneath his aspect grave
   What passions strove in chains.

"He had his share of care and pain,
   No holiday was life to him;
Still in the heirloom cup we drain
   The bitter drop will swim.

"Yet Heaven was kind, and here a bird
   And there a flower beguiled his way;
And, cool, in summer noons, he heard
   The fountains plash and play.

"On all his sad or restless moods
   The patient peace of Nature stole;
The quiet of the fields and woods
   Sank deep into his soul.

"He worshipped as his fathers did,
   And kept the faith of childish days,
And, howsoe'er he strayed or slid,
   He loved the good old ways.

"The simple tastes, the kindly traits,
   The tranquil air, and gentle speech,
The silence of the soul that waits
   For more than man to teach.

"The cant of party, school, and sect,
   Provoked at times his honest scorn,
And Folly, in its gray respect,
   He tossed on satire's horn.

"But still his heart was full of awe
   And reverence for all sacred things;

And, brooding over form and law,
  He saw the Spirit's wings!

"Life's mystery wrapt him like a cloud;
  He heard far voices mock his own,
The sweep of wings unseen, the loud,
  Long roll of waves unknown.

"The arrows of his straining sight
  Fell quenched in darkness; priest and sage,
Like lost guides calling left and right,
  Perplexed his doubtful age.

"Like childhood, listening for the sound
  Of its dropped pebbles in the well,
All vainly down the dark profound
  His brief-lined plummet fell.

"So, scattering flowers with pious pains
  On old beliefs, of later creeds,
Which claimed a place in Truth's domains,
  He asked the title-deeds.

"He saw the old-time's groves and shrines
  In the long distance fair and dim;
And heard, like sound of far-off pines,
  The century-mellowed hymn!

"He dared not mock the Dervish whirl,
  The Brahmin's rite, the Lama's spell;
God knew the heart; Devotion's pearl
  Might sanctify the shell.

"While others trod the altar stairs
  He faltered like the publican;

And, while they praised as saints, his prayers
　　Were those of sinful man.

"For, awed by Sinai's Mount of Law,
　　The trembling faith alone sufficed,
That, through its cloud and flame, he saw
　　The sweet, sad face of Christ!—

"And listening, with his forehead bowed,
　　Heard the Divine compassion fill
The pauses of the trump and cloud
　　With whispers small and still.

"The words he spake, the thoughts he penned,
　　Are mortal as his hand and brain,
But, if they served the Master's end,
　　He has not lived in vain!"

Heaven make thee better than thy name,
　　Child of my friends!—For thee I crave
What riches never bought, nor fame
　　To mortal longing gave.

I pray the prayer of Plato old:
　　God make thee beautiful within,
And let thine eyes the good behold
　　In everything save sin!

Imagination held in check
　　To serve, not rule, thy poiséd mind;
Thy Reason, at the frown or beck
　　Of Conscience, loose or bind.

No dreamer thou, but real all,—
　　Strong manhood crowning vigorous youth;

Life made by duty epical
   And rhythmic with the truth.

So shall that life the fruitage yield
   Which trees of healing only give,
And green-leafed in the Eternal field
   Of God, forever live!

SKIPPER IRESON'S RIDE*

Of all the rides since the birth of time,
Told in story or sung in rhyme,—
On Apuleius's Golden Ass,
Or one-eyed Calendar's horse of brass,
Witch astride of a human back,
Islam's prophet on Al-Borák,—
The strangest ride that ever was sped
Was Ireson's, out of Marblehead!
   Old Floyd Ireson, for his hard heart,
     Tarred and feathered and carried in a cart
      By the women of Marblehead!

Body of turkey, head of owl,
Wings a-droop like a rained-on fowl,
Feathered and ruffled in every part,
Skipper Ireson stood in the cart.
Scores of women, old and young,
Strong of muscle, and glib of tongue,

* Whittier wrote the story as he heard it from a fellow-student at Haverhill Academy. Historian Samuel Eliot Morison comments: "In 1808 occurred the regrettable incident of Skipper Benjamin (not Floyd) Ireson, for his crew's cowardice and lying (not for his hard heart), tarred and feathered and carried in a dory (not cart) by the fishermen (not the women) of Marblehead."

Pushed and pulled up the rocky lane,
Shouting and singing the shrill refrain:
"Here's Flud Oirson, fur his horrd horrt,
Torr'd an' futherr'd an' corr'd in a corrt
By the women o' Morble'ead!"

Wrinkled scolds with hands on hips,
Girls in bloom of cheek and lips,
Wild-eyed, free-limbed, such as chase
Bacchus round some antique vase,
Brief of skirt, with ankles bare,
Loose of kerchief and loose of hair,
With conch-shells blowing and fish-horns' twang,
Over and over the Mænads sang:
"Here's Flud Oirson, fur his horrd horrt,
Torr'd an' futherr'd an' corr'd in a corrt
By the women o' Morble'ead!"

Small pity for him!—He sailed away
From a leaking ship in Chaleur Bay,—
Sailed away from a sinking wreck,
With his own town's-people on her deck!
"Lay by! lay by!" they called to him.
Back he answered, "Sink or swim!
Brag of your catch of fish again!"
And off he sailed through the fog and rain!
Old Floyd Ireson, for his hard heart,
Tarred and feathered and carried in a cart
By the women of Marblehead!

Fathoms deep in dark Chaleur
That wreck shall lie forevermore.
Mother and sister, wife and maid,
Looked from the rocks of Marblehead
Over the moaning and rainy sea,—

Looked for the coming that might not be!
What did the winds and the sea-birds say
Of the cruel captain who sailed away?—
   Old Floyd Ireson, for his hard heart,
    Tarred and feathered and carried in a cart
      By the women of Marblehead!

Through the street, on either side,
Up flew windows, doors swung wide;
Sharp-tongued spinsters, old wives gray,
Treble lent the fish-horn's bray.
Sea-worn grandsires, cripple-bound,
Hulks of old sailors run aground,
Shook head, and fist, and hat, and cane,
And cracked with curses the hoarse refrain:
   "Here's Flud Oirson, fur his horrd horrt,
    Torr'd an' futherr'd an' corr'd in a corrt
      By the women o' Morble'ead!"

Sweetly along the Salem road
Bloom of orchard and lilac showed.
Little the wicked skipper knew
Of the fields so green and the sky so blue.
Riding there in his sorry trim,
Like an Indian idol glum and grim,
Scarcely he seemed the sound to hear
Of voices shouting, far and near:
   "Here's Flud Oirson, fur his horrd horrt,
    Torr'd an' futherr'd an' corr'd in a corrt
      By the women o' Morble'ead!"

"Hear me, neighbors!" at last he cried,—
"What to me is this noisy ride?
What is the shame that clothes the skin
To the nameless horror that lives within?

Waking or sleeping, I see a wreck,
And hear a cry from a reeling deck!
Hate me and curse me,—I only dread
The hand of God and the face of the dead!"
  Said old Floyd Ireson, for his hard heart,
  Tarred and feathered and carried in a cart
    By the women of Marblehead!

Then the wife of the skipper lost at sea
Said, "God has touched him! why should we!"
Said an old wife mourning her only son,
"Cut the rogue's tether and let him run!"
So with soft relentings and rude excuse,
Half scorn, half pity, they cut him loose,
And gave him a cloak to hide him in,
And left him alone with his shame and sin.
  Poor Floyd Ireson, for his hard heart,
  Tarred and feathered and carried in a cart
    By the women of Marblehead!

THE OLD BURYING–GROUND

Our vales are sweet with fern and rose,
  Our hills are maple-crowned;
But not from them our fathers chose
  The village burying-ground.

The dreariest spot in all the land
  To Death they set apart;
With scanty grace from Nature's hand,
  And none from that of Art.

A winding wall of mossy stone,
  Frost-flung and broken, lines
A lonesome acre thinly grown
  With grass and wandering vines.

Without the wall a birch-tree shows
  Its drooped and tasselled head;
Within, a stag-horned sumach grows,
  Fern-leafed, with spikes of red.

There, sheep that graze the neighboring plain
  Like white ghosts come and go,
The farm-horse drags his fetlock chain,
  The cow-bell tinkles slow.

Low moans the river from its bed,
  The distant pines reply;
Like mourners shrinking from the dead,
  They stand apart and sigh.

Unshaded smites the summer sun,
  Unchecked the winter blast;
The school-girl learns the place to shun,
  With glances backward cast.

For thus our fathers testified,—
  That he might read who ran,—
The emptiness of human pride,
  The nothingness of man.

They dared not plant the grave with flowers,
  Nor dress the funeral sod,
Where, with a love as deep as ours,
  They left their dead with God.

The hard and thorny path they kept
    From beauty turned aside;
Nor missed they over those who slept
    The grace to life denied.

Yet still the wilding flowers would blow,
    The golden leaves would fall,
The seasons come, the seasons go,
    And God be good to all.

Above the graves the blackberry hung
    In bloom and green its wreath,
And harebells swung as if they rung
    The chimes of peace beneath.

The beauty Nature loves to share,
    The gifts she hath for all,
The common light, the common air,
    O'ercrept the graveyard's wall.

It knew the glow of eventide,
    The sunrise and the noon,
And glorified and sanctified
    It slept beneath the moon.

With flowers or snow-flakes for its sod,
    Around the seasons ran,
And evermore the love of God
    Rebuked the fear of man.

We dwell with fears on either hand,
    Within a daily strife,
And spectral problems waiting stand
    Before the gates of life.

The doubts we vainly seek to solve,
   The truths we know, are one;
The known and nameless stars revolve
   Around the Central Sun.

And if we reap as we have sown
   And take the dole we deal,
The law of pain is love alone,
   The wounding is to heal.

Unharmed from change to change we glide,
   We fall as in our dreams;
The far-off terror at our side
   A smiling angel seems.

Secure on God's all-tender heart
   Alike rest great and small;
Why fear to lose our little part,
   When he is pledged for all?

O fearful heart and troubled brain!
   Take hope and strength from this,—
That Nature never hints in vain,
   Nor prophesies amiss.

Her wild birds sing the same sweet stave,
   Her lights and airs are given
Alike to playground and the grave;
   And over both is Heaven.

TELLING THE BEES

Here is the place; right over the hill
    Runs the path I took;
You can see the gap in the old wall still,
    And the stepping-stones in the shallow brook.

There is the house, with the gate red-barred,
    And the poplars tall;
And the barn's brown length, and the cattle-yard,
    And the white horns tossing above the wall.

There are the bee hives ranged in the sun;
    And down by the brink
Of the brook are her poor flowers, weed-o'errun,
    Pansy and daffodil, rose and pink.

A year has gone, as the tortoise goes,
    Heavy and slow;
And the same rose blows, and the same sun glows,
    And the same brook sings of a year ago.

There's the same sweet clover-smell in the breeze;
    And the June sun warm
Tangles his wings of fire in the trees,
    Setting, as then, over Fernside farm.

I mind me how with a lover's care
    From my Sunday coat
I brushed off the burrs, and smoothed my hair,
    And cooled at the brookside my brow and throat.

Since we parted, a month had passed,—
    To love, a year;

Down through the beeches I looked at last
   On the little red gate and the well-sweep near.

I can see it all now,—the slantwise rain
   Of light through the leaves,
The sundown's blaze on her window-pane,
   The bloom of her roses under the eaves.

Just the same as a month before,—
   The house and the trees,
The barn's brown gable, the vine by the door,—
   Nothing changed but the hives of bees.

Before them, under the garden wall,
   Forward and back,
Went drearily singing the chore-girl small,
   Draping each hive with a shred of black.

Trembling, I listened: the summer sun
   Had the chill of snow;
For I knew she was telling the bees of one
   Gone on the journey we all must go!

Then I said to myself, "My Mary weeps
   For the dead to-day:
Haply her blind old grandsire sleeps
   The fret and the pain of his age away."

But her dog whined low; on the doorway sill,
   With his cane to his chin,
The old man sat; and the chore-girl still
   Sung to the bees stealing out and in.

And the song she was singing ever since
   In my ear sounds on:—

"Stay at home, pretty bees, fly not hence!
   Mistress Mary is dead and gone!"

FOR RIGHTEOUSNESS' SAKE

Inscribed to Friends under Arrest for
Treason against the Slave Power

The age is dull and mean. Men creep,
   Not walk; with blood too pale and tame
   To pay the debt they owe to shame;
Buy cheap, sell dear; eat, drink, and sleep
   Down-pillowed, deaf to moaning want;
Pay tithes for soul-insurance; keep
   Six days to Mammon, one to Cant.

In such a time, give thanks to God,
   That somewhat of the holy rage
   With which the prophets in their age
On all its decent seemings trod,
   Has set your feet upon the lie,
That man and ox and soul and clod
   Are market stock to sell and buy!

The hot words from your lips, my own,
   To caution trained, might not repeat;
   But if some tares among the wheat
Of generous thought and deed were sown,
   No common wrong provoked your zeal;
The silken gauntlet that is thrown
   In such a quarrel rings like steel.

The brave old strife the fathers saw
   For Freedom calls for men again

Like those who battled not in vain
For England's Charter, Alfred's law;
  And right of speech and trial just
Wage in your name their ancient war
  With venal courts and perjured trust.

God's ways seem dark, but, soon or late,
  They touch the shining hills of day;
  The evil cannot brook delay,
The good can well afford to wait.
  Give ermined knaves their hour of crime;
Ye have the future grand and great,
  The safe appeal of Truth to Time!

MY PLAYMATE

The pines were dark on Ramoth hill,
  Their song was soft and low;
The blossoms in the sweet May wind
  Were falling like the snow.

The blossoms drifted at our feet,
  The orchard birds sang clear;
The sweetest and the saddest day
  It seemed of all the year.

For, more to me than birds or flowers,
  My playmate left her home,
And took with her the laughing spring,
  The music and the bloom.

She kissed the lips of kith and kin,
  She laid her hand in mine:

What more could ask the bashful boy
    Who fed her father's kine?

She left us in the bloom of May:
    The constant years told o'er
Their seasons with as sweet May morns,
    But she came back no more.

I walk, with noiseless feet, the round
    Of uneventful years;
Still o'er and o'er I sow the spring
    And reap the autumn ears.

She lives where all the golden year
    Her summer roses blow;
The dusky children of the sun
    Before her come and go.

There haply with her jewelled hands
    She smooths her silken gown,—
No more the homespun lap wherein
    I shook the walnuts down.

The wild grapes wait us by the brook,
    The brown nuts on the hill,
And still the May-day flowers make sweet
    The woods of Follymill.

The lilies blossom in the pond,
    The bird builds in the tree,
The dark pines sing on Ramoth hill
    The slow song of the sea.

I wonder if she thinks of them,
    And how the old time seems,—

If ever the pines of Ramoth wood
  Are sounding in her dreams.

I see her face, I hear her voice:
  Does she remember mine?
And what to her is now the boy
  Who fed her father's kine?

What cares she that the orioles build
  For other eyes than ours,—
That other hands with nuts are filled,
  And other laps with flowers?

O playmate in the golden time!
  Our mossy seat is green,
Its fringing violets blossom yet,
  The old trees o'er it lean.

The winds so sweet with birch and fern
  A sweeter memory blow;
And there in spring the veeries sing
  The song of long ago.

And still the pines of Ramoth wood
  Are moaning like the sea,—
The moaning of the sea of change
  Between myself and thee!

MONADNOCK FROM WACHUSET

I would I were a painter, for the sake
  Of a sweet picture, and of her who led,
A fitting guide, with reverential tread,

Into that mountain mystery. First a lake
　Tinted with sunset; next the wavy lines
　　Of far receding hills; and yet more far,
　Monadnock lifting from his night of pines
　　His rosy forehead to the evening star.
Beside us, purple-zoned, Wachuset laid
His head against the West, whose warm light made
　　His aureole; and o'er him, sharp and clear,
Like a shaft of lightning in mid-launching stayed,
　A single level cloud-line, shone upon
　By the fierce glances of the sunken sun,
　　Menaced the darkness with its golden spear!

So twilight deepened round us. Still and black
The great woods climbed the mountain at our back;
And on their skirts, where yet the lingering day
On the shorn greenness of the clearing lay,
　The brown old farm-house like a bird's-nest hung.
With home-life sounds the desert air was stirred:
The bleat of sheep along the hill we heard,
The bucket plashing in the cool, sweet well,
The pasture-bars that clattered as they fell;
Dogs barked, fowls fluttered, cattle lowed; the gate
Of the barn-yard creaked beneath the merry weight
　Of sun-brown children, listening, while they swung,
　　The welcome sound of supper-call to hear;
　　And down the shadowy lane, in tinklings clear,
　The pastoral curfew of the cow-bell rung.
Thus soothed and pleased, our backward path we took,
　Praising the farmer's home. He only spake,
　Looking into the sunset o'er the lake,
　　Like one to whom the far-off is most near:
"Yes, most folks think it has a pleasant look;
　I love it for my good old mother's sake,

Who lived and died here in the peace of God!"
The lesson of his words we pondered o'er,
As silently we turned the eastern flank
Of the mountain, where its shadow deepest sank,
Doubling the night along our rugged road:
We felt that man was more than his abode,—
The inward life than Nature's raiment more;
And the warm sky, the sundown-tinted hill,
The forest and the lake, seemed dwarfed and dim
Before the saintly soul, whose human will
Meekly in the Eternal footsteps trod,
Making her homely toil and household ways
An earthly echo of the song of praise
Swelling from angel lips and harps of seraphim.

LAUS DEO! *

It is done!
Clang of bell and roar of gun
Send the tidings up and down.
How the belfries rock and reel!
How the great guns, peal on peal,
Fling the joy from town to town!

Ring, O bells!
Every stroke exulting tells
Of the burial hour of crime.
Loud and long, that all may hear,
Ring for every listening ear
Of Eternity and Time!

* Composed while the bells were ringing to celebrate the passage of the Constitutional Amendment abolishing slavery.

Let us kneel:
God's own voice is in that peal,
And this spot is holy ground.
Lord, forgive us! What are we,
That our eyes this glory see,
That our ears have heard the sound!

For the Lord
On the whirlwind is abroad;
In the earthquake He has spoken:
He has smitten with his thunder
The iron walls asunder,
And the gates of brass are broken!

Loud and long
Lift the old exulting song;
Sing with Miriam by the sea,
He has cast the mighty down;
Horse and rider sink and drown;
"He hath triumphed gloriously!"

Did we dare,
In our agony of prayer,
Ask for more than He has done?
When was ever his right hand
Over any time or land
Stretched as now beneath the sun?

How they pale,
Ancient myth and song and tale,
In this wonder of our days,
When the cruel rod of war
Blossoms white with righteous law,
And the wrath of man is praise!

Blotted out!
All within and all about
Shall a fresher life begin;
Freer breathe the universe
As it rolls its heavy curse
On the dead and buried sin!

It is done!
In the circuit of the sun
Shall the sound thereof go forth.
It shall bid the sad rejoice,
It shall give the dumb a voice,
It shall belt with joy the earth!

Ring and swing,
Bells of joy! On morning's wing
Send the song of praise abroad!
With a sound of broken chains
Tell the nations that He reigns,
Who alone is Lord and God!

SNOW–BOUND*

A WINTER IDYL

The sun that brief December day
Rose cheerless over hills of gray,
And, darkly circled, gave at noon
A sadder light than waning moon.
Slow tracing down the thickening sky

* The scene is the Whittier homestead in East Haverhill. The people described are the members of the family, the district schoolmaster, and a gifted but eccentric young woman named Harriet Livermore.

Its mute and ominous prophecy,
A portent seeming less than threat,
It sank from sight before it set.
A chill no coat, however stout,
Of homespun stuff could quite shut out,
A hard, dull bitterness of cold,
That checked, mid-vein, the circling race
Of life-blood in the sharpened face,
The coming of the snow-storm told.
The wind blew east; we heard the roar
Of Ocean on his wintry shore,
And felt the strong pulse throbbing there
Beat with low rhythm our inland air.

Meanwhile we did our nightly chores,—
Brought in the wood from out of doors,
Littered the stalls, and from the mows
Raked down the herd's-grass for the cows:
Heard the horse whinnying for his corn;
And, sharply clashing horn on horn,
Impatient down the stanchion rows
The cattle shake their walnut bows;
While, peering from his early perch
Upon the scaffold's pole of birch,
The cock his crested helmet bent
And down his querulous challenge sent.

Unwarmed by any sunset light
The gray day darkened into night,
A night made hoary with the swarm
And whirl-dance of the blinding storm,
As zigzag, wavering to and fro,
Crossed and recrossed the wingèd snow:
And ere the early bedtime came

The white drift piled the window-frame,
And through the glass the clothes-line posts
Looked in like tall and sheeted ghosts.

So all night long the storm roared on:
The morning broke without a sun;
In tiny spherule traced with lines
Of Nature's geometric signs,
In starry flake, and pellicle,
All day the hoary meteor fell;
And, when the second morning shone,
We looked upon a world unknown,
On nothing we could call our own.
Around the glistening wonder bent
The blue walls of the firmament,
No cloud above, no earth below,—
A universe of sky and snow!
The old familiar sights of ours
Took marvellous shapes; strange domes and towers
Rose up where sty or corn-crib stood,
Or garden-wall, or belt of wood;
A smooth white mound the brush-pile showed,
A fenceless drift what once was road;
The bridle-post an old man sat
With loose-flung coat and high cocked hat;
The well-curb had a Chinese roof;
And even the long sweep, high aloof,
In its slant splendor, seemed to tell
Of Pisa's leaning miracle.

A prompt, decisive man, no breath
Our father wasted: "Boys, a path!"
Well pleased (for when did farmer boy
Count such a summons less than joy?)
Our buskins on our feet we drew;

With mittened hands, and caps drawn low,
To guard our necks and ears from snow,
We cut the solid whiteness through.
And, where the drift was deepest, made
A tunnel walled and overlaid
With dazzling crystal: we had read
Of rare Aladdin's wondrous cave,
And to our own his name we gave,
With many a wish the luck were ours
To test his lamp's supernal powers.
We reached the barn with merry din,
And roused the prisoned brutes within.
The old horse thrust his long head out,
And grave with wonder gazed about;
The cock his lusty greeting said,
And forth his speckled harem led;
The oxen lashed their tails, and hooked,
And mild reproach of hunger looked;
The hornèd patriarch of the sheep,
Like Egypt's Amun roused from sleep,
Shook his sage head with gesture mute,
And emphasized with stamp of foot.

All day the gusty north-wind bore
The loosening drift its breath before;
Low circling round its southern zone,
The sun through dazzling snow-mist shone.
No church-bell lent its Christian tone
To the savage air, no social smoke
Curled over woods of snow-hung oak.
A solitude made more intense
By dreary-voicèd elements,
The shrieking of the mindless wind,
The moaning tree-boughs swaying blind,
And on the glass the unmeaning beat

Of ghostly finger-tips of sleet.
Beyond the circle of our hearth
No welcome sound of toil or mirth
Unbound the spell, and testified
Of human life and thought outside.
We minded that the sharpest ear
The buried brooklet could not hear,
The music of whose liquid lip
Had been to us companionship,
And, in our lonely life, had grown
To have an almost human tone.

As night drew on, and, from the crest
Of wooded knolls that ridged the west,
The sun, a snow-blown traveller, sank
From sight beneath the smothering bank,
We piled, with care, our nightly stack
Of wood against the chimney-back,—
The oaken log, green, huge, and thick,
And on its top the stout back-stick;
The knotty forestick laid apart,
And filled between with curious art
The ragged brush; then, hovering near,
We watched the first red blaze appear,
Heard the sharp crackle, caught the gleam
On whitewashed wall and sagging beam,
Until the old, rude-furnished room
Burst, flower-like, into rosy bloom;
While radiant with a mimic flame
Outside the sparkling drift became,
And through the bare-boughed lilac-tree
Our own warm hearth seemed blazing free.
The crane and pendent trammels showed,
The Turks' heads on the andirons glowed;
While childish fancy, prompt to tell

The meaning of the miracle,
Whispered the old rhyme: "*Under the tree,*
When fire outdoors burns merrily,
There the witches are making tea."

The moon above the eastern wood
Shone at its full; the hill-range stood
Transfigured in the silver flood,
Its blown snows flashing cold and keen,
Dead white, save where some sharp ravine
Took shadow, or the somber green
Of hemlocks turned to pitchy black
Against the whiteness at their back.
For such a world and such a night
Most fitting that unwarming light,
Which only seemed where'er it fell
To make the coldness visible.

Shut in from all the world without,
We sat the clean-winged hearth about,
Content to let the north-wind roar
In baffled rage at pane and door,
While the red logs before us beat
The frost-line back with tropic heat;
And ever, when a louder blast
Shook beam and rafter as it passed,
The merrier up its roaring draught
The great throat of the chimney laughed;
The house-dog on his paws outspread
Laid to the fire his drowsy head,
The cat's dark silhouette on the wall
A couchant tiger's seemed to fall;
And, for the winter fireside meet,
Between the andirons' straddling feet,
The mug of cider simmered slow,

The apples sputtered in a row,
And, close at hand, the basket stood
With nuts from brown October's wood.

What matter how the night behaved?
What matter how the north-wind raved?
Blow high, blow low, not all its snow
Could quench our hearth-fire's ruddy glow.
O Time and Change!—with hair as gray
As was my sire's that winter day,
How strange it seems, with so much gone
Of life and love, to still live on!
Ah, brother! only I and thou
Are left of all that circle now,—
The dear home faces whereupon
That fitful firelight paled and shone.
Henceforward, listen as we will,
The voices of that hearth are still;
Look where we may, the wide earth o'er,
Those lighted faces smile no more.
We tread the paths their feet have worn,
    We sit beneath their orchard trees,
    We hear, like them, the hum of bees
And rustle of the bladed corn;
We turn the pages that they read,
    Their written words we linger o'er,
But in the sun they cast no shade,
No voice is heard, no sign is made,
    No step is on the conscious floor!
Yet Love will dream, and Faith will trust,
(Since He who knows our need is just,)
That somehow, somewhere, meet we must.
Alas for him who never sees
The stars shine through his cypress-trees!
Who, hopeless, lays his dead away,

Nor looks to see the breaking day
Across the mournful marbles play!
Who hath not learned, in hours of faith,
    The truth to flesh and sense unknown,
That Life is ever lord of Death,
    And Love can never lose its own!

We sped the time with stories old,
Wrought puzzles out, and riddles told,
Or stammered from our school-book lore
"The Chief of Gambia's golden shore."
How often since, when all the land
Was clay in Slavery's shaping hand,
As if a far-blown trumpet stirred
The languorous sin-sick air, I heard:
"*Does not the voice of reason cry,*
    Claim the first right which Nature gave,
From the red scourge of bondage fly,
    Nor deign to live a burdened slave!"
Our father rode again his ride
On Memphremagog's wooded side;
Sat down again to moose and samp
In trapper's hut and Indian camp;
Lived o'er the old idyllic ease
Beneath St. François' hemlock-trees;
Again for him the moonlight shone
On Norman cap and bodiced zone;
Again he heard the violin play
Which led the village dance away,
And mingled in its merry whirl
The grandam and the laughing girl.
Or, nearer home, our steps he led
Where Salisbury's level marshes spread
    Mile-wide as flies the laden bee;
Where merry mowers, hale and strong,

Swept, scythe on scythe, their swaths along
   The low green prairies of the sea.
We shared the fishing off Boar's Head,
   And round the rocky Isles of Shoals
   The hake-broil on the drift-wood coals;
The chowder on the sand-beach made,
Dipped by the hungry, steaming hot,
With spoons of clam-shell from the pot.
We heard the tales of witchcraft old,
And dream and sign and marvel told
To sleepy listeners as they lay
Stretched idly on the salted hay,
Adrift along the winding shores,
When favoring breezes deigned to blow
The square sail of the gundelow
And idle lay the useless oars.

Our mother, while she turned her wheel
Or run the new-knit stocking-heel,
Told how the Indian hordes came down
At midnight on Cocheco town,
And how her own great-uncle bore
His cruel scalp-mark to fourscore.
Recalling, in her fitting phrase,
   So rich and picturesque and free,
   (The common unrhymed poetry
Of simple life and country ways,)
The story of her early days,—
She made us welcome to her home;
Old hearths grew wide to give us room;
We stole with her a frightened look
At the gray wizard's conjuring-book,
The fame whereof went far and wide
Through all the simple country-side;
We heard the hawks at twilight play,

The boat-horn on Piscataqua,
The loon's weird laughter far away;
We fished her little trout-brook, knew
What flowers in wood and meadow grew,
What sunny hillsides autumn-brown
She climbed to shake the ripe nuts down,
Saw where in sheltered cove and bay
The ducks' black squadron anchored lay,
And heard the wild-geese calling loud
Beneath the gray November cloud.

Then, haply, with a look more grave,
And soberer tone, some tale she gave
From painful Sewel's ancient tome,
Beloved in every Quaker home,
Of faith fire-winged by martyrdom,
Or Chalkley's Journal, old and quaint,—
Gentlest of skippers, rare sea-saint!—
Who, when the dreary calms prevailed,
And water-butt and bread-cask failed,
And cruel, hungry eyes pursued
His portly presence mad for food,
With dark hints muttered under breath
Of casting lots for life or death,
Offered, if Heaven withheld supplies,
To be himself the sacrifice.
Then, suddenly, as if to save
The good man from his living grave,
A ripple on the water grew,
A school of porpoise flashed in view.
"Take, eat," he said, "and be content;
These fishes in my stead are sent
By Him who gave the tangled ram
To spare the child of Abraham."

Our uncle, innocent of books,
Was rich in lore of fields and brooks,
The ancient teachers never dumb
Of Nature's unhoused lyceum.
In moons and tides and weather wise,
He read the clouds as prophecies,
And foul or fair could well divine,
By many an occult hint and sign,
Holding the cunning-warded keys
To all the woodcraft mysteries;
Himself to Nature's heart so near
That all her voices in his ear
Of beast or bird had meanings clear,
Like Apollonius of old,
Who knew the tales the sparrows told,
Or Hermes, who interpreted
What the sage cranes of Nilus said;
A simple, guileless, childlike man,
Content to live where life began;
Strong only on his native grounds,
The little world of sights and sounds
Whose girdle was the parish bounds,
Whereof his fondly partial pride
The common features magnified,
As Surrey hills to mountains grew
In White of Selborne's loving view,—
He told how teal and loon he shot,
And how the eagle's eggs he got,
The feats on pond and river done,
The prodigies of rod and gun;
Till, warming with the tales he told,
Forgotten was the outside cold,
The bitter wind unheeded blew,
From ripening corn the pigeons flew,

The partridge drummed i' the wood, the mink
Went fishing down the river-brink.
In fields with bean or clover gay,
The woodchuck, like a hermit gray,
  Peered from the doorway of his cell;
The muskrat plied the mason's trade,
And tier by tier his mud-walls laid;
And from the shagbark overhead
  The grizzled squirrel dropped his shell.

Next, the dear aunt, whose smile of cheer
And voice in dreams I see and hear—
The sweetest woman ever Fate
Perverse denied a household mate,
Who, lonely, homeless, not the less
Found peace in love's unselfishness,
And welcome whereso'er she went,
A calm and gracious element,
Whose presence seemed the sweet income
And womanly atmosphere of home—
Called up her girlhood memories,
The huskings and the apple-bees,
The sleigh-rides and the summer sails,
Weaving through all the poor details
And homespun warp of circumstance
A golden woof-thread of romance.
For well she kept her genial mood
And simple faith of maidenhood;
Before her still a cloud-land lay,
The mirage loomed across her way;
The morning dew, that dries so soon
With others, glistened at her noon;
Through years of toil and soil and care,
From glossy tress to thin gray hair,
All unprofaned she held apart

The virgin fancies of the heart.
Be shame to him of woman born
Who hath for such but thought of scorn.

There, too, our elder sister plied
Her evening task the stand beside;
A full, rich nature, free to trust,
Truthful and almost sternly just,
Impulsive, earnest, prompt to act,
And make her generous thought a fact,
Keeping with many a light disguise
The secret of self-sacrifice.
O heart sore-tried! thou hast the best,
That Heaven itself could give thee,—rest,
Rest from all bitter thoughts and things!
How many a poor one's blessing went
With thee beneath the low green tent
Whose curtain never outward swings!

As one who held herself a part
Of all she saw, and let her heart
Against the household bosom lean,
Upon the motley-braided mat
Our youngest and our dearest sat,
Lifting her large, sweet, asking eyes,
Now bathed in the unfading green
And holy peace of Paradise.
Oh, looking from some heavenly hill,
Or from the shade of saintly palms,
Or silver reach of river calms,
Do those large eyes behold me still?
With me one little year ago:—
The chill weight of the winter snow
For months upon her grave has lain;
And now, when summer south-winds blow

And brier and harebell bloom again,
I tread the pleasant paths we trod,
I see the violet-sprinkled sod
Whereon she leaned, too frail and weak
The hillside flowers she loved to seek,
Yet following me wher'er I went
With dark eyes full of love's content.
The birds are glad; the brier-rose fills
The air with sweetness; all the hills
Stretch green to June's unclouded sky;
But still I wait with ear and eye
For something gone which should be nigh,
A loss in all familiar things,
In flower that blooms, and bird that sings.
And yet, dear heart! remembering thee,
　　Am I not richer than of old?
Safe in thy immortality,
　　What change can reach the wealth I hold?
　　What chance can mar the pearl and gold
Thy love hath left in trust with me?
And while in life's late afternoon,
　　Where cool and long the shadows grow,
I walk to meet the night that soon
　　Shall shape and shadow overflow,
I cannot feel that thou art far,
Since near at need the angels are;
And when the sunset gates unbar,
　　Shall I not see thee waiting stand,
And, white against the evening star,
　　The welcome of thy beckoning hand?

Brisk wielder of the birch and rule,
The master of the district school
Held at the fire his favored place,
Its warm glow lit a laughing face

Fresh-hued and fair, where scarce appeared
The uncertain prophecy of beard.
He teased the mitten-blinded cat,
Played cross-pins on my uncle's hat,
Sang songs, and told us what befalls
In classic Dartmouth's college halls.
Born the wild Northern hills among,
From whence his yeoman father wrung
By patient toil subsistence scant,
Not competence and yet not want,
He early gained the power to pay
His cheerful, self-reliant way;
Could doff at ease his scholar's gown
To peddle wares from town to town;
Or through the long vacation's reach
In lonely lowland districts teach,
Where all the droll experience found
At stranger hearths in boarding round,
The moonlit skater's keen delight,
The sleigh-drive through the frosty night,
The rustic-party, with its rough
Accompaniment of blind-man's-buff,
And whirling-plate, and forfeits paid,
His winter task a pastime made.
Happy the snow-locked homes wherein
He tuned his merry violin,
Or played the athlete in the barn,
Or held the good dame's winding-yarn,
Or mirth-provoking versions told
Of classic legends rare and old,
Wherein the scenes of Greece and Rome
Had all the commonplace of home,
And little seemed at best the odds
'Twixt Yankee pedlers and old gods;
Where Pindus-born Arachthus took

The guise of any grist-mill brook,
And dread Olympus at his will
Became a huckleberry hill.

A careless boy that night he seemed;
    But at his desk he had the look
And air of one who wisely schemed,
    And hostage from the future took
    In trainèd thought and lore of book.
Large-brained, clear-eyed, of such as he
Shall Freedom's young apostles be,
Who, following in War's bloody trail,
Shall every lingering wrong assail;
All chains from limb and spirit strike,
Uplift the black and white alike;
Scatter before their swift advance
The darkness and the ignorance,
The pride, the lust, the squalid sloth,
Which nurtured Treason's monstrous growth,
Made murder pastime, and the hell
Of prison-torture possible;
The cruel lie of caste refute,
Old forms remould, and substitute
For Slavery's lash the freeman's will,
For blind routine, wise-handed skill;
A school-house plant on every hill,
Stretching in radiate nerve-lines thence
The quick wires of intelligence;
Till North and South together brought
Shall own the same electric thought,
In peace a common flag salute,
And, side by side in labor's free
And unresentful rivalry,
Harvest the fields wherein they fought.

Another guest that winter night
Flashed back from lustrous eyes the light.
Unmarked by time, and yet not young,
The honeyed music of her tongue
And words of meekness scarcely told
A nature passionate and bold,
Strong, self-concentred, spurning guide,
Its milder features dwarfed beside
Her unbent will's majestic pride.
She sat among us, at the best,
A not unfeared, half-welcome guest,
Rebuking with her cultured phrase
Our homeliness of words and ways.
A certain pard-like, treacherous grace
Swayed the lithe limbs and dropped the lash,
Lent the white teeth their dazzling flash;
And under low brows, black with night,
Rayed out at times a dangerous light;
The sharp heat-lightnings of her face
   Presaging ill to him whom Fate
   Condemned to share her love or hate.
A woman tropical, intense
In thought and act, in soul and sense,
She blended in a like degree
The vixen and the devotee,
Revealing with each freak or feint
   The temper of Petruchio's Kate,
The raptures of Siena's saint.
Her tapering hand and rounded wrist
Had facile power to form a fist;
The warm, dark languish of her eyes
Was never safe from wrath's surprise.
Brows saintly calm and lips devout
Knew every change of scowl and pout;

And the sweet voice had notes more high
And shrill for social battle-cry.

Since then what old cathedral town
Has missed her pilgrim staff and gown,
What convent-gate has held its lock
Against the challenge of her knock!
Through Smyrna's plague-hushed thoroughfares,
Up sea-set Malta's rocky stairs,
Gray olive slopes of hills that hem
Thy tombs and shrines, Jerusalem,
Or startling on her desert throne
The crazy Queen of Lebanon
With claims fantastic as her own,
Her tireless feet have held their way;
And still, unrestful, bowed, and gray,
She watches under Eastern skies,
    With hope each day renewed and fresh,
    The Lord's quick coming in the flesh,
Whereof she dreams and prophesies!

Where'er her troubled path may be,
    The Lord's sweet pity with her go!
The outward wayward life we see,
    The hidden springs we may not know.
Nor is it given us to discern
    What threads the fatal sisters spun,
    Through what ancestral years has run
The sorrow with the woman born,
What forged her cruel chain of moods,
What set her feet in solitudes,
    And held the love within her mute,
What mingled madness in the blood,
    A life-long discord and annoy,
    Water of tears with oil of joy,

And hid within the folded bud
  Perversities of flower and fruit.
It is not ours to separate
The tangled skein of will and fate,
To show what metes and bounds should stand
Upon the soul's debatable land,
And between choice and Providence
Divide the circle of events;
But He who knows our frame is just,
Merciful and compassionate,
And full of sweet assurances
And hope for all the language is,
That He remembereth we are dust!

At last the great logs, crumbling low,
Sent out a dull and duller glow,
The bull's-eye watch that hung in view,
Ticking its weary circuit through,
Pointed with mutely warning sign
Its black hand to the hour of nine.
That sign the pleasant circle broke:
My uncle ceased his pipe to smoke,
Knocked from its bowl the refuse gray,
And laid it tenderly away;
Then roused himself to safely cover
The dull red brands with ashes over.
And while, with care, our mother laid
The work aside, her steps she stayed
One moment, seeking to express
Her grateful sense of happiness
For food and shelter, warmth and health,
And love's contentment more than wealth,
With simple wishes (not the weak,
Vain prayers which no fulfilment seek,
But such as warm the generous heart,

O'er-prompt to do with Heaven its part)
That none might lack, that bitter night,
For bread and clothing, warmth and light.

Within our beds awhile we heard
The wind that round the gables roared,
With now and then a ruder shock,
Which made our very bedsteads rock.
We heard the loosened clapboards tost,
The board-nails snapping in the frost;
And on us, through the unplastered wall,
Felt the light sifted snow-flakes fall.
But sleep stole on, as sleep will do
When hearts are light and life is new;
Faint and more faint the murmurs grew,
Till in the summer-land of dreams
They softened to the sound of streams,
Low stir of leaves, and dip of oars,
And lapsing waves on quiet shores.

Next morn we wakened with the shout
Of merry voices high and clear;
And saw the teamsters drawing near
To break the drifted highways out.
Down the long hillside treading slow
We saw the half-buried oxen go,
Shaking the snow from heads uptost,
Their straining nostrils white with frost.
Before our door the straggling train
Drew up, an added team to gain.
The elders threshed their hands a-cold,
    Passed, with the cider-mug, their jokes
    From lip to lip; the younger folks
Down the loose snow-banks, wrestling, rolled,
Then toiled again the cavalcade

O'er windy hill, through clogged ravine,
   And woodland paths that wound between
Low drooping pine-boughs winter-weighed.
From every barn a team afoot,
At every house a new recruit,
Where, drawn by Nature's subtlest law,
Haply the watchful young men saw
Sweet doorway pictures of the curls
And curious eyes of merry girls,
Lifting their hands in mock defence
Against the snow-ball's compliments,
And reading in each missive tost
The charm with Eden never lost.

We heard once more the sleigh-bells' sound;
   And, following where the teamsters led,
The wise old Doctor went his round,
Just pausing at our door to say,
In the brief autocratic way
Of one who, prompt at Duty's call,
Was free to urge her claim on all,
   That some poor neighbor sick abed
At night our mother's aid would need.
For, one in generous thought and deed,
   What mattered in the sufferer's sight
   The Quaker matron's inward light,
The Doctor's mail of Calvin's creed?
All hearts confess the saints elect
   Who, twain in faith, in love agree,
And melt not in an acid sect
   The Christian pearl of charity!

So days went on: a week had passed
Since the great world was heard from last.
The Almanac we studied o'er,

Read and reread our little store
Of books and pamphlets, scarce a score;
One harmless novel, mostly hid
From younger eyes, a book forbid,
And poetry, (or good or bad,
A single book was all we had,)
Where Ellwood's meek, drab-skirted Muse,
   A stranger to the heathen Nine,
   Sang, with a somewhat nasal whine,
The wars of David and the Jews.
At last the floundering carrier bore
The village paper to our door.
Lo! broadening outward as we read,
To warmer zones the horizon spread;
In panoramic length unrolled
We saw the marvels that it told.
Before us passed the painted Creeks,
   And daft McGregor on his raids
   In Costa Rica's everglades.
And up Taygetos winding slow
Rode Ypsilanti's Mainote Greeks,
A Turk's head at each saddle-bow!
Welcome to us its week-old news,
Its corner for the rustic Muse,
   Its monthly gauge of snow and rain,
Its record, mingling in a breath
The wedding bell and dirge of death:
Jest, anecdote, and love-lorn tale,
The latest culprit sent to jail;
Its hue and cry of stolen and lost,
Its vendue sales and goods at cost,
   And traffic calling loud for gain.
We felt the stir of hall and street,
The pulse of life that round us beat;
The chill embargo of the snow

Was melted in the genial glow;
Wide swung again our ice-locked door,
And all the world was ours once more!

Clasp, Angel of the backward look
    And folded wings of ashen gray
    And voice of echoes far away,
The brazen covers of thy book;
The weird palimpsest old and vast,
Wherein thou hid'st the spectral past;
Where, closely mingling, pale and glow
The characters of joy and woe;
The monographs of outlived years,
Or smile-illumed or dim with tears,
    Green hills of life that slope to death,
And haunts of home, whose vistaed trees
Shade off to mournful cypresses
    With the white amaranths underneath.
Even while I look, I can but heed
    The restless sands' incessant fall,
Importunate hours that hours succeed,
Each clamorous with its own sharp need,
    And duty keeping pace with all.
Shut down and clasp the heavy lids;
I hear again the voice that bids
The dreamer leave his dream midway
For larger hopes and graver fears:
Life greatens in these later years,
The century's aloe flowers to-day!

Yet, haply, in some lull of life,
Some Truce of God which breaks its strife,
The worldling's eyes shall gather dew,
    Dreaming in throngful city ways
Of winter joys his boyhood knew;

And dear and early friends—the few
Who yet remain—shall pause to view
   These Flemish pictures of old days;
Sit with me by the homestead hearth,
And stretch the hands of memory forth
   To warm them at the wood-fire's blaze!
And thanks untraced to lips unknown
Shall greet me like the odors blown
From unseen meadows newly mown,
Or lilies floating in some pond,
Wood-fringed, the wayside gaze beyond;
The traveller owns the grateful sense
Of sweetness near, he knows not whence,
And, pausing, takes with forehead bare
The benediction of the air.

ABRAHAM DAVENPORT

In the old days (a custom laid aside
With breeches and cocked hats) the people sent
Their wisest men to make the public laws.
And so, from a brown homestead, where the Sound
Drinks the small tribute of the Mianas,
Waved over by the woods of Rippowams,
And hallowed by pure lives and tranquil deaths,
Stamford sent up to the councils of the State
Wisdom and grace in Abraham Davenport.

'Twas on a May-day of the far old year
Seventeen hundred eighty, that there fell
Over the bloom and sweet life of the Spring,
Over the fresh earth and the heaven of noon,

A horror of great darkness, like the night
In day of which the Norland sagas tell,—
The Twilight of the Gods. The low-hung sky
Was black with ominous clouds, save where its rim
Was fringed with a dull glow, like that which climbs
The crater's sides from the red hell below.
Birds ceased to sing, and all the barnyard fowls
Roosted; the cattle at the pasture bars
Lowed, and looked homeward; bats on leathern wings
Flitted abroad; the sounds of labor died;
Men prayed, and women wept; all ears grew sharp
To hear the doom-blast of the trumpet shatter
The black sky, that the dreadful face of Christ
Might look from the rent clouds, not as he looked
A loving guest at Bethany, but stern
As Justice and inexorable Law.

Meanwhile in the old State House, dim as ghosts,
Sat the lawgivers of Connecticut,
Trembling beneath their legislative robes.
"It is the Lord's Great Day! Let us adjourn,"
Some said; and then, as if with one accord,
All eyes were turned to Abraham Davenport.
He rose, slow cleaving with his steady voice
The intolerable hush. "This well may be
The Day of Judgment which the world awaits;
But be it so or not, I only know
My present duty, and my Lord's command
To occupy till he come. So at the post
Where he hath set me in his providence,
I choose, for one, to meet him face to face,—
No faithless servant frightened from my task,
But ready when the Lord of the harvest calls;
And therefore, with all reverence, I would say,

Let God do his work, we will see to ours.
Bring in the candles." And they brought them in.

Then by the flaring lights the Speaker read,
Albeit with husky voice and shaking hands,
An act to amend an act to regulate
The shad and alewive fisheries. Whereupon
Wisely and well spake Abraham Davenport,
Straight to the question, with no figures of speech
Save the ten Arab signs, yet not without
The shrewd dry humor natural to the man:
His awe-struck colleagues listening all the while,
Between the pauses of his argument,
To hear the thunder of the wrath of God
Break from the hollow trumpet of the cloud.

And there he stands in memory to this day,
Erect, self-poised, a rugged face, half seen
Against the background of unnatural dark,
A witness to the ages as they pass,
That simple duty hath no place for fear.

From AMONG THE HILLS

PRELUDE

Along the roadside, like the flowers of gold
That tawny Incas for their gardens wrought,
Heavy with sunshine droops the goldenrod,
And the red pennons of the cardinal-flowers
Hang motionless upon their upright staves.
The sky is hot and hazy, and the wind,
Wing-weary with its long flight from the south,

Unfelt; yet, closely scanned, yon maple leaf
With faintest motion, as one stirs in dreams,
Confesses it. The locust by the wall
Stabs the noon-silence with his sharp alarm.
A single hay-cart down the dusty road
Creaks slowly, with its driver fast asleep
On the load's top. Against the neighboring hill,
Huddled along the stone wall's shady side,
The sheep show white, as if a snowdrift still
Defied the dog-star. Through the open door
A drowsy smell of flowers—gray heliotrope,
And white sweet clover, and shy mignonette—
Comes faintly in, and silent chorus lends
To the pervading symphony of peace.

No time is this for hands long overworn
To task their strength: and (unto Him be praise
Who giveth quietness!) the stress and strain
Of years that did the work of centuries
Have ceased, and we can draw our breath once more
Freely and full. So, as yon harvesters
Make glad their nooning underneath the elms
With tale and riddle and old snatch of song,
I lay aside grave themes, and idly turn
The leaves of memory's sketch-book, dreaming o'er
Old summer pictures of the quiet hills,
And human life, as quiet, at their feet.

And yet not idly all. A farmer's son,
Proud of field-lore and harvest craft, and feeling
All their fine possibilities, how rich
And restful even poverty and toil
Become when beauty, harmony, and love
Sit at their humble hearth as angels sat
At evening in the patriarch's tent, when man

Makes labor noble, and his farmer's frock
The symbol of a Christian chivalry
Tender and just and generous to her
Who clothes with grace all duty; still, I know
Too well the picture has another side,—
How wearily the grind of toil goes on
Where love is wanting, how the eye and ear
And heart are starved amidst the plenitude
Of nature, and how hard and colorless
Is life without an atmosphere. I look
Across the lapse of half a century,
And call to mind old homesteads, where no flower
Told that the spring had come, but evil weeds,
Nightshade and rough-leaved burdock in the place
Of the sweet doorway greeting of the rose
And honeysuckle, where the house walls seemed
Blistering in sun, without a tree or vine
To cast the tremulous shadow of its leaves
Across the curtainless windows from whose panes
Fluttered the signal rags of shiftlessness;
Within, the cluttered kitchen-floor, unwashed
(Broom-clean I think they called it); the best room
Stifling with cellar damp, shut from the air
In hot midsummer, bookless, pictureless
Save the inevitable sampler hung
Over the fireplace, or a mourning piece,
A green-haired woman, peony-cheeked, beneath
Impossible willows; the wide-throated hearth
Bristling with faded pine-boughs half concealing
The piled-up rubbish at the chimney's back;
And, in sad keeping with all things about them,
Shrill, querulous women, sour and sullen men,
Untidy, loveless, old before their time,
With scarce a human interest save their own
Monotonous round of small economies,

Or the poor scandal of the neighborhood;
Blind to the beauty everywhere revealed,
Treading the May-flowers with regardless feet;
For them the song-sparrow and the bobolink
Sang not, nor winds made music in the leaves;
For them in vain October's holocaust
Burned, gold and crimson, over all the hills,
The sacramental mystery of the woods.
Church-goers, fearful of the unseen Powers,
But grumbling over pulpit-tax and pew-rent,
Saving, as shrewd economists, their souls
And winter pork with the least possible outlay
Of salt and sanctity; in daily life
Showing as little actual comprehension
Of Christian charity and love and duty,
As if the Sermon on the Mount had been
Outdated like a last year's almanac:
Rich in broad woodlands and in half-tilled fields,
And yet so pinched and bare and comfortless,
The veriest straggler limping on his rounds,
The sun and air his sole inheritance,
Laughed at a poverty that paid its taxes,
And hugged his rags in self-complacency!

Not such should be the homesteads of a land
Where whoso wisely wills and acts may dwell
As king and lawgiver, in broad-acred state,
With beauty, art, taste, culture, books, to make
His hour of leisure richer than a life
Of fourscore to the barons of old time,
Our yeoman should be equal to his home
Set in the fair, green valleys, purple walled,
A man to match his mountains, not to creep
Dwarfed and abased below them. I would fain
In this light way (of which I needs must own

With the knife-grinder of whom Canning sings,
"Story, God bless you! I have none to tell you!")
Invite the eye to see and heart to feel
The beauty and the joy within their reach,—
Home, and home loves, and the beatitudes
Of nature free to all. Haply in years
That wait to take the places of our own,
Heard where some breezy balcony looks down
On happy homes, or where the lake in the moon
Sleeps dreaming of the mountains, fair as Ruth,
In the old Hebrew pastoral, at the feet
Of Boaz, even this simple lay of mine
May seem the burden of a prophecy,
Finding its late fulfilment in a change
Slow as the oak's growth, lifting manhood up
Through broader culture, finer manners, love,
And reverence, to the level of the hills.

O Golden Age, whose light is of the dawn,
And not of sunset, forward, not behind,
Flood the new heavens and earth, and with thee bring
All the old virtues, whatsoever things
Are pure and honest and of good repute,
But add thereto whatever bard has sung
Or seer has told of when in trance and dream
They saw the Happy Isles of prophecy!
Let Justice hold her scale, and Truth divide
Between the right and wrong; but give the heart
The freedom of its fair inheritance;
Let the poor prisoner, cramped and starved so long,
At Nature's table feast his ear and eye
With joy and wonder; let all harmonies
Of sound, form, color, motion, wait upon
The princely guest, whether in soft attire
Of leisure clad, or the coarse frock of toil,

And, lending life to the dead form of faith,
Give human nature reverence for the sake
Of One who bore it, making it divine
With the ineffable tenderness of God;
Let common need, the brotherhood of prayer,
The heirship of an unknown destiny,
The unsolved mystery round about us, make
A man more precious than the gold of Ophir.
Sacred, inviolate, unto whom all things
Should minister, as outward types and signs
Of the eternal beauty which fulfils
The one great purpose of creation, Love,
The sole necessity of Earth and Heaven!

MY TRIUMPH

The autumn-time has come;
On woods that dream of bloom,
And over purpling vines,
The low sun fainter shines.

The aster-flower is failing,
The hazel's gold is paling;
Yet overhead more near
The eternal stars appear!

And present gratitude
Insures the future's good,
And for the things I see
I trust the things to be;

That in the paths untrod,
And the long days of God,

My feet shall still be led,
My heart be comforted.

O living friends who love me!
O dear ones gone above me!
Careless of other fame,
I leave to you my name.

Hide it from idle praises,
Save it from evil phrases:
Why, when dear lips that spake it
Are dumb, should strangers wake it?

Let the thick curtain fall;
I better know than all
How little I have gained,
How vast the unattained.

Not by the page word-painted
Let life be banned or sainted:
Deeper than written scroll
The colors of the soul.

Sweeter than any sung
My songs that found no tongue;
Nobler than any fact
My wish that failed of act.

Others shall sing the song,
Others shall right the wrong,—
Finish what I begin,
And all I fail of win.

What matter, I or they?
Mine or another's day,

So the right word be said
And life the sweeter made?

Hail to the coming singers!
Hail to the brave light-bringers!
Forward I reach and share
All that they sing and dare.

The airs of heaven blow o'er me;
A glory shines before me
Of what mankind shall be,—
Pure, generous, brave, and free.

A dream of man and woman
Diviner but still human,
Solving the riddle old,
Shaping the Age of Gold!

The love of God and neighbor;
An equal-handed labor;
The richer life, where beauty
Walks hand in hand with duty.

Ring, bells in unreared steeples,
The joy of unborn peoples!
Sound, trumpets far off blown,
Your triumph is my own!

Parcel and part of all,
I keep the festival,
Fore-reach the good to be,
And share the victory.

I feel the earth move sunward,
I join the great march onward,

And take, by faith, while living,
My freehold of thanksgiving.

THE BREWING OF SOMA

"These libations mixed with milk have been prepared for In-
dra: offer Soma to the drinker of Soma."
VASHISTA, Trans. by MAX MULLER.

The fagots blazed, the caldron's smoke
    Up through the green wood curled;
"Bring honey from the hollow oak,
Bring milky sap," the brewers spoke,
    In the childhood of the world.

And brewed they well or brewed they ill,
    The priests thrust in their rods,
First tasted, and then drank their fill,
And shouted, with one voice and will,
    "Behold the drink of gods!"

They drank, and lo! in heart and brain
    A new, glad life began;
The gray of hair grew young again,
The sick man laughed away his pain,
    The cripple leaped and ran.

"Drink, mortals, what the gods have sent,
    Forget your long annoy."
So sang the priests. From tent to tent
The Soma's sacred madness went,
    A storm of drunken joy.

Then knew each rapt inebriate
   A winged and glorious birth,
Soared upward, with strange joy elate,
Beat, with dazed head, Varuna's gate,
   And, sobered, sank to earth.

The land with Soma's praises rang;
   On Gihon's banks of shade
Its hymns the dusky maidens sang;
In joy of life or mortal pang
   All men to Soma prayed.

The morning twilight of the race
   Sends down these matin psalms;
And still with wondering eyes we trace
The simple prayers to Soma's grace,
   That Vedic verse embalms.

As in that child-world's early year,
   Each after age has striven
By music, incense, vigils drear,
And trance, to bring the skies more near,
   Or lift men up to heaven!—

Some fever of the blood and brain,
   Some self-exalting spell,
The scourger's keen delight of pain,
The Dervish dance, the Orphic strain,
   The wild-haired Bacchant's yell,—

The desert's hair-grown hermit sunk
   The saner brute below;
The naked Santon, hashish-drunk,
The cloister madness of the monk,
   The fakir's torture-show!

And yet the past comes round again,
   And new doth old fulfil;
In sensual transports wild as vain
We brew in many a Christian fane
   The heathen Soma still!

Dear Lord and Father of mankind,
   Forgive our foolish ways!
Reclothe us in our rightful mind,
In purer lives thy service find,
   In deeper reverence, praise.

In simple trust like theirs who heard
   Beside the Syrian sea
The gracious calling of the Lord,
Let us, like them, without a word,
   Rise up and follow thee.

O Sabbath rest by Galilee!
   O calm of hills above,
Where Jesus knelt to share with thee
The silence of eternity
   Interpreted by love!

With that deep hush subduing all
   Our words and works that drown
The tender whisper of thy call,
As noiseless let thy blessing fall
   As fell thy manna down.

Drop thy still dews of quietness,
   Till all our strivings cease;
Take from our souls the strain and stress,
And let our ordered lives confess
   The beauty of thy peace.

Breathe through the heats of our desire
   Thy coolness and thy balm;
Let sense be dumb, let flesh retire;
Speak through the earthquake, wind, and fire,
   O still, small voice of calm!

SUNSET ON THE BEARCAMP

A gold fringe on the purpling hem
   Of hills the river runs
As down its long, green valley falls
   The last of summer's suns.
Along its tawny gravel-bed
   Broad-flowing, swift, and still,
As if its meadow levels felt
   The hurry of the hill,
Noiseless between its banks of green
   From curve to curve it slips;
The drowsy maple-shadows rest
   Like fingers on its lips.

A waif from Carroll's wildest hills,
   Unstoried and unknown;
The ursine legend of its name
   Prowls on its banks alone,
Yet flowers as fair its slopes adorn
   As ever Yarrow knew,
Or, under rainy Irish skies,
   By Spenser's Mulla grew;
And through the gaps of leaning trees
   Its mountain cradle shows:
The gold against the amethyst,
   The green against the rose.

Touched by a light that hath no name,
   A glory never sung,
Aloft on sky and mountain wall
   Are God's great pictures hung.
How changed the summits vast and old!
   No longer granite-browed,
They melt in rosy mist; the rock
   Is softer than the cloud;
The valley holds its breath; no leaf
   Of all its elms is twirled:
The silence of eternity
   Seems falling on the world.

The pause before the breaking seals
   Of mystery is this;
Yon miracle-play of night and day
   Makes dumb its witnesses.
What unseen altar crowns the hills
   That reach up stair on stair?
What eyes look through, what white wings fan
   These purple veils of air?
What Presence from the heavenly heights
   To those of earth stoops down?
Not vainly Hellas dreamed of gods
   On Ida's snowy crown!

Slow fades the vision of the sky,
   The golden water pales,
And over all the valley-land
   A gray-winged vapor sails.
I go the common way of all;
   The sunset fires will burn,
The flowers will blow, the river flow,
   When I no more return.
No whisper from the mountain pine

Nor lapsing stream shall tell
The stranger, treading where I tread,
Of him who loved them well.

But beauty seen is never lost,
God's colors all are fast;
The glory of this sunset heaven
Into my soul has passed,—
A sense of gladness unconfined
To mortal date or clime;
As the soul liveth, it shall live
Beyond the years of time.
Beside the mystic asphodels
Shall bloom the home-born flowers,
And new horizons flush and glow
With sunset hues of ours.

Farewell! these smiling hills must wear
Too soon their wintry frown,
And snow-cold winds from off them shake
The maple's red leaves down.
But I shall see a summer sun
Still setting broad and low;
The mountain slopes shall blush and bloom,
The golden water flow.
A lover's claim is mine on all
I see to have and hold,—
The rose-light of perpetual hills,
And sunsets never cold!

THE DEAD FEAST OF THE KOL–FOLK*

We have opened the door,
   Once, twice, thrice!
We have swept the floor,
   We have boiled the rice.
Come hither, come hither!
Come from the far lands,
Come from the star lands,
   Come as before!
We lived long together,
We loved one another;
   Come back to our life.
Come father, come mother,
Come sister and brother,
   Child, husband, and wife,
For you we are sighing.
Come take your old places,
Come look in our faces,
The dead on the dying,
      Come home!

We have opened the door,
   Once, twice, thrice!
We have kindled the coals,
   And we boil the rice
For the feast of souls.
   Come hither, come hither!
Think not we fear you,
Whose hearts are so near you.
Come tenderly thought on,
Come all unforgotten,

* Based on an account of the burial customs of a primitive tribe at Chota Naypur, Assam.

Come from the shadow-lands,
From the dim meadow-lands
Where the pale grasses bend
  Low to our sighing.
Come father, come mother,
Come sister and brother,
Come husband and friend,
  The dead to the dying,
    Come home!

We have opened the door
  You entered so oft;
For the feast of souls
We have kindled the coals,
  And we boil the rice soft.
Come you who are dearest
To us who are nearest,
Come hither, come hither,
From out the wild weather;
The storm clouds are flying,
The peepul is sighing;
  Come in from the rain.
Come father, come mother,
Come sister and brother,
Come husband and lover,
Beneath our roof-cover.
  Look on us again,
The dead on the dying,
    Come home!

We have opened the door!
For the feast of souls
We have kindled the coals
  We may kindle no more!
Snake, fever, and famine,

The curse of the Brahmin,
  The sun and the dew,
They burn us, they bite us,
They waste us and smite us;
  Our days are but few!
In strange lands far yonder
To wonder and wander
  We hasten to you.
List then to our sighing,
  While yet we are here:
Nor seeing nor hearing,
We wait without fearing,
  To feel you draw near.
O dead to the dying
  Come home!

AT LAST

When on my day of life the night is falling,
  And, in the winds from unsunned spaces blown,
I hear far voices out of darkness calling
  My feet to paths unknown,

Thou who hast made my home of life so pleasant,
  Leave not its tenant when its walls decay;
O Love Divine, O Helper ever present,
  Be Thou my strength and stay!

Be near me when all else is from me drifting:
  Earth, sky, home's pictures, days of shade and shine,
And kindly faces to my own uplifting
  The love which answers mine.

I have but Thee, my Father! let Thy spirit
  Be with me then to comfort and uphold;
No gate of pearl, no branch of palm I merit,
  Nor street of shining gold.

Suffice it if—my good and ill unreckoned,
  And both forgiven through Thy abounding grace—
I find myself by hands familiar beckoned
  Unto my fitting place.

Some humble door among Thy many mansions,
  Some sheltering shade where sin and striving cease,
And flows forever through heaven's green expansions
  The river of Thy peace.

There, from the music round about me stealing,
  I fain would learn the new and holy song,
And find at last, beneath Thy trees of healing,
  The life for which I long.

Oliver Wendell Holmes

1809-1894

THE BALLAD OF THE OYSTERMAN

It was a tall young oysterman lived by the river-side,
His shop was just upon the bank, his boat was on the tide;
The daughter of a fisherman, that was so straight and slim,
Lived over on the other bank, right opposite to him.

It was the pensive oysterman that saw a lovely maid,
Upon a moonlight evening, a sitting in the shade;
He saw her wave her handkerchief, as much as if to say,
"I'm wide awake, young oysterman, and all the folks away."

Then up arose the oysterman, and to himself said he,
"I guess I'll leave the skiff at home, for fear that folks should see;
I read it in the story-book, that, for to kiss his dear,
Leander swam the Hellespont,—and I will swim this here."

And he has leaped into the waves, and crossed the shining
    stream,
And he has clambered up the bank, all in the moonlight gleam;
O there were kisses sweet as dew, and words as soft as rain,—
But they have heard her father's step, and in he leaps again!

Out spoke the ancient fisherman,—"O what was that, my
    daughter?"
" 'Twas nothing but a pebble, sir, I threw into the water."
"And what is that, pray tell me, love, that paddles off so fast?"
"It's nothing but a porpoise, sir, that's been a swimming past."

Out spoke the ancient fisherman,—"Now bring me my harpoon!
I'll get into my fishing-boat, and fix the fellow soon."

Down fell that pretty innocent, as falls a snow-white lamb,
Her hair drooped round her pallid cheeks, like seaweed
    on a clam.

Alas for those two loving ones! she waked not from her swound,
And he was taken with the cramp, and in the waves was
    drowned;
But Fate has metamorphosed them, in pity of their woe,
And now they keep an oyster-shop for mermaids down below.

OLD IRONSIDES*

Ay, tear her tattered ensign down!
    Long has it waved on high,
And many an eye has danced to see
    That banner in the sky;
Beneath it rung the battle shout,
    And burst the cannon's roar;—
The meteor of the ocean air
    Shall sweep the clouds no more.

Her deck, once red with heroes' blood,
    Where knelt the vanquished foe,
When winds were hurrying o'er the flood,
    And waves were white below,
No more shall feel the victor's tread,
    Or know the conquered knee;—
The harpies of the shore shall pluck
    The eagle of the sea!

* In consequence of this poem, which was copied all over the country, the
U.S. frigate *Constitution* was preserved from destruction.

Oh, better that her shattered hulk
  Should sink beneath the wave;
Her thunders shook the mighty deep,
  And there should be her grave;
Nail to the mast her holy flag,
  Set every threadbare sail,
And give her to the god of storms,
  The lightning and the gale!

THE LAST LEAF

I saw him once before,
As he passed by the door,
  And again
The pavement stones resound,
As he totters o'er the ground
  With his cane.

They say that in his prime,
Ere the pruning-knife of Time
  Cut him down,
Not a better man was found
By the Crier on his round
  Through the town.

But now he walks the streets,
And he looks at all he meets
  Sad and wan,
And he shakes his feeble head,
That it seems as if he said,
  "They are gone."

The mossy marbles rest
On the lips that he has prest

In their bloom,
And the names he loved to hear
Have been carved for many a year
  On the tomb.

My grandmamma has said—
Poor old lady, she is dead
  Long ago—
That he had a Roman nose,
And his cheek was like a rose
  In the snow.

But now his nose is thin,
And it rests upon his chin
  Like a staff,
And a crook is in his back,
And a melancholy crack
  In his laugh.

I know it is a sin
For me to sit and grin
  At him here;
But the old three-cornered hat,
And the breeches, and all that,
  Are so queer!

And if I should live to be
The last leaf upon the tree
  In the spring,
Let them smile, as I do now,
At the old forsaken bough
  Where I cling.

MY AUNT

My aunt! my dear unmarried aunt!
    Long years have o'er her flown;
Yet still she strains the aching clasp
    That binds her virgin zone;
I know it hurts her,—though she looks
    As cheerful as she can;
Her waist is ampler than her life,
    For life is but a span.

My aunt! my poor deluded aunt!
    Her hair is almost gray;
Why will she train that winter curl
    In such a spring-like way?
How can she lay her glasses down,
    And say she reads as well,
When, through a double convex lens,
    She just makes out to spell?

Her father—grandpapa! forgive
    This erring lip its smiles—
Vowed she should make the finest girl
    Within a hundred miles;
He sent her to a stylish school;
    'Twas in her thirteenth June;
And with her, as the rules required,
    "Two towels and a spoon."

They braced my aunt against a board,
    To make her straight and tall;
They laced her up, they starved her down,
    To make her light and small;
They pinched her feet, they singed her hair,
    They screwed it up with pins;—

O never mortal suffered more
   In penance for her sins.

So, when my precious aunt was done,
   My grandsire brought her back;
(By daylight, lest some rabid youth
   Might follow on the track;)
"Ah!" said my grandsire, as he shook
   Some powder in his pan,
"What could this lovely creature do
   Against a desperate man!"

Alas! nor chariot, nor barouche,
   Nor bandit cavalcade,
Tore from the trembling father's arms
   His all-accomplished maid.
For her how happy had it been!
   And Heaven had spared to me
To see one sad, ungathered rose
   On my ancestral tree.

A SONG

For the Centennial Celebration of Harvard College, 1836

When the Puritans came over,
   Our hills and swamps to clear,
The woods were full of catamounts,
   And Indians red as deer,
With tomahawks and scalping-knives,
   That make folks' heads look queer;—
Oh the ship from England used to bring
   A hundred wigs a year!

The crows came cawing through the air
    To pluck the Pilgrims' corn,
The bears came snuffing round the door
    Whene'er a babe was born,
The rattlesnakes were bigger round
    Than the butt of the old ram's horn
The deacon blew at meeting time
    On every "Sabbath" morn.

But soon they knocked the wigwams down,
    And pine-tree trunk and limb
Began to sprout among the leaves
    In shape of steeples slim;
And out the little wharves were stretched
    Along the ocean's rim,
And up the little school-house shot
    To keep the boys in trim.

And when at length the College rose,
    The sachem cocked his eye
At every tutor's meagre ribs
    Whose coat-tails whistled by:
But when the Greek and Hebrew words
    Came tumbling from his jaws,
The copper-colored children all
    Ran screaming to the squaws.

And who was on the Catalogue
    When college was begun?
Two nephews of the President,
    And *the* Professor's son;
(They turned a little Indian by,
    As brown as any bun;)
Lord! how the seniors knocked about
    The freshman class of one!

They had not then the dainty things
   That commons now afford,
But *succotash* and *hominy*
   Were smoking on the board;
They did not rattle round in gigs,
   Or dash in long-tailed blues,
But always on Commencement days
   The tutors blacked their shoes.

God bless the ancient Puritans!
   Their lot was hard enough;
But honest hearts make iron arms,
   And tender maids are tough;
So love and faith have formed and fed
   Our true-born Yankee stuff,
And keep the kernel in the shell
   The British found so rough!

THE DEACON'S MASTERPIECE

Or, the Wonderful "One-Hoss Shay": a Logical Story

Have you heard of the wonderful one-hoss shay,
That was built in such a logical way
It ran a hundred years to a day,
And then, of a sudden, it—ah, but stay,
I'll tell you what happened without delay,
Scaring the parson into fits,
Frightening people out of their wits,—
Have you ever heard of that, I say?

Seventeen hundred and fifty-five.
Georgius Secundus was then alive,—

Snuffy old drone from the German hive.
That was the year when Lisbon-town
Saw the earth open and gulp her down,
And Braddock's army was done so brown,
Left without a scalp to its crown.
It was on the terrible Earthquake-day
That the Deacon finished the one-hoss shay.

Now in building of chaises, I tell you what
There is always *somewhere* a weakest spot,—
In hub, tire, felloe, in spring or thill,
In panel, or crossbar, or floor, or sill,
In screw, bolt, thoroughbrace,—lurking still,
Find it somewhere you must and will,—
Above or below, or within or without,—
And that's the reason, beyond a doubt,
That a chaise *breaks down*, but doesn't *wear out*.

But the Deacon swore (as Deacons do,
With an "I dew vum," or an "I tell *yeou*,")
He would build one shay to beat the taown
'N' the keounty 'n' all the kentry raoun';
It should be so built that it *couldn'* break daown:
"Fur," said the Deacon, " 't's mighty plain
Thut the weakes' place mus' stan' the strain;
'N' the way t' fix it, uz I maintain,
Is only jest
T' make that place uz strong uz the rest."

So the Deacon inquired of the village folk
Where he could find the strongest oak,
That couldn't be split nor bent nor broke,—
That was for spokes and floor and sills;
He sent for lancewood to make the thills;
The crossbars were ash, from the straightest trees;

The panels of white-wood, that cuts like cheese,
But lasts like iron for things like these;
The hubs of logs from the "Settler's ellum,"—
Last of its timber,—they couldn't sell 'em,
Never an axe had seen their chips,
And the wedges flew from between their lips,
Their blunt ends frizzled like celery-tips;
Step and prop-iron, bolt and screw,
Spring, tire, axle, and linchpin too,
Steel of the finest, bright and blue;
Thoroughbrace bison-skin, thick and wide;
Boot, top, dasher, from tough old hide
Found in the pit when the tanner died.
That was the way he "put her through."
"There!" said the Deacon, "naow she'll dew!"

Do! I tell you, I rather guess
She was a wonder, and nothing less!
Colts grew horses, beards turned gray,
Deacon and deaconess dropped away,
Children and grandchildren—where were they?
But there stood the stout old one-hoss shay
As fresh as on Lisbon-earthquake-day!

EIGHTEEN HUNDRED;—it came and found
The Deacon's masterpiece strong and sound.
Eighteen hundred increased by ten;—
"Hahnsum kerridge" they called it then.
Eighteen hundred and twenty came;—
Running as usual; much the same.
Thirty and forty at last arrive,
And then come fifty, and FIFTY-FIVE.

Little of all we value here
Wakes on the morn of its hundredth year

Without both feeling and looking queer.
In fact, there's nothing that keeps its youth,
So far as I know, but a tree and truth.
(This is a moral that runs at large;
Take it.—You're welcome.—No extra charge.)

FIRST OF NOVEMBER,—the Earthquake-day.—
There are traces of age in the one-hoss shay,
A general flavor of mild decay,
But nothing local, as one may say.
There couldn't be,—for the Deacon's art
Had made it so like in every part
That there wasn't a chance for one to start.
For the wheels were just as strong as the thills,
And the floor was just as strong as the sills,
And the panels just as strong as the floor,
And the whipple-tree neither less nor more,
And the back crossbar as strong as the fore,
And spring and axle and hub *encore.*
And yet, *as a whole,* it is past a doubt
In another hour it will be *worn out!*

First of November, 'Fifty-five!
This morning the parson takes a drive.
Now, small boys, get out of the way!
Here comes the wonderful one-horse shay,
Drawn by a rat-tailed, ewe-necked bay.
"Huddup!" said the parson.—Off went they.
The parson was working his Sunday's text,—
Had got to *fifthly,* and stopped perplexed
At what the—Moses—was coming next.
All at once the horse stood still,
Close by the meet'n'-house on the hill.
First a shiver, and then a thrill,
Then something decidedly like a spill,—

And the parson was sitting upon a rock,
At half-past nine by the meet'n'-house clock,—
Just the hour of the Earthquake shock!
What do you think the parson found,
When he got up and stared around?
The poor old chaise in a heap or mound,
As if it had been to the mill and ground!
You see, of course, if you're not a dunce,
How it went to pieces all at once,—
All at once and nothing first,—
Just as bubbles do when they burst.

End of the wonderful one-hoss shay.
Logic is logic. That's all I say.

THE CHAMBERED NAUTILUS

This is the ship of pearl, which, poets feign,
　　Sails the unshadowed main,—
　　The venturous bark that flings
On the sweet summer wind its purpled wings
In gulfs enchanted, where the Siren sings,
　　And coral reefs lie bare,
Where the cold sea-maids rise to sun their streaming hair.

Its webs of living gauze no more unfurl;
　　Wrecked is the ship of pearl!
　　And every chambered cell,
Where its dim dreaming life was wont to dwell,
As the frail tenant shaped his growing shell,
　　Before thee lies revealed,—
Its irised ceiling rent, its sunless crypt unsealed!

Year after year beheld the silent toil
   That spread his lustrous coil;
   Still, as the spiral grew,
He left the past year's dwelling for the new,
Stole with soft step its shining archway through,
   Built up its idle door,
Stretched in his last-found home, and knew the old no more.

Thanks for the heavenly message brought by thee,
   Child of the wandering sea,
   Cast from her lap, forlorn!
From thy dead lips a clearer note is born
Than ever Triton blew from wreathéd horn!
   While on mine ear it rings,
Through the deep caves of thought I hear a voice that sings:—

Build thee more stately mansions, O my soul,
   As the swift seasons roll!
   Leave thy low-vaulted past!
Let each new temple, nobler than the last,
Shut thee from heaven with a dome more vast,
   Till thou at length art free,
Leaving thine outgrown shell by life's unresting sea!

BROTHER JONATHAN'S LAMENT FOR SISTER CAROLINE *

She has gone,—she has left us in passion and pride,—
Our stormy-browed sister, so long at our side!
She has torn her own star from our firmament's glow,
And turned on her brother the face of a foe!

* Occasioned by the secession of South Carolina.

O Caroline, Caroline, child of the sun,
We can never forget that our hearts have been one,—
Our foreheads both sprinkled in Liberty's name,
From the fountain of blood with the finger of flame!

You were always too ready to fire at a touch;
But we said, "She is hasty,—she does not mean much."
We have scowled, when you uttered some turbulent threat;
But Friendship still whispered, "Forgive and forget!"

Has our love all died out? Have its altars grown cold?
Has the curse come at last which the fathers foretold?
Then Nature must teach us the strength of the chain
That her petulant children would sever in vain.

They may fight till the buzzards are gorged with their spoil,
Till the harvest grows black as it rots in the soil,
Till the wolves and the catamounts troop from their caves,
And the shark tracks the pirate, the lord of the waves:

In vain is the strife! When its fury is past,
Their fortunes must flow in one channel at last,
As the torrents that rush from the mountains of snow
Roll mingled in peace through the valleys below.

Our Union is river, lake, ocean, and sky:
Man breaks not the medal, when God cuts the die!
Though darkened with sulphur, though cloven with steel,
The blue arch will brighten, the waters will heal!

O Caroline, Caroline, child of the sun,
There are battles with Fate that can never be won!
The star-flowering banner must never be furled,
For its blossoms of light are the hope of the world!

Go, then, our rash sister! afar and aloof,
Run wild in the sunshine away from our roof;
But when your heart aches and your feet have grown sore,
Remember the pathway that leads to our door!

THE MORAL BULLY

Yon whey-faced brother, who delights to wear
A weedy flux of ill-conditioned hair,
Seems of the sort that in a crowded place
One elbows freely into smallest space;
A timid creature, lax of knee and hip,
Whom small disturbance whitens round the lip;
One of those harmless spectacled machines,
The Holy-Week of Protestants convenes;
Whom school-boys question if their walk transcends
The last advices of maternal friends;
Whom John, obedient to his master's sign,
Conducts, laborious, up to *ninety-nine*,
While Peter, glistening with luxurious scorn,
Husks his white ivories like an ear of corn;
Dark in the brow and bilious in the cheek,
Whose yellowish linen flowers but once a week,
Conspicuous, annual, in their threadbare suits,
And the laced high-lows which they call their boots,
Well mayst thou *shun* that dingy front severe,
But him, O stranger, him thou canst not *fear!*

Be slow to judge, and slower to despise,
Man of broad shoulders and heroic size!
The tiger, writhing from the boa's rings,
Drops at the fountain where the cobra stings.

In that lean phantom, whose extended glove
Points to the text of universal love,
Behold the master that can tame thee down
To crouch, the vassal of his Sunday frown;
His velvet throat against thy corded wrist,
His loosened tongue against thy doubled fist!

The MORAL BULLY, though he never swears,
Nor kicks intruders down his entry stairs,
Though meekness plants his backward-sloping hat,
And non-resistance ties his white cravat,
Though his black broadcloth glories to be seen
In the same plight with Shylock's gaberdine,
Hugs the same passion to his narrow breast
That heaves the cuirass on the trooper's chest,
Hears the same hell-hounds yelling in his rear
That chase from port the maddened buccaneer,
Feels the same comfort while his acrid words
Turn the sweet milk of kindness into curds,
Or with grim logic prove, beyond debate,
That all we love is worthiest of our hate,
As the scarred ruffian of the pirate's deck,
When his long swivel rakes the staggering wreck!

Heaven keep us all! Is every rascal clown
Whose arm is stronger free to knock us down?
Has every scarecrow, whose cachectic soul
Seems fresh from Bedlam, airing on parole,
Who, though he carries but a doubtful trace
Of angel visits on his hungry face,
From lack of marrow or the coins to pay,
Has dodged some vices in a shabby way,
The right to stick us with his cutthroat terms,
And bait his homilies with his brother worms?

A SUN–DAY HYMN

Lord of all being! throned afar,
Thy glory flames from sun and star;
Centre and soul of every sphere,
Yet to each loving heart how near!

Sun of our life, thy quickening ray
Sheds on our path the glow of day;
Star of our hope, thy softened light
Cheers the long watches of the night.

Our midnight is thy smile withdrawn;
Our noontide is thy gracious dawn;
Our rainbow arch thy mercy's sign;
All, save the clouds of sin, are thine!

Lord of all life, below, above,
Whose light is truth, whose warmth is love,
Before thy ever-blazing throne
We ask no lustre of our own.

Grant us thy truth to make us free,
And kindling hearts that burn for thee,
Till all thy living altars claim
One holy light, one heavenly flame!

BILL AND JOE *

Come, dear old comrade, you and I
Will steal an hour from days gone by,
The shining days when life was new,

* Written for a reunion of the class of 1829 at Harvard College.

And all was bright with morning dew,
The lusty days of long ago,
When you were Bill and I was Joe.

Your name may flaunt a titled trail
Proud as a cockerel's rainbow tail,
And mine as brief appendix wear
As Tam O'Shanter's luckless mare;
To-day, old friend, remember still
That I am Joe and you are Bill.

You've won the great world's envied prize,
And grand you look in people's eyes,
With H O N. and L L. D.
In big brave letters, fair to see,—
Your fist, old fellow! off they go!—
How are you, Bill? How are you, Joe?

You've worn the judge's ermined robe;
You've taught your name to half the globe;
You've sung mankind a deathless strain;
You've made the dead past live again:
The world may call you what it will,
But you and I are Joe and Bill.

The chaffing young folks stare and say
"See those old buffers, bent and gray,—
They talk like fellows in their teens!
Mad, poor old boys! That's what it means,"—
And shake their heads; they little know
The throbbing hearts of Bill and Joe!—

How Bill forgets his hour of pride,
While Joe sits smiling at his side;
How Joe, in spite of time's disguise,

Finds the old schoolmate in his eyes,—
Those calm, stern eyes that melt and fill
As Joe looks fondly up at Bill.

Ah, pensive scholar, what is fame?
A fitful tongue of leaping flame;
A giddy whirlwind's fickle gust,
That lifts a pinch of mortal dust;
A few swift years, and who can show
Which dust was Bill and which was Joe?

The weary idol takes his stand,
Holds out his bruised and aching hand,
While gaping thousands come and go,—
How vain it seems, this empty show!
Till all at once his pulses thrill;—
'Tis poor old Joe's "God bless you, Bill!"

And shall we breathe in happier spheres
The names that pleased our mortal ears;
In some sweet lull of harp and song
For earth-born spirits none too long,
Just whispering of the world below
Where this was Bill, and that was Joe?

No matter; while our home is here
No sounding name is half so dear;
When fades at length our lingering day,
Who cares what pompous tombstones say?
Read on the hearts that love us still,
Hic jacet Joe. *Hic jacet* Bill.

DOROTHY Q.

A FAMILY PORTRAIT

Grandmother's mother: her age, I guess,
Thirteen summers, or something less;
Girlish bust, but womanly air;
Smooth, square forehead with uprolled hair,
Lips that lover has never kissed;
Taper fingers and slender wrist;
Hanging sleeves of stiff brocade;
So they painted the little maid.

On her hand a parrot green
Sits unmoving and broods serene.
Hold up the canvas full in view,—
Look! there's a rent the light shines through,
Dark with a century's fringe of dust,—
That was a Red-Coat's rapier-thrust!
Such is the tale the lady old,
Dorothy's daughter's daughter, told.

Who the painter was none may tell,—
One whose best was not over well;
Hard and dry, it must be confessed,
Flat as a rose that has long been pressed;
Yet in her cheek the hues are bright,
Dainty colors of red and white,
And in her slender shape are seen
Hint and promise of stately mien.

Look not on her with eyes of scorn,—
Dorothy Q. was a lady born!
Ay! since the galloping Normans came,
England's annals have known her name;

And still to the three-hilled rebel town
Dear is that ancient name's renown,
For many a civic wreath they won,
The youthful sire and the gray-haired son.

O Damsel Dorothy! Dorothy Q.!
Strange is the gift that I owe to you;
Such a gift as never a king
Save to daughter or son might bring,—
All my tenure of heart and hand,
All my title to house and land;
Mother and sister and child and wife
And joy and sorrow and death and life!

What if a hundred years ago
Those close-shut lips had answered No,
When forth the tremulous question came
That cost the maiden her Norman name,
And under the folds that look so still
The bodice swelled with the bosom's thrill?
Should I be I, or would it be
One tenth another, to nine tenths me?

Soft is the breath of a maiden's YES:
Not the light gossamer stirs with less;
But never a cable that holds so fast
Through all the battles of wave and blast,
And never an echo of speech or song
That lives in the babbling air so long!
There were tones in the voice that whispered then
You may hear to-day in a hundred men.

O lady and lover, how faint and far
Your images hover,—and here we are,
Solid and stirring in flesh and bone,—

Edward's and Dorothy's—all their own,—
A goodly record for Time to show
Of a syllable spoken so long ago!—
Shall I bless you, Dorothy, or forgive
For the tender whisper that bade me live?

It shall be a blessing, my little maid!
I will heal the stab of the Red-Coat's blade,
And freshen the gold of the tarnished frame,
And gild with a rhyme your household name;
So you shall smile on us brave and bright
As first you greeted the morning's light,
And live untroubled by woes and fears
Through a second youth of a hundred years.

AT THE "ATLANTIC" DINNER

December 15, 1874

I suppose it's myself that you're making allusion to
And bringing the sense of dismay and confusion to.
Of course *some* must speak,—they are always selected to,
But pray what's the reason that I am expected to?
I'm not fond of wasting my breath as those fellows do
That want to be blowing forever as bellows do;
Their legs are uneasy, but why will you jog any
That long to stay quiet beneath the mahogany?

Why, why call *me* up with your battery of flatteries?
You say "He writes poetry,"—that's what the matter is!
"It costs him no trouble—a pen full of ink or two
And the poem is done in the time of a wink or two;
As for thoughts—never mind—take the ones that lie uppermost,
And the rhymes used by Milton and Byron and Tupper most;

The lines come so easy! at one end he jingles 'em,
At the other with capital letters he shingles 'em,—
Why, the thing writes itself, and before he's half done with it
He hates to stop writing he has such good fun with it!"

Ah, that is the way in which simple ones go about
And draw a fine picture of things they don't know about!
We all know a kitten, but come to a catamount
The beast is a stranger when grown up to that amount,
(A stranger we rather prefer shouldn't visit us,
A *felis* whose advent is far from felicitous.)
The boy who can boast that his trap has just got a mouse
Mustn't draw it and write underneath "hippopotamus";
Or say unveraciously, "this is an elephant"—
Don't think, let me beg, these examples irrelevant—
What they mean is just this—that a thing to be painted well
Should always be something with which we're acquainted well.

You call on your victim for "things he has plenty of,—
Those copies of verses no doubt at least twenty of;
His desk is crammed full, for he always keeps writing 'em
And reading to friends as his way of delighting 'em!"—
I tell you this writing of verses means business,—
It makes the brain whirl in a vortex of dizziness:
You think they are scrawled in the languor of laziness—
I tell you they're squeezed by a spasm of craziness,
A fit half as bad as the staggering vertigos
That seize a poor fellow and down in the dirt he goes!

And therefore it chimes with the word's etymology
That the sons of Apollo are great on apology,
For the writing of verse is a struggle mysterious
And the gayest of rhymes is a matter that's serious.
For myself, I'm relied on by friends in extremities,
And I don't mind so much if a comfort to them it is;

'Tis a pleasure to please, and the straw that can tickle us
Is a source of enjoyment though slightly ridiculous.

I am up for a—something—and since I've begun with it,
I must give you a toast now before I have done with it.
Let me pump at my wits as they pumped the Cochituate
That moistened—it may be—the very last bit you ate.
—Success to our publishers, authors and editors;
To our debtors good luck,—pleasant dreams to our creditors;
May the monthly grow yearly, till all we are groping for
Has reached the fulfilment we're all of us hoping for;
Till the bore through the tunnel—it makes me let off a sigh
To think it may possibly ruin my prophecy—
Has been punned on so often 'twill never provoke again
One mild adolescent to make the old joke again;
Till abstinent, all-go-to-meeting society
Has forgotten the sense of the word inebriety;
Till the work that poor Hannah and Bridget and Phillis do
The humanized, civilized female gorillas do;
Till the roughs, as we call them, grown loving and dutiful,
Shall worship the true and the pure and the beautiful,
And, preying no longer as tiger and vulture do,
All read the "Atlantic" as persons of culture do!

TO JOHN GREENLEAF WHITTIER

On His Eightieth Birthday

1 8 8 7

Friend, whom thy fourscore winters leave more dear
Than when life's roseate summer on thy cheek
Burned in the flush of manhood's manliest year,
Lonely, how lonely! is the snowy peak

Thy feet have reached, and mine have climbed so near!
Close on thy footsteps 'mid the landscape drear
I stretch my hand thine answering grasp to seek,
Warm with the love no rippling rhymes can speak!
Look backward! From thy lofty height survey
Thy years of toil, of peaceful victories won,
Of dreams made real, largest hopes outrun!
Look forward! Brighter than earth's morning ray
Streams the pure light of Heaven's unsetting sun,
The unclouded dawn of life's immortal day!

Jones Very

1813 – 1880

TO THE CANARY BIRD

I cannot hear thy voice with others' ears,
Who make of thy lost liberty a gain;
And in a tale of blighted hopes and fears
Feel not that every note is born with pain.
Alas! that with thy music's gentle swell
Past days of joy should through thy memory throng,
And each to thee their words of sorrow tell,
While ravished sense forgets thee in thy song.
The heart that on the past and future feeds,
And pours in human words its thoughts divine,
Though at each birth the spirit inly bleeds,
Its song may charm the listening ear like thine,
And men with gilded cage and praise will try
To make the bard, like thee, forget his native sky.

THE TREE

I love thee when thy swelling buds appear
And one by one their tender leaves unfold,
As if they knew that warmer suns were near,
Nor longer sought to hide from winter's cold;
And when with darker growth thy leaves are seen
To veil from view the early robin's nest,
I love to lie beneath thy waving screen
With limbs by summer's heat and toil opprest;
And when the autumn winds have stript thee bare,
And round thee lies the smooth untrodden snow,

When nought is thine that made thee once so fair,
I love to watch thy shadowy form below,
And through thy leafless arms to look above
On stars that brighter beam when most we need their love. 1

THE PRESENCE

I sit within my room, and joy to find
That Thou who always lov'st art with me here,
That I am never left by Thee behind,
But by thyself Thou keep'st me ever near;
The fire burns brighter when with Thee I look,
And seems a kinder servant sent to me;
With gladder heart I read Thy holy book,
Because Thou art the eyes by which I see;
This aged chair, that table, watch and door
Around in ready service ever wait;
Nor can I ask of Thee a menial more
To fill the measure of my large estate,
For Thou thyself, with all a father's care,
Where'er I turn, art ever with me there.

THE DEAD

I see them,—crowd on crowd they walk the earth,
Dry leafless trees no autumn wind laid bare;
And in their nakedness find cause for mirth,
And all unclad would winter's rudeness dare;
No sap doth through their clattering branches flow,
Whence springing leaves and blossoms bright appear;
Their hearts the living God have ceased to know

Who gives the spring time to th' expectant year;
They mimic life, as if from him to steal
The glow of health to paint the livid cheek;
They borrow words for thoughts they cannot feel,
That with a seeming heart their tongue may speak;
And in their show of life more dead they live
Than those that to the earth with many tears they give.

THY BROTHER'S BLOOD

I have no Brother,—they who meet me now
Offer a hand with their own wills defiled,
And, while they wear a smooth unwrinkled brow,
Know not that Truth can never be beguiled;
Go wash the hand that still betrays thy guilt;
Before the spirit's gaze what stain can hide?
Abel's red blood upon the earth is spilt,
And by thy tongue it cannot be denied;
I hear not with the ear,—the heart doth tell
Its secret deeds to me untold before;
Go, all its hidden plunder quickly sell,
Then shalt thou cleanse thee from thy brother's gore,
Then will I take thy gift; that bloody stain
Shall not be seen upon thy hand again.

THE CALL

Why art thou not awake, my son?
The morning breaks I formed for thee;
And I thus early by thee stand,
Thy new-awakening life to see.

Why art thou not awake, my son?
The birds upon the bough rejoice;
And I thus early by thee stand
To hear with theirs thy tuneful voice.

Why sleep'st thou still? the laborers all
Are in My vineyard; hear them toil,
As for the poor with harvest song
They treasure up the wine and oil.

I come to wake thee; haste, arise,
Or thou no share with Me can find;
Thy sandals seize, gird on thy clothes,
Or I must leave thee here behind.

THE PRAYER

Wilt Thou not visit me?
The plant beside me feels Thy gentle dew;
And every blade of grass I see,
From Thy deep earth its quickening moisture drew.

Wilt Thou not visit me?
Thy morning calls on me with cheering tone;
And every hill and tree
Lends but one voice, the voice of Thee alone.

Come, for I need Thy love,
More than the flower the dew, or grass the rain;
Come, gently as Thy holy dove;
And let me in thy sight rejoice to live again.

I will not hide from them,
When Thy storms come, though fierce may be their wrath;
But bow with leafy stem,
And strengthened follow on Thy chosen path.

Yes, Thou wilt visit me,
Nor plant nor tree Thine eye delights so well,
As when from sin set free
My spirit loves with Thine in peace to dwell.

YOURSELF

'Tis to yourself I speak; you cannot know
Him whom I call in speaking such an one,
For thou beneath the earth liest buried low,
Which he alone as living walks upon;
Thou mayst at times have heard him speak to you,
And often wished perchance that you were he;
And I must ever wish that it were true,
For then thou couldst hold fellowship with me;
But now thou hear'st us talk as strangers, met
Above the room wherein thou liest abed;
A word perhaps loud spoken thou mayst get,
Or hear our feet when heavily they tread;
But he who speaks, or him who's spoken to,
Must both remain as strangers still to you.

THE HAND AND FOOT

The hand and foot that stir not, they shall find
Sooner than all the rightful place to go;

Now in their motion free as roving wind,
Though first no snail more limited and slow;
I mark them full of labor all the day,
Each active motion made in perfect rest;
They cannot from their path mistaken stray,
Though 'tis not theirs, yet in it they are blest;
The bird has not their hidden track found out,
Nor cunning fox, though full of art he be;
It is the way unseen, the certain route,
Where ever bound, yet thou art ever free;
The path of Him, whose perfect law of love
Bids spheres and atoms in just order move.

THE LOST

The fairest day that ever yet has shone
Will be when thou the day within shalt see;
The fairest rose that ever yet has blown,
When thou the flower thou lookest on shalt be;
But thou art far away amidst Time's toys;
Thyself the day thou lookest for in them,
Thyself the flower that now thine eye enjoys;
But wilted now thou hang'st upon thy stem;
The bird thou hearest on the budding tree
Thou hast made sing with thy forgotten voice;
But when it swells again to melody,
The song is thine in which thou wilt rejoice;
And thou new risen 'midst these wonders live,
That now to them dost all thy substance give.

THE ABSENT

Thou art not yet at home in thine own house,
But to one room I see thee now confined;
Having one hole like rat or skulking mouse,
And as a mole to all the others blind;
Does the great Day find preference when he shines
In at each window, lighting every room?
No selfish wish the moon's bright glance confines,
And each in turn the stars' faint rays illume;
Within thy sleeping room thou dost abide,
And thou the social parlor dost prefer;
All other wilt thou in the cupboard hide,
And this or that's the room for him or her;
But the same sun, and moon with silver face,
Look in on all, and lighten every place.

THE CREATED

There is nought for thee by thy haste to gain;
'Tis not the swift with Me that win the race;
Through long endurance of delaying pain,
Thine opened eye shall see thy Father's face;
Nor here nor there, where now thy feet would turn,
Thou wilt find Him who ever seeks for thee;
But let obedience quench desires that burn,
And where thou art, thy Father too will be!
Behold! as day by day the spirit grows,
Thou see'st by inward light things hid before;
Till what God is, thyself His image shows;
And thou dost wear the robe that first thou wore,
When, bright with radiance from His forming hand,
He saw the lord of all his creatures stand.

HOW LONG?

'Tis all a great show,
　The world that we're in,
None can tell when 'twas finished,
　None saw it begin;
Men wander and gaze through
　Its courts and its halls,
Like children whose love is
　The picture-hung walls.

There are flowers in the meadow,
　There are clouds in the sky,
Songs pour from the woodland,
　The waters glide by;
Too many, too many,
　For eye or for ear,
The sights that we see
　And the sounds that we hear.

A weight as of slumber
　Comes down on the mind;
So swift is life's train
　To its objects we're blind;
I myself am but one
　In the fleet-gliding show,
Like others I walk,
　But know not where I go.

One saint to another
　I heard say "How long?"
I listened, but nought more
　I heard of his song.
The shadows are walking
　Through city and plain,

How long shall the night
  And its shadows remain!

How long ere shall shine
  In this glimmer of things
The light of which prophet
  In prophecy sings;
And the gates of that city
  Be open, whose sun
No more in the west
  In its circuit shall run?

THE LAMENT OF THE FLOWERS

I looked to find Spring's early flowers,
  In spots where they were wont to bloom;
But they had perished in their bowers;
  The haunts they loved had proved their tomb!

The alder, and the laurel green,
  Which sheltered them, had shared their fate;
And but the blackened ground was seen
  Where hid their swelling buds of late.

From the bewildered, homeless bird,
  Whose half-built nest the flame destroys,
A low complaint of wrong I heard,
  Against the thoughtless, ruthless boys.

Sadly I heard its notes complain,
  And ask the young its haunts to spare;
Prophetic seemed the sorrowing strain,
  Sung o'er its home, but late so fair!

"No more with hues like ocean shell
    The delicate wind-flower here shall blow;
The spot that loved its form so well
    Shall ne'er again its beauty know.

"Or, if it bloom, like some pale ghost
    'Twill haunt the black and shadeless dell,
Where once it bloomed a numerous host,
    Of its once pleasant bowers to tell.

"And coming years no more shall find
    The laurel green upon the hills;
The frequent fire leaves naught behind,
    But e'en the very roots it kills.

"No more upon the turnpike's side
    The rose shall shed its sweet perfume;
The traveler's joy, the summer's pride,
    Will share with them a common doom.

"No more shall these returning fling
    Round childhood's home a heavenly charm,
With song of bird in early spring,
    To glad the heart and save from harm."

THE FALLING LEAF

Fall, yellow leaf, for thy brief work is done,
    The work for which thy beauteous form was made;
No more thou'lt glisten in the morning sun,
    No more thou'lt darken with the evening shade.

Thy work is done! No more the parent tree
   Shall need thy aid, for winter-time is near;
No more upon its boughs thy form we'll see,
   Through the long winter months to charm and cheer.

But though thy work is done, to outward sight,
   And thou art trodden 'neath the feet of men,
Still to the memory thou shalt bring delight,
   And in thy beauty seem to live again.

Thy work can never cease, while thought shall bring
   Some pleasant memories of days gone by,
When, wandering in the woods, in early spring,
   Thy brilliant green first caught the admiring eye;

Or when, in summer, from the glare and heat
   We sought the shelter of the quiet grove,
And found beneath its shade a cool retreat,
   To pass the sultry hours with friends we love;

Or when, in autumn, midst her changing bowers
   I mused upon the lessons which they taught;
Forgetful of the swiftly passing hours,
   Lost in a dream of sweet yet solemn thought.

Thy work shall never cease while thou shalt be
   A thought the springs of memory to control,
A power the mind of man from sense to free,
   A joy and teaching to the deathless soul!

SHIP ROCK

With a sudden sweet surprise
  Bursts the prospect on our eyes;
Far the city's spires are seen,
  Hills and fields and woods between.

Farther still, the ocean blue
  Fitly bounds the charming view;
Where, on the horizon clear,
  Noble ships their courses steer.

By the pond beneath the hill,
  Silent stands the noisy mill;
While the brook with laugh and song
  Through the meadow glides along.

Science may thy birth explore,
  On the far-off Arctic shore,
And thy various wanderings show
  In the ages long ago;

With more interest here I trace
  Backward my own name and race;
From thy top the scene behold
  Where they lived and toiled of old.

Here the wooded fields they cleared,
  And their humble homesteads reared;
Here they planted, gathered here
  Harvests ripe from year to year.

Here they worshiped Him, whose word
  In their father-land they heard;

Him, who o'er the ocean wide
  Was their Hope, their Strength, their Guide.

Here in sweet and holy trust
  They committed dust to dust;
Minding where the soul's conveyed
  More than where the body's laid.

Still their orchard-lot I see,
  Here and there a moss-grown tree;
Here their dwelling's site is known,
  Now by shrubs and vines o'ergrown.

Sacred is this spot to me,
  Rock and brook and lofty tree;
For amid the scenes I tread
  Rests the dust of kindred dead!

Christopher Pearse Cranch

1813 – 1892

THE FLOWER AND THE BEE

Love me as the flower loves the bee.
Ask no monopoly of sympathy.
　　I must flit by,
Nor stay to heave too deep a sigh,
Nor dive too deep into thy charms.
Untwine thy prisoning arms;
　　Let the truth-garnering bee
　　Pass ever free!

Yield all the thymy fragrance I can draw
　From out thy soul's rich sweetness. Not forever
Can lovers see one truth, obey one law,
　Though they spend long endeavor.
Give me thy blossoming heart;
I can but take thereof that part
　　Which grand Economy
　　Permitteth me to see.

Friendship and love may last in name,
　As lamps outlive their flame;
An earthly tie may bind our hands;
　The spirit snaps the bands.
If Nature made us different,
Our compliments in vain are spent;
But if alike, ah, then I rest in thee
As in the flower's full heart the sated bee.

IN THE GARDEN

With rose and orange scents this place was laden;
  The summer air was quivering thick with birds.
In these cool garden walks I met the maiden
  Whose beauty robs her praisers' tongues of words.

A crimson rose was in her hand. She held it
  Close to my lips,—in truth, a flower divine;
But I looked in her eyes and scarcely smelled it,
  But took the flower and hand in both of mine.

These are the shades where arm in arm for hours
  We walked,—brief hours of throbbing pain and bliss.
Here drank love's bitter-sweet, deep hid in flowers;
  Here gave and took our last despairing kiss.

And where is she, the fair light-footed comer?
  I pace these lonely garden walks in vain.
O long-lost joy! O Rose of love and summer!
  That day ye bloomed will never come again!

THE PINES AND THE SEA

Beyond the low marsh-meadows and the beach,
Seen through the hoary trunks of windy pines,
The long blue level of the ocean shines.
The distant surf, with hoarse, complaining speech,
Out from its sandy barrier seems to reach;
And while the sun behind the woods declines,
The moaning sea with sighing boughs combines,
And waves and pines make answer, each to each.
O melancholy soul, whom far and near,

In life, faith, hope, the same sad undertone
Pursues from thought to thought! thou needs must hear
An old refrain, too much, too long thine own:
'Tis thy mortality infects thine ear;
The mournful strain was in thyself alone.

DECEMBER

No more the scarlet maples flash and burn
   Their beacon-fires from hilltop and from plain;
The meadow-grasses and the woodland fern
   In the bleak woods lie withered once again.

The trees stand bare, and bare each stony scar
   Upon the cliffs; half frozen glide the rills;
The steel-blue river like a scimitar
   Lies cold and curved between the dusky hills.

Over the upland farm I take my walk,
   And miss the flaunting flocks of golden-rod;
Each autumn flower a dry and leafless stalk,
   Each mossy field a track of frozen sod.

I hear no more the robin's summer song
   Through the gray network of the wintry woods;
Only the cawing crows that all day long
   Clamor about the windy solitudes.

Like agate stones upon earth's frozen breast,
   The little pools of ice lie round and still;
While sullen clouds shut downward east and west
   In marble ridges stretched from hill to hill.

Come once again, O southern wind,—once more
   Come with thy wet wings flapping at my pane;
Ere snow-drifts pile their mounds about my door,
   One parting dream of summer bring again.

Ah, no! I hear the windows rattle fast;
   I see the first flakes of the gathering snow,
That dance and whirl before the northern blast.
   No countermand the march of days can know.

December drops no weak, relenting tear,
   By our fond summer sympathies ensnared;
Nor from the perfect circle of the year
   Can even winter's crystal gems be spared.

GNOSIS

Thought is deeper than all speech,
   Feeling deeper than all thought:
Souls to souls can never teach
   What unto themselves was taught.

We are spirits clad in veils;
   Man by man was never seen;
All our deep communing fails
   To remove the shadowy screen.

Heart to heart was never known;
   Mind with mind did never meet;
We are columns left alone
   Of a temple once complete.

Like the stars that gem the sky,
    Far apart though seeming near,
In our light we scattered lie;
    All is thus but starlight here.

What is social company
    But a babbling summer stream?
What our wise philosophy
    But the glancing of a dream?

Only when the Sun of Love
    Melts the scattered stars of thought,
Only when we live above
    What the dim-eyed world hath taught,

Only when our souls are fed
    By the Fount which gave them birth,
And by inspiration led
    Which they never drew from earth,

We, like parted drops of rain,
    Swelling till they meet and run,
Shall be all absorbed again,
    Melting, flowing into one.

SO FAR, SO NEAR

Thou, so far, we grope to grasp thee—
Thou, so near, we cannot clasp thee—
Thou, so wise, our prayers grow heedless—
Thou, so loving, they are needless!
In each human soul thou shinest;

Human-best is thy divinest.
In each deed of love thou warmest;
Evil into good transformest.
Soul of all, and moving centre
Of each moment's life we enter.
Breath of breathing—light of gladness—
Infinite antidote of sadness;—
All-preserving ether flowing
Through the worlds, yet past our knowing.
Never past our trust and loving,
Nor from thine our life removing.
Still creating, still inspiring,
Never of thy creatures tiring.
Artist of thy solar spaces,
And thy humble human faces;
Mighty glooms and splendors voicing;
In thy plastic work rejoicing;
Through benignant law connecting
Best with best—and all perfecting,
Though all human races claim thee,
Thought and language fail to name thee,
Mortal lips be dumb before thee,
Silence only can adore thee!

HUMAN HELPERS

Praise, praise ye the prophets, the sages
Who lived and who died for the ages;
The grand and magnificent dreamers;
The heroes, and mighty redeemers;
The martyrs, reformers, and leaders;
The voices of mystical Vedas;
The bibles of races long shrouded

Who left us their wisdom unclouded;
The truth that is old as their mountains,
But fresh as the rills from their fountains.

And praise ye the poets whose pages
Give solace and joy to the ages;
Who have seen in their marvellous trances
Of thought and of rhythmical fancies,
The manhood of Man in all errors;
The triumph of hope over terrors;
The great human heart ever pleading
Its kindred divine, though misleading
Fate held it aloof from the heaven
That to spirits untempted was given.

The creeds of the past that have bound us,
With visions of terror around us
Like dungeons of stone that have crumbled,
Beneath us lie shattered and humbled.
The tyranny mitred and crested,
Flattered and crowned and detested;
The blindness that trod upon Science;
    The bigotry Ignorance cherished;
The armed and the sainted alliance
    Of conscience and hate—they have perished,
Have melted like mists in the splendor
    Of life and of beauty supernal—
Of love ever watchful and tender,
    Of law ever one and eternal.

Henry David Thoreau

1817 – 1862

PRAYER

Great God, I ask thee for no meaner pelf
Than that I may not disappoint myself,
That in my action I may soar as high,
As I can now discern with this clear eye.

And next in value, which thy kindness lends,
That I may greatly disappoint my friends,
Howe'er they think or hope that it may be,
They may not dream how thou'st distinguished me.

That my weak hand may equal my firm faith,
And my life practice more than my tongue saith;
That my low conduct may not show,
Nor my relenting lines,
That I thy purpose did not know,
Or overrated thy designs.

SMOKE IN WINTER

The sluggish smoke curls up from some deep dell,
The stiffened air exploring in the dawn,
And making slow acquaintance with the day;
Delaying now upon its heavenward course,
In wreathéd loiterings dallying with itself,
With as uncertain purpose and slow deed,
As its half-wakened master by the hearth,

327

Whose mind still slumbering and sluggish thoughts
Have not yet swept into the onward current
Of the new day;—and now it streams afar,
The while the chopper goes with step direct,
And mind intent to swing the early axe.

   First in the dusky dawn he sends abroad
His early scout, his emissary, smoke,
The earliest, latest pilgrim from the roof,
To feel the frosty air, inform the day;
And while he crouches still beside the hearth,
Nor musters courage to unbar the door,
It has gone down the glen with the light wind,
And o'er the plain unfurled its venturous wreath,
Draped the tree tops, loitered upon the hill,
And warmed the pinions of the early bird;
And now, perchance, high in the crispy air,
Has caught sight of the day o'er the earth's edge,
And greets its master's eye at his low door,
As some refulgent cloud in the upper sky.

HAZE

Woof of the sun, ethereal gauze,
Woven of Nature's richest stuffs,
Visible heat, air-water, and dry sea,
Last conquest of the eye;
Toil of the day displayed, sun-dust,
Aerial surf upon the shores of earth,
Ethereal estuary, frith of light,
Breakers of air, billows of heat,
Fine summer spray on inland seas;
Bird of the sun, transparent-winged

Owlet of noon, soft-pinioned,
From heath or stubble rising without song;
Establish thy serenity o'er the fields.

LOW–ANCHORED CLOUD

Low-anchored cloud,
Newfoundland air,
Fountain-head and source of rivers,
Dew-cloth, dream drapery,
And napkin spred by fays;
Drifting meadow of the air,
Where bloom the daisied banks and violets,
And in whose fenny labyrinth
The bittern booms and heron wades;
Spirit of lakes and seas and rivers,
Bear only perfumes and the scent
Of healing herbs to just men's fields!

LIGHT–WINGED SMOKE

Light-wingéd Smoke, Icarian bird,
Melting thy pinions in thy upward flight,
Lark without song, and messenger of dawn,
Circling above the hamlets as thy nest;
Or else, departing dream, and shadowy form
Of midnight vision, gathering up thy skirts;
By night star-veiling, and by day
Darkening the light and blotting out the sun;
Go thou my incense upward from this hearth,
And ask the gods to pardon this clear flame.

WHEN WINTER FRINGES EVERY BOUGH

When Winter fringes every bough
    With his fantastic wreath,
And puts the seal of silence now
    Upon the leaves beneath;

When every stream in its pent-house
    Goes gurgling on its way,
And in his gallery the mouse
    Nibbleth the meadow hay;

Methinks the summer still is nigh,
    And lurketh underneath,
As that same meadow mouse doth lie
    Snug in the last year's heath.

And if perchance the chicadee
    Lisp a faint note anon,
The snow is summer's canopy,
    Which she herself put on.

Fair blossoms deck the cheerful trees,
    And dazzling fruits depend,
The north wind sighs a summer breeze,
    The nipping frosts to fend,

Bringing glad tidings unto me,
    The while I stand all ear,
Of a serene eternity,
    Which need not winter fear.

Out on the silent pond straightway
    The restless ice doth crack,

And pond sprites merry gambles play
  Amid the deafening rack.

Eager I hasten to the vale,
  As if I heard brave news,
How nature held high festival,
  Which it were hard to lose.

I gambol with my neighbor ice,
  And sympathizing quake,
As each new crack darts in a trice
  Across the gladsome lake.

One with the cricket in the ground,
  And faggot on the hearth,
Resounds the rare domestic sound
  Along the forest path.

MEN SAY

Men say they know many things;
But lo! they have taken wings,—
The arts and sciences,
And a thousand appliances;
The wind that blows
Is all that any body knows.

WHAT'S THE RAILROAD

What's the railroad to me?
I never go to see

Where it ends.
It fills a few hollows,
And makes banks for the swallows,
It sets the sand a-blowing,
And the blackberries a-growing.

THE RESPECTABLE FOLKS

The respectable folks,—
Where dwell they?
They whisper in the oaks,
And they sigh in the hay;
Summer and winter, night and day,
Out on the meadow, there dwell they.
They never die,
Nor snivel, nor cry,
Nor ask our pity
With a wet eye.
A sound estate they ever mend,
To every asker readily lend;
To the ocean wealth,
To the meadow health,
To Time his length,
To the rocks strength,
To the stars light,
To the weary night,
To the busy day,
To the idle play;
And so their good cheer never ends,
For all are their debtors, and all their friends.

TO THE MAIDEN IN THE EAST

Low in the eastern sky
Is set thy glancing eye;
And though its gracious light
Ne'er riseth to my sight,
Yet every star that climbs
Above the gnarled limbs
    Of yonder hill
Conveys thy gentle will.

Believe I knew thy thought,
And that the zephyrs brought
Thy kindest wishes through,
As mine they bear to you,
That some attentive cloud
Did pause amid the crowd
    Over my head,
While gentle things were said.

Believe the thrushes sung,
And that the flower-bells rung,
That herbs exhaled their scent,
And beasts knew what was meant,
The trees a welcome waved,
And lakes their margins laved,
    When thy free mind
To my retreat did wind.

It was a summer's eve,
The air did gently heave
While yet a low-hung cloud
Thy eastern skies did shroud;
The lightning's silent gleam,

Startling my drowsy dream,
        Seemed like the flash
Under thy dark eyelash.

Still will I strive to be
As if thou wert with me;
Whatever path I take,
It shall be for thy sake,
Of gentle slope and wide,
As thou wert by my side,
        Without a root
To trip thy gentle foot.

I'll walk with gentle pace,
And choose the smoothest place,
And careful dip the oar,
And shun the winding shore,
And gently steer my boat
Where water-lilies float,
        And cardinal flowers
Stand in their sylvan bowers.

THE OFFER

I make ye an offer,
Ye gods, hear the scoffer,
The scheme will not hurt you,
If ye will find goodness, I will find virtue.
Though I am your creature,
And child of your nature,
I have pride still unbended,
And blood undescended,
Some free independence,
And my own descendants.

I cannot toil blindly,
Though ye behave kindly,
And I swear by the rood,
I'll be slave to no God.
If ye will deal plainly,
I will strive mainly,
If ye will discover
Great plans to your lover,
And give him a sphere
Somewhat larger than here.

CONSCIENCE

Conscience is instinct bred in the house,
Feeling and Thinking propagate the sin
By an unnatural breeding in and in.
I say, Turn it out doors,
Into the moors.
I love a life whose plot is simple,
And does not thicken with every pimple,
A soul so sound no sickly conscience binds it,
That makes the universe no worse than't finds it.
I love an earnest soul,
Whose mighty joy and sorrow
Are not drowned in a bowl,
And brought to life to-morrow;
That lives one tragedy,
And not seventy;
A conscience worth keeping,
Laughing not weeping;
A conscience wise and steady,
And forever ready;
Not changing with events,

Dealing in compliments;
A conscience exercised about
Large things, where one *may* doubt.
I love a soul not all of wood,
Predestinated to be good,
But true to the backbone
Unto itself alone,
And false to none;
Born to its own affairs,
Its own joys and own cares;
By whom the work which God begun
Is finished, and not undone;
Taken up where he left off,
Whether to worship or to scoff;
If not good, why then evil,
If not good god, good devil.
Goodness! you hypocrite, come out of that,
Live your life, do your work, then take your hat.
I have no patience towards
Such conscientious cowards.
Give me simple laboring folk,
Who love their work,
Whose virtue is a song
To cheer God along.

THOUGH ALL THE FATES SHOULD PROVE UNKIND

Though all the fates should prove unkind,
Leave not your native land behind.
The ship, becalmed, at length stands still;
The steed must rest beneath the hill;
But swiftly still our fortunes pace
To find us out in every place.

The vessel, though her masts be firm,
Beneath her copper bears a worm;
Around the cape, across the line,
Till fields of ice her course confine;
It matters not how smooth the breeze,
How shallow or how deep the seas,
Whether she bears Manilla twine,
Or in her hold Madeira wine,
Or China teas, or Spanish hides,
In port or quarantine she rides;
Far from New England's blustering shore,
New England's worm her hulk shall bore,
And sink her in the Indian seas,
Twine, wine, and hides, and China teas.

RUMORS FROM AN AEOLIAN HARP

There is a vale which none hath seen,
Where foot of man has never been,
Such as here lives with toil and strife,
An anxious and a sinful life.

There every virtue has its birth,
Ere it descends upon the earth,
And thither every deed returns,
Which in the generous bosom burns.

There love is warm, and youth is young,
And poetry is yet unsung,
For Virtue still adventures there,
And freely breathes her native air.

And ever, if you hearken well,
You still may hear its vesper bell,
And tread of high-souled men go by,
Their thoughts conversing with the sky.

MAN'S LITTLE ACTS

Man's little acts are grand,
Beheld from land to land,
There as they lie in time,
Within their native clime.
  Ships with the noontide weigh,
  And glide before its ray
  To some retired bay,
  Their haunt,
  Whence, under tropic sun,
  Again they run,
  Bearing gum Senegal and Tragicant.
For this was ocean meant,
For this the sun was sent,
And moon was lent,
And winds in distant caverns pent.

EPIGRAMS

1

I'm contented you should stay
  For ever and aye
If you can take yourself away
  Any day.

2

Die and be buried who will,
    I mean to live here still;
My nature grows ever more young
    The primitive pines among.

3

Upon the lofty elm tree sprays
The vireo rings the changes sweet,
During the trivial summer days,
Striving to lift our thoughts above the street.

4

The deeds of king and meanest hedger
Stand side by side in heaven's ledger.

5

My life has been the poem I would have writ,
But I could not both live and utter it.

THE ATLANTIDES

The smothered streams of love, which flow
More bright than Phlegethon, more low,
Island us ever, like the sea,
In an Atlantic mystery.
Our fabled shores none ever reach,
No mariner has found our beach,
Scarcely our mirage now is seen,
And neighboring waves with floating green,
Yet still the oldest charts contain

Some dotted outline of our main;
In ancient times midsummer days
Unto the western islands gaze,
To Teneriffe and the Azores,
Have shown our faint and cloud-like shores.

But sink not yet, ye desolate isles,
Anon your coast with commerce smiles,
And richer freights ye'll furnish far
Than Africa or Malabar.
Be fair, be fertile evermore,
Ye rumored but untrodden shore,
Princes and monarchs will contend
Who first unto your land shall send,
And pawn the jewels of the crown
To call your distant soil their own.

MY LOVE MUST BE AS FREE

My love must be as free
    As is the eagle's wing,
Hovering o'er land and sea
    And everything.

I must not dim my eye
    In thy saloon,
I must not leave my sky
    And nightly moon.

Be not the fowler's net
    Which stays my flight,
And craftily is set
    T' allure the sight.

But be the favoring gale
  That bears me on,
And still doth fill my sail
  When thou art gone.

I cannot leave my sky
  For thy caprice,
True love would soar as high
  As heaven is.

The eagle would not brook
  Her mate thus won,
Who trained his eye to look
  Beneath the sun.

FRIENDSHIP

"Friends, Romans, Countrymen, and Lovers"

Let such pure hate still underprop
Our love, that we may be
Each other's conscience,
And have our sympathy
Mainly from thence.

We'll one another treat like gods,
And all the faith we have
In virtue and in truth, bestow
On either, and suspicion leave
To gods below.

Two solitary stars,—
Unmeasured systems far

Between us roll,
But by our conscious light we are
Determined to one pole.

What need confound the sphere,—
Love can afford to wait,
For it no hour's too late
That witnesseth one duty's end,
Or to another doth beginning lend.

It will subserve no use,
More than the tints of flowers,
Only the independent guest
Frequents its bowers,
Inherits its bequest.

No speech though kind has it,
But kinder silence doles
Unto its mates,
By night consoles,
By day congratulates.

What saith the tongue to tongue?
What heareth ear of ear?
By the decrees of fate
From year to year,
Does it communicate.

Pathless the gulf of feeling yawns,—
No trivial bridge of words,
Or arch of boldest span,
Can leap the moat that girds
The sincere man.

No show of bolts and bars
Can keep the foeman out,
Or 'scape his secret mine
Who entered with the doubt
That drew the line.

No warder at the gate
Can let the friendly in,
But, like the sun, o'er all
He will the castle win,
And shine along the wall.

There's nothing in the world I know
That can escape from love,
For every depth it goes below,
And every height above.
It waits as waits the sky,
Until the clouds go by,
Yet shines serenely on
With an eternal day,
Alike when they are gone,
And when they stay.

Implacable is Love,—
Foes may be bought or teased
From their hostile intent,
But he goes unappeased
Who is on kindness bent.

THE INWARD MORNING

Packed in my mind lie all the clothes
    Which outward nature wears,

And in its fashion's hourly change
　　It all things else repairs.

In vain I look for change abroad,
　　And can no difference find,
Till some new ray of peace uncalled
　　Illumes my inmost mind.

What is it gilds the trees and clouds,
　　And paints the heavens so gay,
But yonder fast-abiding light
　　With its unchanging ray.

Lo, when the sun streams through the wood,
　　Upon a winter's morn,
Where'er his silent beams intrude
　　The murky night is gone.

How could the patient pine have known
　　The morning breeze would come,
Or humble flowers anticipate
　　The insect's noonday hum,—

Till the new light with morning cheer
　　From far streamed through the aisles,
And nimbly told the forest trees
　　For many stretching miles?

I've heard within my inmost soul
　　Such cheerful morning news,
In the horizon of my mind
　　Have seen such orient hues,

As in the twilight of the dawn,
　　When the first birds awake,

Are heard within some silent wood,
    Where they the small twigs break,

Or in the eastern skies are seen,
    Before the sun appears,
The harbingers of summer heats
    Which from afar he bears.

MY BOOKS I'D FAIN CAST OFF

My books I'd fain cast off, I cannot read,
'Twixt every page my thoughts go stray at large
Down in the meadow, where is richer feed,
And will not mind to hit their proper targe.

Plutarch was good, and so was Homer too,
Our Shakespeare's life were rich to live again,
What Plutarch read, that was not good nor true,
Nor Shakespeare's books, unless his books were men.

Here while I lie beneath this walnut bough,
What care I for the Greeks or for Troy town,
If juster battles are enacted now
Between the ants upon this hummock's crown?

Bid Homer wait till I the issue learn,
If red or black the gods will favor most,
Or yonder Ajax will the phalanx turn,
Struggling to heave some rock against the host.

Tell Shakespeare to attend some leisure hour,
For now I've business with this drop of dew,

And see you not, the clouds prepare a shower,—
I'll meet him shortly when the sky is blue.

This bed of herd's-grass and wild oats was spread
Last year with nicer skill than monarchs use,
A clover tuft is pillow for my head,
And violets quite overtop my shoes.

And now the cordial clouds have shut all in,
And gently swells the wind to say all's well,
The scattered drops are falling fast and thin,
Some in the pool, some in the flower-bell.

I am well drenched upon my bed of oats;
But see that globe come rolling down its stem,
Now like a lonely planet there it floats,
And now it sinks into my garment's hem.

Drip drip the trees for all the country round,
And richness rare distils from every bough,
The wind alone it is makes every sound,
Shaking down crystals on the leaves below.

For shame the sun will never show himself,
Who could not with his beams e'er melt me so,
My dripping locks,—they would become an elf,
Who in a beaded coat does gayly go.

SIC VITA

I am a parcel of vain strivings tied
    By a chance bond together,
      Dangling this way and that, their links

Were made so loose and wide,
    Methinks,
  For milder weather.

A bunch of violets without their roots,
    And sorrel intermixed,
  Encircled by a wisp of straw
    Once coiled about their shoots,
        The law
      By which I'm fixed.

A nosegay which Time clutched from out
    Those fair Elysian fields,
  With weeds and broken stems, in haste,
    Doth make the rabble rout
        That waste
      The day he yields.

And here I bloom for a short hour unseen,
    Drinking my juices up,
  With no root in the land
    To keep my branches green,
        But stand
      In a bare cup.

Some tender buds were left upon my stem
    In mimicry of life,
  But ah! the children will not know,
    Till time has withered them,
        The woe
      With which they're rife.

But now I see I was not plucked for naught,
    And after in life's vase

Of glass set while I might survive,
  But by a kind hand brought
      Alive
    To a strange place.

That stock thus thinned will soon redeem its hours,
    And by another year,
Such as God knows, with freer air,
    More fruits and fairer flowers
        Will bear,
      While I droop here.

LOVE

We two that planets erst had been
Are now a double star,
And in the heavens may be seen,
Where that we fixéd are.

Yet whirled with subtle power along,
Into new space we enter,
And evermore with spheral song
Revolve about one centre.

INDEPENDENCE

My life more civil is and free
    Than any civil polity.

Ye princes, keep your realms
    And circumscribèd power,

Not wide as are my dreams,
    Nor rich as is this hour.

What can ye give which I have not?
What can you take which I have got?
    Can ye defend the dangerless?
    Can ye inherit nakedness?

To all true wants Time's ear is deaf,
Penurious States lend no relief
    Out of their pelf:
  But a free soul—thank God—
    Can help itself.

  Be sure your fate
Doth keep apart its state,
Not linked with any band,
Even the noblest of the land;

In tented fields with cloth of gold
    No place doth hold,
But is more chivalrous than they are,
And sigheth for a nobler war;
A finer strain its trumpet rings,
A brighter gleam its armor flings.

The life that I aspire to live
    No man proposeth me;
No trade upon the street
    Wears its emblazonry.

INDEED INDEED, I CANNOT TELL

Indeed indeed, I cannot tell,
Though I ponder on it well,
Which were easier to state,
All my love or all my hate.
Surely, surely, thou wilt trust me
When I say thou dost disgust me.
O, I hate thee with a hate
That would fain annihilate;
Yet sometimes against my will,
My dear friend, I love thee still.
It were treason to our love,
And a sin to God above,
One iota to abate
Of a pure impartial hate.

From INSPIRATION

If with light head erect I sing,
    Though all the Muses lend their force,
From my poor love of any thing,
    The verse is weak and shallow as its source.

But if with bended neck I grope,
    Listening behind me for my wit,
With faith superior to hope,
    More anxious to keep back than forward it,—

Making my soul accomplice there
    Unto the flame my heart hath lit,—
Then will the verse forever wear:
    Time cannot bend the line which God hath writ.

Always the general show of things
    Floats in review before my mind,
And such true love and reverence brings,
    That sometimes I forget that I am blind.

But now there comes, unsought, unseen,
    Some clear divine electuary,
And I, who had but sensual been,
    Grow sensible, and as God is, am wary.

I hearing get, who had but ears,
    And sight, who had but eyes before;
I moments live, who lived but years,
    And truth discern, who knew but learning's lore.

I hear beyond the range of sound,
    I see beyond the range of sight,
New earths and skies and seas around,
    And in my day the sun doth pale his light.

A clear and ancient harmony
    Pierces my soul through all its din,
As through its utmost melody,—
    Farther behind than they, farther within.

More swift its bolt than lightning is,
    Its voice than thunder is more loud,
It doth expand my privacies
    To all, and leave me single in the crowd.

It speaks with such authority,
    With so serene and lofty tone,
That idle Time runs gadding by,
    And leaves me with Eternity alone.

Now chiefly is my natal hour,
    And only now my prime of life;
Of manhood's strength it is the flower,
    'Tis peace's end, and war's beginning strife.

*All your
whole life is lived
for the Supreme
moment*

A WINTER AND SPRING SCENE

The willows droop,
The alders stoop,
The pheasants group
    Beneath the snow;
The fishes glide
From side to side,
In the clear tide,
    The ice below.

The ferret weeps,
The marmot sleeps,
The owlet keeps
    In his snug nook.
The rabbit leaps,
The mouse out-creeps,
The flag out-peeps,
    Beside the brook.

The snow-dust falls,
The otter crawls,
The partridge calls
    Far in the wood;
The traveller dreams,
The tree-ice gleams,
The blue jay screams
    In angry mood.

The apples thaw,
The ravens caw,
The squirrels gnaw
　　The frozen fruit;
To their retreat
I track the feet
Of mice that eat
　　The apple's root.

The axe resounds,
And bay of hounds,
And tinkling sounds
　　Of wintry fame;
The hunter's horn
Awakes the dawn
On field forlorn,
　　And frights the game.

The tinkling air
Doth echo bear
To rabbit's lair,
　　With dreadful din;
She scents the air,
And far doth fare,
Returning where
　　She did begin.

The fox stands still
Upon the hill
Not fearing ill
　　From trackless wind.
But to his foes
The still wind shows
In treacherous snows
　　His tracks behind.

Now melts the snow
In the warm sun.
The meadows flow,
The streamlets run.
The spring is born,
The wild bees bum,
The insects hum,
The trees drop gum.
And winter's gone,
And summer's come.

The chic-a-dee
Lisps in the tree,
The winter bee
    Not fearing frost;
The small nuthatch
The bark doth scratch
Some worm to catch
    At any cost.

The catkins green
Cast o'er the scene
A summer sheen,
A genial glow.

I melt, I flow,
    And rippling run,
Like melting snow
    In this warm sun.

William Ellery Channing

1818–1901

A POET'S HOPE

Flying,—flying beyond all lower regions,
Beyond the light called day, and night's repose,
Where the untrammelled soul, on her wind-pinions
Fearlessly sweeping, defies my earthly woes;—
There,—there, upon that infinitest sea,
Lady, thy hope,—so fair a hope, summons me.

Fall off, ye garments of my misty weather,
Drop from my eyes, ye scales of time's applying;
Am I not godlike? meet not here together
A past and future infinite, defying,
The cold, still, callous moment of to-day?
Am I not master of the calm alway?

Would I could summon from the deep, deep mine,
Glutted with shapely jewels, glittering bright,
One echo of that splendor, call it thine,
And weave it in the strands of living light;
For it is in me, and the sea smiles fair,
And thitherward I rage, on whirling air.

Unloose me, demons of dull care and want,
I will not stand your slave, I am your king;
Think not within your meshes vile I pant
For the wild liberty of an unclipt wing;
My empire is myself, and I defy
The eternal; yes! I rule the whole, or die.

All music that the fullest breeze can play
In its melodious whisperings in the wood,
All modulations which entrance the day
And deify a sunlight solitude;
All anthems that the waves sing to the ocean
Are mine for song, and yield to my devotion.

And mine the soft glaze of a loving eye,
And mine the pure shapes of the human form,
And mine the bitterest sorrow's witchery,
And spells enough to make a snow-king warm;
For an undying hope thou breathest me,—
Hope which can ride the tossing, foaming sea.

Lady, there is a hope that all men have,
Some mercy for their faults, a grassy place
To rest in, and a flower-strewn, gentle grave;
Another hope which purifies our race,
That when that fearful bourne forever past,
They may find rest,—and rest *so* long to last.

I seek it not, I ask no rest for ever,
My path is onward to the farthest shores,—
Upbear me in your arms, unceasing river,
That from the soul's clear fountain swiftly pours,
Motionless not, until the end is won,
Which now I feel hath scarcely felt the sun.

To feel, to know, to soar unlimited,
Mid throngs of light-winged angels sweeping far,
And pore upon the realms unvisited,
That tesselate the unseen unthought star,
To be the thing that now I feebly dream
Flashing within my faintest, deepest gleam.

Ah! caverns of my soul! how thick your shade,
Where flows that life by which I faintly see,—
Wave your bright torches, for I need your aid,
Golden-eyed demons of my ancestry!
Your son though blinded hath a light within,
A heavenly fire which ye from suns did win.

And, lady, in thy hope my life will rise
Like the air-voyager, till I upbear
These heavy curtains of my filmy eyes,
Into a lighter, more celestial air;
A mortal's hope shall bear me safely on,
Till I the higher region shall have won.

O Time! O death! I clasp you in my arms,
For I can soothe an infinite cold sorrow,
And gaze contented on your icy charms,
And that wild snow-pile, which we call to-morrow;
Sweep on, O soft, and azure-lidded sky,
Earth's waters to your gentle gaze reply.

I am not earth-born, though I here delay;
Hope's child, I summon infiniter powers,
And laugh to see the mild and sunny day
Smile on the shrunk and thin autumnal hours;
I laugh, for hope hath happy place with me,
If my bark sinks, 'tis to another sea.

THE RIVER

There is an inward voice, that in the stream
Sends forth its spirit to the listening ear,
And in a calm content it floweth on,

Like wisdom, welcome with its own respect.
Clear in its breast lie all these beauteous thoughts.
It doth receive the green and graceful trees,
And the gray rocks smile in its peaceful arms,
And over all floats a serenest blue,
Which the mild heaven sheds down on it like rain.
O fair, sweet stream, thy undisturbed repose
Me beckons to thy front, and thou vexed world,
Thou other turbulent sphere where I have dwelt,
Diminished into distance touch'st no more
My feelings here, than does the swaying soft,
(Made by the delicate wave parted in front,
As through the gentle element we move
Like shadows gliding through untroubled realms,)
Disturb these lily circles, these white bells,
And yet on thee shall wind come fiercely down,
Hail pelt thee with dull words, ice bind thee up;
And yet again when the fierce rage is o'er,
O smiling river, shalt thou smile once more,
And, as it were, even in thy depths revere
The sage security thy nature wears.

THE POOR

I do not mourn my friends are false,
    I dare not grieve for sins of mine,
I weep for those who pine to death,
    Great God! in this rich world of thine.

So many trees there are to see,
    And fields go waving broad with grain,
And yet,—what utter misery!—
    Our very brothers lie in pain.

These by their darkened hearth-stones sit,
   Their children shivering idly round,
As true as liveth God, 'twere fit
   For these poor men to curse the ground.

And those who daily bread have none,
   Half starved the long, long winter's day,
Fond parents gazing on their young,
   Too wholly sad one word to say.

To them it seems, their God has cursed
   This race of ours since they were born;
Willing to toil, and yet deprived
   Of common wood, or store of corn.

I do not weep for my own woes,
   They are as nothing in my eye;
I weep for them who, starved and froze,
   Do curse their God, and long to die.

FOR A WOOD SCENE IN WINTER

Around this spot the trees have fallen,—the path
Leads its rude way o'er the decaying trunks
Of prostrate pines. Above, against the sky,
A massy wall of splintered rock soars up,
Once gay with those green plants that smile in shade,
The broad-leaved ferns. How still it is,—how lone.
You seem to hear the silence whispering—hush!
But in the spring I heard, as here I stood,
A loud and hissing stream, and in the fall
The wind plies its wild fingers, and plucks off
The sere and crimson foliage of the ash.

Life's winter, like the silent season, mute,
Crowned by a wreath of snow as white as this,
That hangs so loosely on the leafless trees,
Like this calm place still brightens in the sun;
And winter should be dear to man, as he
In his most venerable aspect, this
Does imitate.

From SONNETS

II

Thou art like that which is most sweet and fair,
A gentle morning in the youth of spring,
When the few early birds begin to sing
Within the delicate depths of the fine air.

Yet shouldst thou those dear beauties much impair,
Since thou art better than is every thing
Which or the woods, or skies, or green fields bring,
And finer thoughts hast thou than they can wear.

In the proud sweetness of thy grace I see,
What lies within, a pure and steadfast mind,
Which its own mistress is of sanctity,

And to all gentleness hath been refined;
So that thy least breath falleth upon me
As the soft breathing of midsummer wind.

IX

In those bright, laughing days that pierce the fall,
With sunny spears forged from the summer's glow,

The crimson leaves sail slowly on the pall
Of the warm fitful air; but there will blow

At sunset a cool breeze; then the leaves flow
In heaped-up multitudes beneath the wall;
Thus drifts of bodies to the graveyard go,
And the pinched foliage in their times recall.

That fall's warm wind is first affection's tear,
And near remembrance, with its fiery thought;
That frosty breeze is memory, all grown sere,

And consolation, curiously wrought;
That pile of sapless sheaths the hosts who died,
And those we lately added to their side.

THE LONELY ROAD

No track had worn the lone deserted road,
Save where the Fox had leapt from wall to wall;
There were the swelling, glittering piles of snow,
Up even with the walls, and save the Crow
Who lately had been pecking Barberries,
No other signs of life beyond ourselves.
We strayed along, beneath our feet the lane
Creaked at each pace, and soon we stood content
Where the old cellar of the house had been,
Out of which now a fruit-tree wags its top.
Some scraggy orchards hem the landscape round,
A forest of sad Apple-trees unpruned,
And then a newer orchard pet of him,
Who in his dotage kept this lonely place.
In this wild scene, and shut-in Orchard dell,

Men like ourselves, once dwelt by roaring fires,
Loved this still spot, nor had a further wish.
A little wall half falling bounds a square
Where choicer fruit-trees showed the Garden's pride,
Now crimsoned by the Sumach, whose red cones
Displace the colors of the cultured growth.
I know not how it is, that in these scenes
There is a desolation so complete,
It tarries with me after I have passed,
And the dense growth of woodland, or a sight
Of distant Cottages or landscapes wide,
Cannot obscure the dreary, cheerless thought.
But why should I remember those once there,
And think of childish voices, or that kind
Caressing hands of tender parents gone,
Have twined themselves in that soft golden hair,
All fled, and silent as an unlit Cave.
Why should I stand and muse upon their lives,
Who for me truly never had more life,
Than in the glancing mind's eye; or in Fancy
Wear this irrespective form, thus fleeting.
I people the void scene with Fancy's eye,
Her children do not live too long for me,
They vibrate in the house whose walls I rear,
The mansion as themselves, the fugitives
Of my Intent in this soft Winter day.
Nor will I scatter these faint images,
Idle as shadows that the tall reeds cast
Over the silent ice, beneath the moon,
For in these lonely haunts where Fancy dwells,
And evermore creating weaves a veil
In which all this that we call life abides,
There must be deep retirement from the day,
And in these shadowy vistas we shall meet,
Sometime the very Phantom of ourselves.—

A long Farewell, thou dim and silent spot,
Where serious Winter sleeps, or the soft hour,
Of some half dreamy Autumn afternoon;
And may no idle feet tread thy domain,
But only men to Contemplation vowed,
Still as ourselves, creators of the Past.

THE GLADE

A green and vaporous cloud of buds, the Larch
Folds in soft drapery above the glade,
Where deeper foliaged Pines high over-arch,
And dignify the heavy, stooping shade,
There yellow violets spring, in rarest show,
And golden rods in secret clusters blow.
There piping Hylas fill the helpless air,
And chattering Black-birds hold their gossip by,
And near I saw the tender maiden-hair,
With the fine, breeze-born, white anemone;
The Glade, though undisturbed by human art,
Has richer treasures than the busy mart.*

HYMN OF THE EARTH

My highway is unfeatured air,
My consorts are the sleepless stars,
And men my giant arms upbear,
My arms unstained and free from scars.

* Section VI of "Poems of the Heart."

I rest forever on my way,
Rolling around the happy sun,
My children love the sunny day,
But noon and night to me are one.

My heart has pulses like their own,
I am their Mother, and my veins
Though built of the enduring stone,
Thrill as do theirs with godlike pains.

The forests and the mountains high,
The foaming ocean and the springs,
The plains,—O pleasant company,
My voice through all your anthems rings.

Ye are so cheerful in your minds,
Content to smile, content to share,
My being in your chorus finds
The echo of the spheral air.

No leaf may fall, no pebble roll,
No drop of water lose the road,
The issues of the general Soul
Are mirrored in its round abode.

FLIGHT OF THE WILD GEESE

Rambling along the marshes,
On the bank of the Assabet,
Sounding myself as to how it went,
Praying that I might not forget,
And all uncertain

Whether I was in the right,
Toiling to lift Time's curtain,
And if I burnt the strongest light;
Suddenly,
High in the air,
I heard the travelled geese
Their overture prepare.

Stirred above the patent ball,
The wild geese flew,
Nor near so wild as that doth me befall,
Or, swollen Wisdom, you.

In the front there fetched a leader,
Him behind the line spread out,
And waved about,
As it was near night,
When these air-pilots stop their flight.

Cruising off the shoal dominion
Where we sit,
Depending not on their opinion,
Nor hiving sops of wit;
Geographical in tact,
Naming not a pond or river,
Pulled with twilight down in fact,
In the reeds to quack and quiver,
There they go,
Spectators at the play below,
Southward in a row.

The indifferent geese
Cannot land and map the stars,
Nor taste the sweetmeats in odd jars,

Nor speculate and freeze;
Raucid weasands need be well,
Feathers glossy, quills in order,
Starts this train, yet rings no bell;
Steam is raised without recorder.

"Up, my feathered fowl, all,"—
Saith the goose commander,
"Brighten your bills, and flirt your pinions,
My toes are nipped,—let us render
Ourselves in soft Guatemala,
Or suck puddles in Campeachy,
Spitzbergen-cake cuts very frosty,
And the tipple is not leechy.

"Let's brush loose for any creek,
There lurk fish and fly,
Condiments to fat the weak,
Inundate the pie.
Flutter not about the place,
Ye concomitants of space!"

Mute the listening nations stand
On that dark receding land;
How faint their villages and towns,
Scattered on the misty downs!
A meeting-house
Appears no bigger than a mouse.
How long?
Never is a question asked,
While a throat can lift the song,
Or a flapping wing be tasked.

All the grandmothers about
Hear the orators of Heaven,

Then put on their woolens stout,
And cower o'er the hearth at even;
And the children stare at sky,
And laugh to see the long black line so high!

Then once more I heard them say,—
" 'Tis a smooth, delightful road,
Difficult to lose the way,
And a trifle for a load.

" 'Twas our forte to pass for this,
Proper sack of sense to borrow,
Wings and legs, and bills that clatter,
And the horizon of To-morrow."

James Russell Lowell

1819–1891

REMEMBERED MUSIC

A FRAGMENT

Thick-rushing, like an ocean vast
  Of bisons the far prairie shaking,
The notes crowd heavily and fast
As surfs, one plunging while the last
  Draws seaward from its foamy breaking.

Or in low murmurs they began,
  Rising and rising momently,
As o'er a harp Æolian
A fitful breeze, until they ran
  Up to a sudden ecstasy.

And then, like minute-drops of rain
  Ringing in water silverly,
They lingering dropped and dropped again,
Till it was almost like a pain
  To listen when the next would be.

TO THE SPIRIT OF KEATS

Great soul, thou sittest with me in my room,
Uplifting me with thy vast, quiet eyes,
On whose full orbs, with kindly lustre, lies
The twilight warmth of ruddy ember-gloom:
Thy clear, strong tones will oft bring sudden bloom

Of hope secure, to him who lonely cries,
Wrestling with the young poet's agonies,
Neglect and scorn, which seem a certain doom.
Yes! the few words which, like great thunder-drops,
Thy large heart down to earth shook doubtfully,
Thrilled by the inward lightning of its might,
Serene and pure, like gushing joy of light,
Shall track the eternal chords of Destiny,
After the moon-led pulse of ocean stops.

HEBE

I saw the twinkle of white feet,
I saw the flash of robes descending;
　Before her ran an influence fleet,
That bowed my heart like barley bending.

　As, in bare fields, the searching bees
Pilot to blooms beyond our finding,
　It led me on, by sweet degrees
Joy's simple honey-cells unbinding.

　Those Graces were that seemed grim Fates;
With nearer love the sky leaned o'er me;
　The long-sought Secret's golden gates
On musical hinges swung before me.

　I saw the brimmed bowl in her grasp
Thrilling with godhood; like a lover
　I sprang the proffered life to clasp;—
The beaker fell; the luck was over.

The Earth has drunk the vintage up;
What boots it patch the goblet's splinters?
    Can Summer fill the icy cup,
Whose treacherous crystal is but Winter's?

O spendthrift haste! await the Gods;
Their nectar crowns the lips of Patience;
    Haste scatters on unthankful sods
The immortal gift in vain libations.

Coy Hebe flies from those that woo,
And shuns the hands would seize upon her;
    Follow thy life, and she will sue
To pour for thee the cup of honor.

From THE BIGLOW PAPERS, *First Series*

HOSEA BIGLOW TO THE RECRUITING SERGEANT

Thrash away, you'll *hev* to rattle
    On them kittle-drums o' yourn,—
'Taint a knowin' kind o' cattle
    Thet is ketched with mouldy corn;
Put in stiff, you fifer feller,
    Let folks see how spry you be,—
Guess you'll toot till you are yeller
    'Fore you git ahold o' me!

Thet air flag's a leetle rotten,
    Hope it aint your Sunday's best;—
Fact! it takes a sight o' cotton
    To stuff out a soger's chest:
Sence we farmers hev to pay fer 't,

Ef you must wear humps like these,
Sposin' you should try salt hay fer 't,
 It would du ez slick ez grease.

'Twould n't suit them Southun fellers,
 They're a dreffle graspin' set,
We must ollers blow the bellers
 Wen they want their irons het;
May be it's all right ez preachin',
 But *my* narves it kind o' grates,
Wen I see the overreachin'
 O' them nigger-drivin' States.

Them thet rule us, them slave-traders,
 Haint they cut a thunderin' swarth
(Helped by Yankee renegaders),
 Thru the vartu o' the North!
We begin to think it's nater
 To take sarse an' not be riled;—
Who'd expect to see a tater
 All on eend at bein' biled?

Ez fer war, I call it murder,—
 There you hev it plain an' flat;
I don't want to go no furder
 Than my Testyment fer that;
God hez sed so plump an' fairly,
 It's ez long ez it is broad,
An' you've gut to git up airly
 Ef you want to take in God.

'Taint your eppyletts an' feathers
 Make the thing a grain more right;
'Taint afollerin' your bell-wethers
 Will excuse ye in His sight;

Ef you take a sword an' dror it,
　　An' go stick a feller thru,
Guv'ment aint to answer for it,
　　God'll send the bill to you.

Wut's the use o' meetin'-goin'
　　Every Sabbath, wet or dry,
Ef it's right to go amowin'
　　Feller-men like oats an' rye?
I dunno but wut it's pooty
　　Trainin' round in bobtail coats,—
But it's curus Christian dooty
　　This 'ere cuttin' folks's throats.

They may talk o' Freedom's airy
　　Tell they're pupple in the face,—
It's a grand gret cemetary
　　Fer the barthrights of our race;
They jest want this Californy
　　So's to lug new slave-states in
To abuse ye, an' to scorn ye,
　　An' to plunder ye like sin.

Aint it cute to see a Yankee
　　Take sech everlastin' pains,
All to git the Devil's thankee
　　Helpin' on 'em weld their chains?
Wy, it's jest ez clear ez figgers,
　　Clear ez one an' one makes two,
Chaps thet make black slaves o' niggers
　　Want to make wite slaves o' you.

Tell ye jest the eend I've come to
　　Arter cipherin' plaguy smart,
An' it makes a handy sum, tu,

Any gump could larn by heart;
Laborin' man an' laborin' woman
   Hev one glory an' one shame.
Ev'y thin' thet's done inhuman
   Injers all on 'em the same.

'Taint by turnin' out to hack folks
   You're agoin' to git your right,
Nor by lookin' down on black folks
   Coz you're put upon by wite;
Slavery aint o' nary color,
   'Taint the hide thet makes it wus,
All it keers fer in a feller
   'S jest to make him fill its pus.

Want to tackle *me* in, du ye?
   I expect you'll hev to wait;
Wen cold lead puts daylight thru ye
   You'll begin to kal'late;
S'pose the crows wun't fall to pickin'
   All the carkiss from your bones,
Coz you helped to give a lickin'
   To them poor half-Spanish drones?

Jest go home an' ask our Nancy
   Wether I'd be sech a goose
Ez to jine ye,—guess you'd fancy
   The etarnal bung wuz loose!
She wants me fer home consumption,
   Let alone the hay's to mow,—
Ef you're arter folks o' gumption,
   You've a darned long row to hoe.

Take them editors thet's crowin'
   Like a cockerel three months old,—

Don't ketch any on 'em goin',
  Though they *be* so blasted bold;
Aint they a prime lot o' fellers?
  'Fore they think on't guess they'll sprout
(Like a peach thet's got the yellers),
  With the meanness bustin' out.

Wal, go 'long to help 'em stealin'
  Bigger pens to cram with slaves,
Help the men thet's ollers dealin'
  Insults on your fathers' graves;
Help the strong to grind the feeble,
  Help the many agin the few,
Help the men thet call your people
  Witewashed slaves an' peddlin' crew!

Massachusetts, God forgive her,
  She's akneelin' with the rest,
She, thet ough' to ha' clung ferever
  In her grand old eagle-nest;
She thet ough' to stand so fearless
  W'ile the wracks are round her hurled,
Holdin' up a beacon peerless
  To the oppressed of all the world!

Ha'n't they sold your colored seamen?
  Ha'n't they made your env'ys w'iz?
Wut'll make ye act like freemen?
  Wut'll git your dander riz?
Come, I'll tell ye wut I'm thinkin'
  Is our dooty in this fix,
They 'd ha' done 't ez quick ez winkin'
  In the days o' seventy-six.

Clang the bells in every steeple,
    Call all true men to disown
The tradoocers of our people,
    The enslavers o' their own;
Let our dear old Bay State proudly
    Put the trumpet to her mouth,
Let her ring this messidge loudly
    In the ears of all the South:—

"I'll return ye good fer evil
    Much ez we frail mortils can,
But I wun't go help the Devil
    Makin' man the cus o' man;
Call me coward, call me traiter,
    Jest ez suits your mean idees,—
Here I stand a tyrant-hater,
    An' the friend o' God an' Peace!"

Ef I'd *my* way I hed ruther
    We should go to work an' part,—
They take one way, we take t' other,
    Guess it wouldn't break my heart;
Man hed ough' to put asunder
    Them thet God has noways jined;
An' I shouldn't gretly wonder
    Ef there's thousands o' my mind.

From THE BIGLOW PAPERS, *Second Series*

THE COURTIN'

God makes sech nights, all white an' still
    Fur 'z you can look or listen,

Moonshine an' snow on field an' hill,
　All silence an' all glisten.

Zekle crep' up quite unbeknown
　An' peeked in thru' the winder,
An' there sot Huldy all alone,
　'ith no one nigh to hender.

A fireplace filled the room's one side
　With half a cord o' wood in—
There warn't no stoves (tell comfort died)
　To bake ye to a puddin'.

The wa'nut logs shot sparkles out
　Towards the pootiest, bless her,
An' leetle flames danced all about
　The chiny on the dresser.

Agin the chimbley crook-necks hung,
　An' in amongst 'em rusted
The ole queen's-arm thet gran'ther Young
　Fetched back from Concord busted.

The very room, coz she was in,
　Seemed warm from floor to ceilin',
An' she looked full ez rosy agin
　Ez the apples she was peelin'.

'T was kin' o' kingdom-come to look
　On sech a blessed cretur,
A dogrose blushin' to a brook
　Ain't modester nor sweeter.

He was six foot o' man, A 1,
　Clear grit an' human natur';

None could n't quicker pitch a ton
  Nor dror a furrer straighter.

He 'd sparked it with full twenty gals,
  Hed squired 'em, danced 'em, druv 'em,
Fust this one, an' then thet, by spells—
  All is, he could n't love 'em.

But long o' her his veins 'ould run
  All crinkly like curled maple,
The side she breshed felt full o' sun
  Ez a south slope in Ap'il.

She thought no v'ice hed sech a swing
  Ez hisn in the choir;
My! when he made Ole Hunderd ring,
  She *knowed* the Lord was nigher.

An' she 'd blush scarlit, right in prayer,
  When her new meetin'-bunnet
Felt somehow thru' its crown a pair
  O' blue eyes sot upon it.

Thet night, I tell ye, she looked *some!*
  She seemed to 've gut a new soul,
For she felt sartin-sure he 'd come,
  Down to her very shoe-sole.

She heered a foot, an' knowed it tu,
  A-raspin' on the scraper,—
All ways to once her feelins flew
  Like sparks in burnt-up paper.

He kin' o' l'itered on the mat,
  Some doubtfle o' the sekle.

His heart kep' goin' pity-pat,
   But hern went pity Zekle.

An' yit she gin her cheer a jerk
   Ez though she wished him furder,
An' on her apples kep' to work,
   Parin' away like murder.

"You want to see my Pa, I s'pose?"
   "Wal . . . . no . . . . I come dasignin' "—
"To see my Ma? She 's sprinklin clo'es
   Agin to-morrer's i'nin'."

To say why gals acts so or so,
   Or don't, 'ould be presumin';
Mebby to mean *yes* an' say *no*
   Comes nateral to women.

He stood a spell on one foot fust,
   Then stood a spell on t' other,
An' on which one he felt the wust
   He could n't ha' told ye nuther.

Says he, "I 'd better call agin";
   Says she, "Think likely, Mister":
Thet last word pricked him like a pin,
   An' . . . . Wal, he up an' kist her.

When Ma bimeby upon 'em slips,
   Huldy sot pale ez ashes,
All kin' o' smily roun' the lips
   An' teary roun' the lashes.

For she was jes' the quiet kind
   Whose naturs never vary,

Like streams that keep a summer mind
   Snowhid in Jenooary.

The blood clost roun' her heart felt glued
   Too tight for all expressin',
Tell mother see how metters stood,
   An' gin 'em both her blessin'.

Then her red come back like the tide
   Down to the Bay o' Fundy,
An' all I know is they was cried
   In meetin' come nex' Sunday.

MR. HOSEA BIGLOW TO THE EDITOR
OF THE ATLANTIC MONTHLY

Dear sir,—Your letter come to han'
   Requestin' me to please be funny;
But I ain't made upon a plan
   Thet knows wut 's comin', gall or honey:
Ther' 's times the world doos look so queer,
   Odd fancies come afore I call 'em;
An' then agin, for half a year,
   No preacher 'thout a call 's more solemn.

You 're 'n want o' sunthin' light an' cute,
   Rattlin' an' shrewd an' kin' o' jingleish,
An' wish, pervidin' it 'ould suit,
   I 'd take an' citify my English.
I *ken* write long-tailed, ef I please,—
   But when I 'm jokin', no, I thankee;
Then, 'fore I know it, my idees
   Run helter-skelter into Yankee.

Sence I begun to scribble rhyme,
   I tell ye wut, I hain't ben foolin';
The parson's books, life, death, an' time
   Hev took some trouble with my schoolin';
Nor th' airth don't git put out with me,
   Thet love her 'z though she wuz a woman;
Why, th' ain't a bird upon the tree
   But half forgives my bein' human.

An' yit I love th' unhighschooled way
   Ol' farmers hed when I wuz younger;
Their talk wuz meatier, an' 'ould stay,
   While book-froth seems to whet your hunger;
For puttin' in a downright lick
   'twixt Humbug's eyes, ther' 's few can metch it,
An' then it helves my thoughts ez slick
   Ez stret-grained hickory doos a hetchet.

But when I can't, I can't, thet 's all,
   For Natur' won't put up with gullin';
Idees you hev to shove an' haul
   Like a druv pig ain't wuth a mullein:
Live thoughts ain't sent for; thru all rifts
   O' sense they pour an' resh ye onwards,
Like rivers when south-lyin' drifts
   Feel thet th' old airth 's a-wheelin' sunwards.

Time wuz, the rhymes come crowdin' thick
   Ez office-seekers arter 'lection,
An' into ary place 'ould stick
   Without no bother nor objection;
But sence the war my thoughts hang back
   Ez though I wanted to enlist 'em,
An' subs'tutes,—*they* don't never lack,
   But then they 'll slope afore you 've mist 'em.

Nothin' don't seem like wut it wuz;
  I can't see wut there is to hender,
An' yit my brains jes' go buzz, buzz,
  Like bumblebees agin a winder;
'fore these times come, in all airth's row,
  Ther' wuz one quiet place, my head in,
Where I could hide an' think,—but now
  It 's all one teeter, hopin', dreadin'.

Where 's Peace? I start, some clear-blown night,
  When gaunt stone walls grow numb an' number,
An', creakin' 'cross the snow-crus' white,
  Walk the col' starlight into summer;
Up grows the moon, an' swell by swell
  Thru the pale pasturs silvers dimmer
Than the last smile thet strives to tell
  O' love gone heavenward in its shimmer.

I hev ben gladder o' sech things
  Than cocks o' spring or bees o' clover,
They filled my heart with livin' springs,
  But now they seem to freeze 'em over;
Sights innercent ez babes on knee,
  Peaceful ez eyes o' pastur'd cattle,
Jes' coz they be so, seem to me
  To rile me more with thoughts o' battle.

In-doors an' out by spells I try;
  Ma'am Natur' keeps her spin-wheel goin',
But leaves my natur' stiff and dry
  Ez fiel's o' clover arter mowin';
An' her jes' keepin' on the same,
  Calmer 'n a clock, an' never carin',
An' findin' nary thing to blame,
  Is wus than ef she took to swearin'.

Snow-flakes come whisperin' on the pane
   The charm makes blazin' logs so pleasant,
But I can't hark to wut they 're say'n',
   With Grant or Sherman ollers present;
The chimbleys shudder in the gale,
   Thet lulls, then suddin takes to flappin'
Like a shot hawk, but all 's ez stale
   To me ez so much sperit-rappin'.

Under the yaller-pines I house,
   When sunshine makes 'em all sweet scented,
An' hear among their furry boughs
   The baskin' west-wind purr contented,
While 'way o'erhead, ez sweet an' low
   Ez distant bells thet ring for meetin',
The wedged wil' geese their bugles blow,
   Further an' further South retreatin'.

Or up the slippery knob I strain
   An' see a hundred hills like islan's
Lift their blue woods in broken chain
   Out o' the sea o' snowy silence;
The farm-smokes, sweetes' sight on airth,
   Slow thru the winter air a-shrinkin'
Seem kin' o' sad, an' roun' the hearth
   Of empty places set me thinkin'.

Beaver roars hoarse with meltin' snows,
   An' rattles di'mon's from his granite;
Time wuz, he snatched away my prose,
   An' into psalms or satires ran it;
But he, nor all the rest thet once
   Started my blood to country-dances,
Can't set me goin' more 'n a dunce
   Thet hain't no use for dreams an' fancies.

Rat-tat-tat-tattle thru the street
  I hear the drummers makin' riot,
An' I set thinkin' o' the feet
  Thet follered once an' now are quiet,—
White feet ez snowdrops innercent,
  Thet never knowed the paths o' Satan,
Whose comin' step ther' 's ears thet won't,
  No, not lifelong, leave off awaitin'.

Why, hain't I held 'em on my knee?
  Did n't I love to see 'em growin',
Three likely lads ez wal could be,
  Hahnsome an' brave an' not tu knowin'?
I set an' look into the blaze
  Whose natur', jes' like theirn, keeps climbin',
Ez long 'z it lives, in shinin' ways,
  An' half despise myself for rhymin'.

Wut's words to them whose faith an' truth
  On War's red techstone rang true metal,
Who ventered life an' love an' youth
  For the gret prize o' death in battle?
To him who, deadly hurt, agen
  Flashed on afore the charge's thunder,
Tippin' with fire the bolt of men
  Thet rived the Rebel line asunder?

'T ain't right to hev the young go fust,
  All throbbin' full o' gifts an' graces,
Leavin' life's paupers dry ez dust
  To try an' make b'lieve fill their places:
Nothin' but tells us wut we miss,
  Ther' 's gaps our lives can't never fay in,
An' *thet* world seems so fur from this
  Lef' for us loafers to grow gray in!

My eyes cloud up for rain; my mouth
    Will take to twitchin' roun' the corners;
I pity mothers, tu, down South,
    For all they sot among the scorners:
I 'd sooner take my chance to stan'
    At Jedgment where your meanest slave is,
Than at God's bar hol' up a han'
    Ez drippin' red ez yourn, Jeff Davis!

Come, Peace! not like a mourner bowed
    For honor lost an' dear ones wasted,
But proud, to meet a people proud,
    With eyes thet tell o' triumph tasted!
Come, with han' grippin' on the hilt,
    An' step thet proves ye Victory's daughter!
Longin' for you, our sperits wilt
    Like shipwrecked men's on raf's for water.

Come, while our country feels the lift
    Of a gret instinct shoutin' forwards,
An' knows thet freedom ain't a gift
    Thet tarries long in han's o' cowards!
Come, sech ez mothers prayed for, when
    They kissed their cross with lips thet quivered,
An' bring fair wages for brave men,
    A nation saved, a race delivered!

ODE RECITED AT THE HARVARD
COMMEMORATION

July 21, 1865

I

Weak-winged is song,
Nor aims at that clear-ethered height
Whither the brave deed climbs for light:
    We seem to do them wrong,
Bringing our robin's-leaf to deck their hearse
Who in warm life-blood wrote their nobler verse,
Our trivial song to honor those who come
With ears attuned to strenuous trump and drum,
And shaped in squadron-strophes their desire,
Live battle-odes whose lines were steel and fire:
    Yet sometimes feathered words are strong,
A gracious memory to buoy up and save
From Lethe's dreamless ooze, the common grave
    Of the unventurous throng.

II

To-day our Reverend Mother welcomes back
    Her wisest Scholars, those who understood
The deeper teaching of her mystic tome,
    And offered their fresh lives to make it good:
        No lore of Greece or Rome,
No science peddling with the names of things,
Or reading stars to find inglorious fates,
        Can lift our life with wings
Far from Death's idle gulf that for the many waits,
        And lengthen out our dates
With that clear fame whose memory sings
In manly hearts to come, and nerves them and dilates:

Nor such thy teaching, Mother of us all!
 Not such the trumpet-call
 Of thy diviner mood,
 That could thy sons entice
From happy homes and toils, the fruitful nest
Of those half-virtues which the world calls best,
 Into War's tumult rude;
 But rather far that stern device
The sponsors chose that round thy cradle stood
 In the dim, unventured wood,
 The VERITAS that lurks beneath
 The letter's unprolific sheath,
 Life of whate'er makes life worth living,
Seed-grain of high emprise, immortal food,
 One heavenly thing whereof earth hath the giving.

III

Many loved Truth, and lavished life's best oil
 Amid the dust of books to find her,
Content at last, for guerdon of their toil,
 With the cast mantle she hath left behind her.
 Many in sad faith sought for her,
 Many with crossed hands sighed for her;
 But these, our brothers, fought for her
 At life's dear peril wrought for her,
 So loved her that they died for her,
 Tasting the raptured fleetness
 Of her divine completeness:
  Their higher instinct knew
Those love her best who to themselves are true,
And what they dare to dream of, dare to do;
 They followed her and found her
 Where all may hope to find,
Not in the ashes of the burnt-out mind,

But beautiful, with danger's sweetness round her.
    Where faith made whole with deed
    Breathes its awakening breath
    Into the lifeless creed,
    They saw her plumed and mailed,
    With sweet, stern face unveiled,
And all-repaying eyes, look proud on them in death.

IV

Our slender life runs rippling by, and glides
    Into the silent hollow of the past;
      What is there that abides
    To make the next age better for the last?
      Is earth too poor to give us
    Something to live for here that shall outlive us?
      Some more substantial boon
Than such as flows and ebbs with Fortune's fickle moon?
      The little that we see
      From doubt is never free;
      The little that we do
      Is but half-nobly true;
      With our laborious hiving
What men call treasure, and the gods call dross,
    Life seems a jest of Fate's contriving,
    Only secure in every one's conniving,
A long account of nothings paid with loss,
Where we poor puppets, jerked by unseen wires,
    After our little hour of strut and rave,
With all our pasteboard passions and desires,
Loves, hates, ambitions, and immortal fires,
    Are tossed pell-mell together in the grave.
    But stay! no age was e'er degenerate,
    Unless men held it at too cheap a rate,
    For in our likeness still we shape our fate.

Ah, there is something here
Unfathomed by the cynic's sneer,
Something that gives our feeble light
A high immunity from Night,
Something that leaps life's narrow bars
To claim its birthright with the hosts of heaven;
A seed of sunshine that doth leaven
Our earthly dulness with the beams of stars,
And glorify our clay
With light from fountains elder than the Day;
A conscience more divine than we,
A gladness fed with secret tears,
A vexing, forward-reaching sense
Of some more noble permanence;
A light across the sea,
Which haunts the soul and will not let it be,
Still beaconing from the heights of undegenerate years.

v

Whither leads the path
To ampler fates that leads?
Not down through flowery meads,
To reap an aftermath
Of youth's vainglorious weeds,
But up the steep, amid the wrath
And shock of deadly-hostile creeds,
Where the world's best hope and stay
By battle's flashes gropes a desperate way,
And every turf the fierce foot clings to bleeds.
Peace hath her not ignoble wreath,
Ere yet the sharp, decisive word
Light the black lips of cannon, and the sword
Dreams in its easeful sheath;
But some day the live coal behind the thought,

Whether from Baäl's stone obscene,
Or from the shrine serene
Of God's pure altar brought,
Bursts up in flame; the war of tongue and pen
Learns with what deadly purpose it was fraught,
And, helpless in the fiery passion caught,
Shakes all the pillared state with shock of men:
Some day the soft Ideal that we wooed
Confronts us fiercely, foe-beset, pursued,
And cries reproachful: "Was it, then, my praise,
And not myself was loved? Prove now thy truth;
I claim of thee the promise of thy youth;
Give me thy life, or cower in empty phrase,
The victim of thy genius, not its mate!"
Life may be given in many ways,
And loyalty to Truth be sealed
As bravely in the closet as the field,
So bountiful is Fate;
But then to stand beside her,
When craven churls deride her,
To front a lie in arms and not to yield,
This shows, methinks, God's plan
And measure of a stalwart man,
Limbed like the old heroic breeds,
Who stands self-poised on manhood's solid earth,
Not forced to frame excuses for his birth,
Fed from within with all the strength he needs.

VI

Such was he, our Martyr-Chief,
Whom late the Nation he had led,
With ashes on her head,
Wept with the passion of an angry grief:
Forgive me, if from present things I turn

To speak what in my heart will beat and burn,
And hang my wreath on his world-honored urn.

Nature, they say, doth dote,
And cannot make a man
Save on some worn-out plan,
Repeating us by rote:
For him her Old-World moulds aside she threw,
And, choosing sweet clay from the breast
Of the unexhausted West,
With stuff untainted shaped a hero new,
Wise, steadfast in the strength of God, and true.

How beautiful to see
Once more a shepherd of mankind indeed,
Who loved his charge, but never loved to lead;
One whose meek flock the people joyed to be,
Not lured by any cheat of birth,
But by his clear-grained human worth,
And brave old wisdom of sincerity!
They knew that outward grace is dust;
They could not choose but trust
In that sure-footed mind's unfaltering skill,
And supple-tempered will
That bent like perfect steel to spring again and thrust.
His was no lonely mountain-peak of mind,
Thrusting to thin air o'er our cloudy bars,
A sea-mark now, now lost in vapors blind;
Broad prairie rather, genial, level-lined,
Fruitful and friendly for all human kind,
Yet also nigh to heaven and loved of loftiest stars.

Nothing of Europe here,
Or, then, of Europe fronting mornward still,
Ere any names of Serf and Peer
Could Nature's equal scheme deface
And thwart her genial will;
Here was a type of the true elder race,

And one of Plutarch's men talked with us face to face.
  I praise him not; it were too late;
And some innative weakness there must be
In him who condescends to victory
Such as the Present gives, and cannot wait,
  Safe in himself as in a fate.
    So always firmly he:
    He knew to bide his time,
    And can his fame abide,
Still patient in his simple faith sublime,
    Till the wise years decide.
  Great captains, with their guns and drums,
  Disturb our judgment for the hour,
    But at last silence comes;
  These all are gone, and, standing like a tower,
  Our children shall behold his fame,
    The kindly-earnest, brave, foreseeing man,
Sagacious, patient, dreading praise, not blame,
  New birth of our new soil, the first American.

VII

Long as man's hope insatiate can discern
  Or only guess some more inspiring goal
  Outside of Self, enduring as the pole,
Along whose course the flying axles burn
Of spirits bravely-pitched, earth's manlier brood;
  Long as below we cannot find
The meed that stills the inexorable mind;
So long this faith to some ideal Good,
Under whatever mortal names it masks,
Freedom, Law, Country, this ethereal mood
That thanks the Fates for their severer tasks,
  Feeling its challenged pulses leap,
  While others skulk in subterfuges cheap,

And, set in Danger's van, has all the boon it asks,
   Shall win man's praise and woman's love,
   Shall be a wisdom that we set above
All other skills and gifts to culture dear,
   A virtue round whose forehead we inwreathe
   Laurels that with a living passion breathe
When other crowns grow, while we twine them, sear.
   What brings us thronging these high rites to pay,
And seal these hours the noblest of our year,
   Save that our brothers found this better way?

This To shall pass away

VIII

We sit here in the Promised Land
That flows with Freedom's honey and milk;
But 'twas they won it, sword in hand,
Making the nettle danger soft for us as silk.
   We welcome back our bravest and our best;—
   Ah me! not all! some come not with the rest,
Who went forth brave and bright as any here!
I strive to mix some gladness with my strain,
    But the sad strings complain,
    And will not please the ear:
I sweep them for a pæan, but they wane
    Again and yet again
Into a dirge, and die away, in pain.
In these brave ranks I only see the gaps,
Thinking of dear ones whom the dumb turf wraps,
Dark to the triumph which they died to gain:
   Fitlier may others greet the living,
   For me the past is unforgiving;
    I with uncovered head
    Salute the sacred dead,
Who went, and who return not.—Say not so!
'Tis not the grapes of Canaan that repay,

But the high faith that failed not by the way;
Virtue treads paths that end not in the grave;
No bar of endless night exiles the brave;
    And to the saner mind
We rather seem the dead that stayed behind.
Blow, trumpets, all your exultations blow!
For never shall their aureoled presence lack:
I see them muster in a gleaming row,
With ever-youthful brows that nobler show;
We find in our dull road their shining track;
    In every nobler mood
We feel the orient of their spirit glow,
Part of our life's unalterable good,
Of all our saintlier aspiration;
    They come transfigured back,
Secure from change in their high-hearted ways,
Beautiful evermore, and with the rays
Of morn on their white Shields of Expectation!

IX

    But is there hope to save
  Even this ethereal essence from the grave?
What ever 'scaped Oblivion's subtle wrong
Save a few clarion names, or golden threads of song?
    Before my musing eye
  The mighty ones of old sweep by,
Disvoicèd now and insubstantial things,
As noisy once as we; poor ghosts of kings,
Shadows of empire wholly gone to dust,
And many races, nameless long ago,
To darkness driven by that imperious gust
Of ever-rushing Time that here doth blow:
O visionary world, condition strange,
Where naught abiding is but only Change,

Where the deep-bolted stars themselves still shift and range!
  Shall we to more continuance make pretence?
Renown builds tombs; a life-estate is Wit;
        And, bit by bit,
The cunning years steal all from us but woe;
  Leaves are we, whose decays no harvest sow.
          But, when we vanish hence,
  Shall they lie forceless in the dark below,
  Save to make green their little length of sods,
  Or deepen pansies for a year or two,
  Who now to us are shining-sweet as gods?
  Was dying all they had the skill to do?
  That were not fruitless: but the Soul resents
  Such short-lived service, as if blind events
  Ruled without her, or earth could so endure;
  She claims a more divine investiture
  Of longer tenure than Fame's airy rents;
  Whate'er she touches doth her nature share;
  Her inspiration haunts the ennobled air,
        Gives eyes to mountains blind,
  Ears to the deaf earth, voices to the wind,
  And her clear trump sings succor everywhere
  By lonely bivouacs to the wakeful mind;
  For soul inherits all that soul could dare:
    Yea, Manhood hath a wider span
  And larger privilege of life than man.
  The single deed, the private sacrifice,
  So radiant now through proudly-hidden tears,
  Is covered up erelong from mortal eyes
  With thoughtless drift of the deciduous years;
  But that high privilege that makes all men peers,
  That leap of heart whereby a people rise
        Up to a noble anger's height,
And, flamed on by the Fates, not shrink, but grow more bright,
  That swift validity in noble veins,

Of choosing danger and disdaining shame,
    Of being set on flame
By the pure fire that flies all contact base,
But wraps its chosen with angelic might,
    These are imperishable gains,
  Sure as the sun, medicinal as light,
  These hold great futures in their lusty reins
And certify to earth a new imperial race.

x

    Who now shall sneer?
  Who dare again to say we trace
  Our lines to a plebeian race?
    Roundhead and Cavalier!
Dumb are those names erewhile in battle loud;
Dream-footed as the shadow of a cloud,
    They flit across the ear:
That is best blood that hath most iron in't.
To edge resolve with, pouring without stint
    For what makes manhood dear.
    Tell us not of Plantagenets,
Hapsburgs, and Guelfs, whose thin bloods crawl
Down from some victor in a border-brawl!
    How poor their outworn coronets,
Matched with one leaf of that plain civic wreath
Our brave for honor's blazon shall bequeath,
  Through whose desert a rescued Nation sets
Her heel on treason, and the trumpet hears
Shout victory, tingling Europe's sullen ears
  With vain resentments and more vain regrets!

XI

Not in anger, not in pride,
Pure from passion's mixture rude
Ever to base earth allied,
But with far-heard gratitude,
Still with heart and voice renewed,
To heroes living and dear martyrs dead,
The strain should close that consecrates our brave.
Lift the heart and lift the head!
Lofty be its mood and grave,
Not without a martial ring,
Not without a prouder tread
And a peal of exultation:
Little right has he to sing
Through whose heart in such an hour
Beats no march of conscious power,
Sweeps no tumult of elation!
'Tis no Man we celebrate,
By his country's victories great,
A hero half, and half the whim of Fate,
But the pith and marrow of a Nation
Drawing force from all her men,
Highest, humblest, weakest, all,
For her time of need, and then
Pulsing it again through them,
Till the basest can no longer cower,
Feeling his soul spring up divinely tall,
Touched but in passing by her mantle-hem.
Come back, then, noble pride, for 'tis her dower!
How could poet ever tower,
If his passions, hopes, and fears,
If his triumphs and his tears,
Kept not measure with his people?
Boom, cannon, boom to all the winds and waves!

Clash out, glad bells, from every rocking steeple!
Banners, adance with triumph, bend your staves!
  And from every mountain-peak
  Let beacon-fire to answering beacon speak,
  Katahdin tell Monadnock, Whiteface he,
And so leap on in light from sea to sea,
    Till the glad news be sent
    Across a kindling continent,
Making earth feel more firm and air breathe braver:
"Be proud! for she is saved, and all have helped to save her!
  She that lifts up the manhood of the poor,
  She of the open soul and open door,
  With room about her hearth for all mankind!
  The fire is dreadful in her eyes no more;
  From her bold front the helm she doth unbind,
  Sends all her handmaid armies back to spin,
  And bids her navies, that so lately hurled
  Their crashing battle, hold their thunders in,
  Swimming like birds of calm along the unharmful shore.
  No challenge sends she to the elder world,
  That looked askance and hated; a light scorn
  Plays o'er her mouth, as round her mighty knees
  She calls her children back, and waits the morn
Of nobler day, enthroned between her subject seas."

XII

Bow down, dear Land, for thou hast found release!
  Thy God, in these distempered days,
  Hath taught thee the sure wisdom of His ways,
And through thine enemies hath wrought thy peace!
    Bow down in prayer and praise!
No poorest in thy borders but may now
Lift to the juster skies a man's enfranchised brow,
O Beautiful! my Country! ours once more!

Smoothing thy gold of war-dishevelled hair
O'er such sweet brows as never other wore,
    And letting thy set lips,
    Freed from wrath's pale eclipse,
The rosy edges of their smile lay bare,
What words divine of lover or of poet
Could tell our love and make thee know it,
Among the Nations bright beyond compare?
    What were our lives without thee?
    What all our lives to save thee?
    We reck not what we gave thee;
    We will not dare to doubt thee,
But ask whatever else, and we will dare!

AUSPEX

My heart, I cannot still it,
Nest that had song-birds in it;
And when the last shall go,
The dreary days, to fill it,
Instead of lark or linnet,
Shall whirl dead leaves and snow.

Had they been swallows only,
Without the passion stronger
That skyward longs and sings,—
Woe's me, I shall be lonely
When I can feel no longer
The impatience of their wings!

A moment, sweet delusion,
Like birds the brown leaves hover;

But it will not be long
Before their wild confusion
Fall wavering down to cover
The poet and his song.

Henry Howard Brownell

1820–1872

THE BURIAL OF THE DANE

Blue gulf all around us,
  Blue sky overhead—
Muster all on the quarter,
  We must bury the dead!

It is but a Danish sailor,
  Rugged of front and form;
A common son of the forecastle,
  Grizzled with sun and storm.

His name, and the strand he hailed from
  We know—and there's nothing more!
But perhaps his mother is waiting
  In the lonely Island of Fohr.

Still, as he lay dying,
  Reason drifting awreck,
" 'Tis my watch," he would mutter,
  "I must go up on deck!"

Aye, on deck—by the foremast!—
  But watch and look-out are done;
The Union-Jack laid o'er him,
  How quiet he lies in the sun!

Slow the ponderous engine,
  Stay the hurrying shaft!
Let the roll of the ocean

Cradle our giant craft—
Gather around the grating,
　Carry your messmate aft!

Our captain reads the service,
　(A little spray on his cheeks,)
The grand old words of burial,
　And the trust a true heart seeks—
"We therefore commit his body
　To the deep"—and, as he speaks,

Launched from the weather railing,
　Swift as the eye can mark,
The ghastly, shotted hammock
　Plunges, away from the shark,
Down, a thousand fathoms,
　Down into the dark!

A thousand summers and winters
　The stormy Gulf shall roll
High o'er his canvas coffin,—
　But, silence to doubt and dole!
There's a quiet harbor somewhere
　For the poor a-weary soul.

Free the fettered engine,
　Speed the tireless shaft!
Loose to'gallant and topsail,
　The breeze is fair abaft!

Blue sea all around us,
　Blue sky bright o'erhead—
Every man to his duty!
　We have buried our dead.

NIGHT–QUARTERS

Tang! tang! went the gong's wild roar
    Through the hundred cells of our great Sea-Hive!
Five seconds—it couldn't be more—
    And the whole Swarm was humming and alive—
(We were on an enemy's shore).

    With savage haste, in the dark,
    (Our steerage hadn't a spark,)
Into boot and hose they blundered—
From for'ard came a strange, low roar,
    The dull and smothered racket
    Of lower rig and jacket
Hurried on, by the hundred—
How the berth deck buzzed and swore!

The third of minutes ten,
And half a thousand men,
From the dream-gulf, dead and deep,
Of the seaman's measured sleep,
In the taking of a lunar,
    In the serving of a ration,
    Every man at his station!—
Three and a quarter, or sooner!
    Never a skulk to be seen—
From the look-out aloft to the gunner
    Lurking in his black magazine.

There they stand, still as death,
And, (a trifle out of breath,
    It may be,) we of the Staff,
All on the poop, to a minute,
Wonder if there's anything in it—
    Doubting if to growl or laugh.

But, somehow, every hand
Feels for hilt and brand,
Tries if buckle and frog be tight—
    So, in the chilly breeze, we stand
Peering through the dimness of the night—
    The men, by twos and ones,
    Grim and silent at the guns,
Ready, if a Foe heave in sight!

But, as we looked aloft,
There, all white and soft,
    Floated on the fleecy clouds,
(Stray flocks in heaven's blue croft)—
How they shone, the eternal stars,
'Mid the black masts and spars
    And the great maze of lifts and shrouds!

From ABRAHAM LINCOLN

(Summer, 1865)

Dead is the roll of the drums,
    And the distant thunders die,
    They fade in the far-off sky;
And a lovely summer comes,
    Like the smile of Him on high.

Lulled, the storm and the onset.
    Earth lies in a sunny swoon;
    Stiller splendor of noon,
Softer glory of sunset,
    Milder starlight and moon!

For the kindly Seasons love us;
   They smile over trench and clod,
(Where we left the bravest of us,)—
   There's a brighter green of the sod,
And a holier calm above us
   In the blesséd Blue of God.

The roar and ravage were vain;
   And Nature, that never yields,
Is busy with sun and rain
At her old sweet work again
   On the lonely battle-fields.

How the tall white daisies grow,
   Where the grim artillery rolled!
(Was it only a moon ago?
   It seems a century old,)—

And the bee hums in the clover,
   As the pleasant June comes on;
Aye, the wars are all over,—
   But our good Father is gone.

There was tumbling of traitor fort,
   Flaming of traitor fleet—
Lighting of city and port,
   Clasping in square and street.

There was thunder of mine and gun,
   Cheering by mast and tent,—
When—his dread work all done,
And his high fame full won—
   Died the Good President. . . .

Kindly Spirit!—Ah, when did treason
　Bid such a generous nature cease,
Mild by temper and strong by reason,
　But ever leaning to love and peace?

A head how sober; a heart how spacious;
　A manner equal with high or low;
Rough but gentle, uncouth but gracious,
　And still inclining to lips of woe.

Patient when saddest, calm when sternest,
　Grieved when rigid for justice' sake;
Given to jest, yet ever in earnest
　If aught of right or truth were at stake.

Simple of heart, yet shrewd therewith,
　Slow to resolve, but firm to hold;
Still with parable and with myth
　Seasoning truth, like Them of old!
Aptest humor and quaintest pith!
　(Still we smile o'er the tales he told.)

And if, sometimes, in saddest stress,
　That mind, over-meshed by fate,
　(Ringed round with treason and hate,
And guiding the State by guess,)
　Could doubt and could hesitate—
Who, alas, had done less
　In the world's most deadly strait?

But how true to the Common Cause!
　Of his task how unweary!
How hard he worked, how good he was,
　How kindly and cheery!

How, while it marked redouble
    The howls and hisses and sneers,
That great heart bore our trouble
    Through all these terrible years;

And, cooling passion with state,
    And ever counting the cost,
Kept the Twin World-Robbers in wait
    Till the time for their clutch was lost. . . .

Yet whoso might pierce the guise
    Of mirth in the man we mourn,
Would mark, and with grieved surprise,
    All the great soul had borne,
In the piteous lines, and the kind, sad eyes
    So dreadfully wearied and worn.

And we trusted, (the last dread page
    Once turned, of our Dooms-day Scroll,)
    To have seen him, sunny of soul,
In a cheery, grand old age.

But, Father, 'tis well with thee!
    And since ever, when God draws nigh,
Some grief for the good must be,
    'Twas well, even so to die,—

'Mid the thunder of Treason's fall,
    The yielding of haughty town,
The crashing of cruel wall,
    The trembling of tyrant crown!

The ringing of hearth and pavement
    To the clash of falling chains,—

The centuries of enslavement
  Dead, with their blood-bought gains!

And through trouble weary and long
  Well hadst thou seen the way,
Leaving the State so strong
  It did not reel for a day;

And even in death couldst give
  A token for Freedom's strife—
A proof how republics live,
  And not by a single life,

But the Right Divine of man,
  And the many, trained to be free,—
And none, since the world began,
  Ever was mourned like thee. . . .

Hush! let our heavy souls
  To-day be glad; for agen
The stormy music swells and rolls,
  Stirring the hearts of men.

And under the Nation's Dome,
  They've guarded so well and long,
Our boys come marching home,
  Two hundred thousand strong.

All in the pleasant month of May,
  With war-worn colors and drums,
Still through the livelong summer's day,
  Regiment, regiment comes.

Like the tide, yeasty and barmy,
  That sets on a wild lee-shore,

Surge the ranks of an army
    Never reviewed before!

Who shall look on the like agen,
    Or see such a host of the brave?
A mighty River of marching men
    Rolls the Capital through—
Rank on rank, and wave on wave,
    Of bayonet-crested blue!

How the chargers neigh and champ,
(Their riders weary of camp,)
    With curvet and with caracole!—
The cavalry comes with thunderous tramp,
    And the cannons heavily roll.

And ever, flowery and gay,
The Staff sweeps on in a spray
    Of tossing forelocks and manes;
But each bridle-arm has a weed
Of funeral, black as the steed
    That fiery Sheridan reins.

Grandest of mortal sights
    The sun-browned ranks to view—
The Colors ragg'd in a hundred fights,
    And the dusty Frocks of Blue!

And all day, mile on mile,
With cheer, and waving, and smile,
The war-worn legions defile
    Where the nation's noblest stand;
And the Great Lieutenant looks on,
    With the Flower of a rescued Land,—
For the terrible work is done,

And the Good Fight is won
  For God and for Fatherland. . . .

And our boys had fondly thought,
  To-day, in marching by,
From the ground so dearly bought,
And the fields so bravely fought,
  To have met their Father's eye.

But they may not see him in place,
  Nor their ranks be seen of him;
We look for the well-known face,
  And the splendor is strangely dim.

Perished?—who was it said
  Our Leader had passed away?
Dead? Our President dead?
  He has not died for a day!

We mourn for a little breath
  Such as, late or soon, dust yields;
But the Dark Flower of Death
  Blooms in the fadeless fields.

We looked on a cold, still brow,
  But Lincoln could yet survive;
  He never was more alive,
Never nearer than now.

For the pleasant season found him,
  Guarded by faithful hands,
  In the fairest of Summer Lands;
With his own brave Staff around him,
  There our President stands.

There they are all at his side,
  The noble hearts and true,
  That did all men might do—
Then slept, with their swords, and died. . . .

And lo, from a thousand fields,
  From all the old battle-haunts,
A greater Army than Sherman wields,
  A grander Review than Grant's!

Gathered home from the grave,
  Risen from sun and rain—
Rescued from wind and wave
  Out of the stormy main—
The Legions of our Brave
  Are all in their lines again!

Many a stout Corps that went,
Full-ranked, from camp and tent,
  And brought back a brigade;
Many a brave regiment
  That mustered only a squad.

The lost battalions
  That, when the fight went wrong,
Stood and died at their guns,—
  The stormers steady and strong,

With their best blood that bought
  Scarp, and ravelin, and wall,—
The companies that fought
  Till a corporal's guard was all.

Many a valiant crew,
  That passed in battle and wreck,—

Ah, so faithful and true!
　　They died on the bloody deck,
They sank in the soundless blue.

All the loyal and bold
　　That lay on a soldier's bier,—
　　The stretchers borne to the rear,
The hammocks lowered to the hold.

The shattered wreck we hurried,
　　In death-fight, from deck and port,—
The Blacks that Wagner buried—
　　That died in the Bloody Fort!

Comrades of camp and mess,
　　Left, as they lay, to die,
In the battle's sorest stress,
　　When the storm of fight swept by,—
They lay in the Wilderness,
　　Ah, where did they not lie?

In the tangled swamp they lay,
　　They lay so still on the sward!—
They rolled in the sick-bay,
Moaning their lives away—
　　They flushed in the fevered ward.

They rotted in Libby yonder,
　　They starved in the foul stockade—
Hearing afar the thunder
　　Of the Union cannonade!

But the old wounds all are healed,
　　And the dungeoned limbs are free,—

The Blue Frocks rise from the field,
  The Blue Jackets out of the sea. . .

The armies have broken camp
  On the vast and sunny plain,
  The drums are rolling again;
With steady, measured tramp,
  They're marching all again.

With alignment firm and solemn,—
  Once again they form
In mighty square and column,
  But never for charge and storm.

The Old Flag they died under
  Floats above them on the shore,
And on the great ships yonder
  The ensigns dip once more—
And once again the thunder
  Of the thirty guns and four!

In solid platoons of steel,
  Under heaven's triumphal arch,
The long lines break and wheel—
  And the word is, "Forward, march!"

The Colors ripple o'erhead,
  The drums roll up to the sky,
And with martial time and tread
  The regiments all pass by—
The ranks of our faithful Dead,
  Meeting their President's eye.

With a soldier's quiet pride
  They smiled o'er the perished pain,

For their anguish was not in vain—
For thee, O Father, we died!
  And we did not die in vain.

March on, your last brave mile!
  Salute him, Star and Lace,
Form round him, rank and file,
  And look on the kind, rough face;
But the quaint and homely smile
  Has a glory and a grace
It never had known erewhile—
  Never, in time and space. . . .

Frederick Goddard Tuckerman

1821–1873

SONNETS: Part I

I

Sometimes, when winding slow by brook and bower,
Beating the idle grass,—of what avail,
I ask, are these dim fancies, cares, and fears?
What though from every bank I drew a flower,—
Bloodroot, king-orchis, or the pearlwort pale,—
And set it in my verse with thoughtful tears?
What would it count, though I should sing my death,
And muse and mourn with as poetic breath
As, in damp garden-walks, the autumn gale
Sighs o'er the fallen floriage? What avail
Is the swan's voice, if all the hearers fail,
Or his great flight, that no eye gathereth,
In the blending blue? And yet, depending so,
God were not God, whom knowledge cannot know.

II

Wherefore, with this belief, held like a blade,—
Gathering my strength and purpose, fair and slow,
I wait; resolved to carry it to the heart
Of that dark doubt in one collected blow;
And stand at guard with spirit undismayed,
Nor fear the Opposer's anger, arms, or art;
When, from a hiding near, behold him start
With a fresh weapon of my weakness made;
And goad me with myself, and urge the attack,
While I strike short, and still give back and back

414

While the foe rages. Then from that disgrace
He points to where they sit that have won the race,
Laurel by laurel wreathing, face o'er face,
And leave me lower still; for, ranked in place,

III

And borne with theirs, my proudest thoughts do seem
Bald at the best, and dim; a barren gleam
Among the immortal stars, and faint and brief
As north-light flitting in the dreary north.
"What have thy dreams,—a vague, prospective worth?
An import imminent? or dost thou deem
Thy life so fair, that thou wouldst set it forth
Before the day? or art thou wise in grief,
Has fruitful Sorrow swept thee with her wing?"
Today I heard a sweet voice carolling
In the wood-land paths, with laugh and careless cry,
Leading her happy mates. Apart I stept;
And, while the laugh and song went lightly by,
In the wild bushes I sat down and wept.

IV

Nor looks that backward life so bare to me,
My later youth, and ways I've wandered through;
But touched with innocent grace,—the early bee
On the maple log, the white-heaped cherry tree
That hummed all day in the sun, the April blue!
Yet hardly now one ray the Forward hath
To show where sorrow rests, and rest begins;
Although I check my feet, nor walk to wrath
Through days of crime, and grosser shadowings
Of evil done in the dark; but fearfully,
'Mid unfulfilled yet unrelinquished sins

That hedge me in, and press about my path,
Like purple-poison flowers of stramony,
With their dull opiate-breath, and dragon-wings.

v

And so the day drops by; the horizon draws
The fading sun, and we stand struck in grief;
Failing to find our haven of relief,—
Wide of the way, nor sure to turn or pause;
And weep to view how fast the splendour wanes,
And scarcely heed, that yet some share remains
Of the red after-light, some time to mark,
Some space between the sundown and the dark.
But not for him those golden calms succeed,
Who, while the day is high and glory reigns,
Sees it go by,—as the dim Pampas plain,
Hoary with salt, and gray with bitter weed,
Sees the vault blacken, feels the dark wind strain,
Hears the dry thunder roll, and knows no rain.

How hopeless can you get
to hear the thunder but not get wet.

VI

Not sometimes, but—to him that heeds the whole,
And in the Ample reads his personal page,
Labouring to reconcile, content, assuage,
The vexed conditions of his heritage—
For ever waits an angel at the goal;
And ills seem but as food for spirits sage,
And grief becomes a dark apparelage,
The weed and wearing of the sacred soul.
Might I but count, but here, one watch-light spark!
But vain, oh vain! this turning for the light,—
Vain as a groping hand to rend the dark.
I call, entangled in the night,—a night

Of wind and voices! but the gusty roll
Is vague, nor comes there cheer of pilotage.

VII

Dank fens of cedar; hemlock-branches gray
With tress and trail of mosses wringing-wet;
Beds of the black pitch-pine in dead leaves set
Whose wasted red has wasted to white away;
Remnants of rain, and droppings of decay,—
Why hold ye so my heart, nor dimly let
Through your deep leaves the light of yesterday,
The faded glimmer of a sunshine set?
Is it that in your darkness, shut from strife,
The bread of tears becomes the bread of life?
Far from the roar of day, beneath your boughs
Fresh griefs beat tranquilly, and loves and vows
Grow green in your gray shadows, dearer far
Even than all lovely lights, and roses, are?

VIII

As when, down some broad River dropping, we,
Day after day, behold the assuming shores
Sink and grow dim, as the great Water-course
Pushes his banks apart and seeks the sea;
Benches of pines, high shelf and balcony,
To flats of willow and low sycamores
Subsiding, till where'er the wave we see
Himself is his horizon utterly:
So fades the portion of our early world.
Still on the ambit hangs the purple air;
Yet, while we lean to read the secret there,
The stream that by green shore-sides plashed and purled
Expands, the mountains melt to vapors rare,
And life alone circles out flat and bare.

IX

Yet wear we on; the deep light disallowed
That lit our youth,—in years no longer young,
We wander silently, and brood among
Dead graves, and tease the sun-break and the cloud
For import. Were it not better yet to fly,
To follow those who go before the throng,
Reasoning from stone to star, and easily
Exampling this existence? or shall I—
Who yield slow reverence where I cannot see,
And gather gleams, where'er by chance or choice
My footsteps draw,—though brokenly dispensed,—
Come into light at last?—or suddenly,
Struck to the knees like Saul, one arm against
The overbearing brightness, hear a Voice?

X

An upper chamber in a darkened house,
Where, ere his footsteps reached ripe manhood's brink,
Terror and anguish were his cup to drink,—
I cannot rid the thought, nor hold it close;
But dimly dream upon that man alone;—
Now though the autumn clouds most softly pass;
The cricket chides beneath the doorstep stone,
And greener than the season grows the grass.
Nor can I drop my lids, nor shade my brows,
But there he stands beside the lifted sash;
And, with a swooning of the heart, I think
Where the black shingles slope to meet the boughs,
And—shattered on the roof like smallest snows—
The tiny petals of the mountain-ash.

XI

What profits it to me, though here allowed
Life, sunlight, leisure, if they fail to urge
Me to due motion, or myself to merge
With the onward stream, too humble, or too proud?
That find myself not with the popular surge
Washed off and on, or up to higher reefs
Flung with the foremost, when the rolling crowd
Hoists like a wave, nor strong to speak aloud;
But standing here, gazing on my own griefs,
Dark household woe, and wounds that bleed and smart;
With still lips, and an outcry in the heart!—
Or now, from day to day, I coldly creep
By summer farms and fields, by stream and steep,
Dull, and like one exhausted with deep sleep.

XII

Tall, stately plants, with spikes and forks of gold,
Crowd every slope: my heart repeats its cry,—
A cry for strength, for strength and victory;
The will to strive, the courage overbold
That would have moved me once to turn indeed,
And level with the dust each lordly weed.
But now I weep upon my wayside walks
And sigh for those fair days, when glorying
I stood a boy amid the mullein-stalks,
And dreamed myself like him the Lion-King.
There, where his shield shed arrows, and the clank
Clashed on his helm of battle-axe and brand,
He pushed the battle backward, rank on rank,
Fallen in the sword-swing of his stormy hand.

XIII

As one who walks and weeps by alien brine,
And hears the heavy land-wash break, so I,
Apart from friends, remote in misery,
But brood on pain, and find in heaven no sign:
The lights are strange, and bitter voices by.
So the doomed sailor, left alone to die,
Looks sadly seaward at the day's decline,
And hears his parting comrades' jeers and scoffs;
Or sees, through mists that hinder and deform,
The dewy stars of home,—sees Regulus shine
With a hot flicker through the murky damp,
And setting Sirius twitch and twinge like a lamp
Slung to the mast-head, in a night of storm,
Of lonely vessel labouring in the troughs.

XIV

Not proud of station, nor in worldly pelf
Immoderately rich, nor rudely gay;
Gentle he was, and generous in a way,
And with a wise direction ruled himself.
Large Nature spread his table every day;
And so he lived,—to all the blasts that woo,
Responsible, as yon long locust spray
That waves and washes in the windy blue.
Nor wanted he a power to reach and reap
From hardest things a consequence and use;
And yet this friend of mine, in one small hour
Fell from himself, and was content to weep
For eyes love-dark, red lips, and cheeks in hues
Not red, but rose-dim, like the jacinth-flower!

XV

And she—her beauty never made her cold—
Young-Oread-like, beside the green hill-crest,
And blissfully obeying Love's behest,
She turned to him as to a god of old!
Her smitten soul with its full strength and spring
Retaliating his love: unto that breast,
Ere scarce the arms dared open to infold,
She gave herself as but a little thing!
And now,—to impulse cold, to passion dead,—
With the wild grief of unperfected years,
He kissed her hands, her mouth, her hair, her head;
Gathered her close and closer, to drink up
The odour of her beauty; then in tears,
As for a world, gave from his lips the cup!

XVI

Yet Nature, where the thunder leaves its trace
On the high hemlock pine, or sandstone bank,
Hating all shock of hue, or contrast rank,
With some consenting colour heals the place,
Or o'er it draws her mosses green and dank.
So gentle Time will bring with tender craft
Another day, and other greens ingraft
On the dead soil, so fire-burned now, and blank.
What we have had, we hold; and cannot sink
Remembrance: patience cometh from above.
And now he breathes apart, to daily drink
In tears the bitter ashes of his love,
Yet precious-rich, and a diviner draught
Than Agria or Artemisia drank!

XVII

All men,—the preacher saith,—whate'er or whence
Their increase, walking through this world has been;
Both those that gather out, or after-glean,
Or hold in simple fee of harvests dense;
Or but perhaps a flowerless barren green,
Barren with spots of sorrel, knot-grass, spurge:—
See to one end their differing paths converge,
And all must render answer, here or hence.
"Lo, Death is at the doors," he crieth, "with blows!"
But what to him unto whose feverish sense
The stars tick audibly, and the wind's low surge
In the pine, attended, tolls, and throngs, and grows
On the dread ear,—a thunder too profound
For bearing,—a Niagara of sound!

XVIII

Perchance his own small field some charge demands,—
So full the eternal Choral sobs and swells;
But clear away the weeds, although there lurk
Within the weeds a few dim asphodels,
Flowers of a former day, how fair! how fair!
And yet behold them not, but to the work,
Before the short light darken, set thy hands!
Nor over the surface dip with easy share,
But beam-deep, plough and plunge your parallels,
Breaking in clod and flower! that so may spring
From the deep grain a goodlier growth and kind;
Unstirred of heats that blast, of frosts that bind,
Nor swept aside, ere the seed catch, by wing
Of casual shower, nor any chance of wind.

XIX

Yet vain, perhaps, the fruits our care applaud:
If the Fore-fate decree the harvest fat,
Why should we mind this thing, or matter that,
To sift the seed, and blow the chaff abroad?
But doubt not so the Giver to defraud,
Who will accuse thy labour: spend, nor slack
Of thy best strength and sweetness too, till God,
With a full hand and flowing, pay thee back.
Behold! on rolling zone and zodiac
The spray and scatter of his bounty flung!
And what canst thou, to whom no hands belong
To hasten by one hour the morning's birth?
Or stay one planet at his circle hung,
In the great flight of stars across the earth?

XX

Still craves the spirit: never Nature solves
That yearning which with her first breath began;
And, in its blinder instinct, still devolves
On god or pagod, Manada or man,
Or, lower yet, brute-service, apes and wolves!
By Borneo's surf, the bare Barbarian
Still to the sands beneath him bows to pray:
Give Greek his god, the Bheel his devil-sway;
And what remains to me, who count no odds
Between such Lord and him I saw to-day,—
The farmer mounted on his market-load,
Bundles of wool, and locks of upland hay;
The son of toil, that his own works bestrode,
And him, Ophion, earliest of the gods?

XXI

O Father, God! to whom, in happier days,
My father bade me cry when troubles fall,
Again I come before thy tribunal,
Too faint for prayer, and all too blind for praise;
Yet owning never, through life's dim career,
The eye that would not see, and reckless ear;
Against my head no more thy tempests call!—
Refreshing that wild sorrow of the heart,
And those fierce tears: another morning raise
Upon this vision, now so dimmed and swoln:
Guide me, as once, unto thy feet to flee;
Claiming no price of labour, place, or part,
And only seek, before thy footstool fall'n,
Tears in mine eyes, to lift these hands of me!

XXII

The morning comes; not slow, with reddening gold,
But wildly driven, with windy shower, and sway
As though the wind would blow the dark away!
Voices of wail, of misery multifold,
Wake with the light, and its harsh glare obey;
And yet I walk betimes this day of spring,
Still my own private portion reckoning,
Not to compute, though every tear be told.
Oh, might I on the gale my sorrow fling!
But sweep, sweep on, wild blast! Who bids thee stay?
Across the stormy headlands shriek and sing;
And, earlier than the daytime, bring the day
To pouring eyes, half-quenched with watery sight,
And breaking hearts that hate the morning light!

XXIII

Shall I not see her? Yes: for one has seen
Her in her beauty, since we called her dead,—
One like herself, a fair young mother, led
By her own lot to feel compassion keen;
And unto her last night my Anna came,
And sat within her arms, and spoke her name,
"While the old smile," she said, "like starlight gleamed:
And like herself in fair young bloom," she said,
"Only the white more white, the red more red;
And fainter than the mist her pressure seemed."
And words there were, though vague, yet beautiful,
Which she who heard them could not tell to me.
It is enough! My Anna did not flee
To grief or fear, nor lies in slumber dull.

XXIV

Perhaps a dream; yet surely truth has beamed
Oft from the gate of dreams upon the brain;
As on yon mountain, dark with thunder-rain,
To-day, through cloudy clefts, the glory streamed.
Why do men doubt, and balance, and disdain,
Where she, the gentler spirit, seeks to skim
Light from the vague,—though thick the shadows swim;
Still counting what she may not all explain,—
Not to be lost, or lightly disesteemed,—
Though cloudy of shape it seem, and meaning dim?
Did Manoah's wife doubt ere she showed to him
The angel standing in the golden grain?
Had Deborah fear? Or was that Vision vain
That Actia, Arlotte, and Mandané dreamed?

XXV

By this low fire I often sit to woo
Memory to bring the days forever done;
And call the mountains, where our love begun,
And the dear happy woodlands dipped in dew;
And pore upon the landscape, like a book,
But cannot find her: or there rise to me
Gardens and groves in light and shadow outspread:
Or, on a headland far away, I see
Men marching slow in orderly review;
And bayonets flash, as, wheeling from the sun,
Rank after rank give fire: or, sad, I look
On miles of moonlit brine, with many a bed
Of wave-weed heaving,—there the wet sands shine;
And just awash, the low reef lifts its line.

XXVI

For Nature daily through her grand design
Breathes contradiction where she seems most clear:
For I have held of her the gift to hear;
And felt, indeed, endowed of sense divine,
When I have found, by guarded insight fine,
Cold April flowers in the green end of June;
And thought myself possessed of Nature's ear,
When by the lonely mill-brook, into mine,
Seated on slab, or trunk asunder sawn,
The night-hawk blew his horn at sunny noon;
And in the rainy midnight I have heard
The ground-sparrow's long twitter from the pine,
And the cat-bird's silver song,—the wakeful bird
That to the lighted window sings for dawn.

XXVII

So, to the mind long brooding but on it,—
A haunting theme for anger, joy, or tears,
With ardent eyes,—not what we think appears,
But, hunted home, behold its opposite!
Worn Sorrow breaking in disastrous mirth,
And wild tears wept of laughter, like the drops
Shook by the trampling thunder to the earth;
And each seems either, or but a counterfeit
Of that it would dissemble: hopes are fears,
And love is woe. Nor here the discord stops;
But through all human life runs the account,—
Born into pain, and ending bitterly;
Yet sweet perchance, between-time, like a fount
That rises salt, and freshens to the sea.

XXVIII

Not the round natural world, not the deep mind,
The reconcilement holds: the blue abyss
Collects it not; our arrows sink amiss;
And but in Him may we our import find.
The agony to know, the grief, the bliss
Of toil, is vain and vain! clots of the sod
Gathered in heat and haste, and flung behind
To blind ourselves and others,—what but this
Still grasping dust, and sowing toward the wind?
No more thy meaning seek, thine anguish plead;
But, leaving straining thought, and stammering word,
Across the barren azure pass to God;
Shooting the void in silence, like a bird,—
A bird that shuts his wings for better speed!

Emily Dickinson

1830–1886

I

This is my letter to the world,
  That never wrote to me,—
The simple news that Nature told,
  With tender majesty.

Her message is committed
  To hands I cannot see;
For love of her, sweet countrymen,
  Judge tenderly of me! *

II

I'm nobody! Who are you?
Are you nobody, too?
Then there's a pair of us—don't tell!
They'd banish us, you know.

How dreary to be somebody!
How public, like a frog
To tell your name the livelong day
To an admiring bog!

III

The soul selects her own society,
Then shuts the door;

---

* Except where otherwise noted these poems are taken from *Poems by Emily Dickinson* (1890) and *Poems: Second Series* (1891), edited by Mabel Loomis Todd and Thomas Wentworth Higginson.

On her divine majority
Obtrude no more.

Unmoved, she notes the chariot's pausing
At her low gate;
Unmoved, an emperor is kneeling
Upon her mat.

I've known her from an ample nation
Choose one;
Then close the valves of her attention
Like stone.

IV

Some keep the Sabbath going to church;
I keep it staying at home,
With a bobolink for a chorister,
And an orchard for a dome.

Some keep the Sabbath in surplice;
I just wear my wings,
And instead of tolling the bell for church,
Our little sexton sings.

God preaches,—a noted clergyman,—
And the sermon is never long;
So instead of getting to heaven at last,
I'm going all along!

V

The heart asks pleasure first,
And then, excuse from pain;

And then, those little anodynes
That deaden suffering;

And then, to go to sleep;
And then, if it should be
The will of its Inquisitor,
The liberty to die.

VI

(handwritten note: Poem about a drunk)

I taste a liquor never brewed,
From tankards scooped in pearl;
Not all the vats upon the Rhine
Yield such an alcohol!

Inebriate of air am I,
And debauchee of dew,
Reeling, through endless summer days,
From inns of molten blue.

When landlords turn the drunken bee
Out of the foxglove's door,
When butterflies renounce their drams,
I shall but drink the more!

Till seraphs swing their snowy hats,
And saints to windows run,
To see the little tippler
Leaning against the sun!

VII

SUCCESS

(handwritten note: I do see Tell you what victory means because he has been defeated.)

Success is counted sweetest
By those who ne'er succeed.

To comprehend a nectar
Requires sorest need.

Not one of all the purple host
Who took the flag to-day
Can tell the definition,
So clear, of victory,

As he, defeated, dying,
On whose forbidden ear
The distant strains of triumph
Break, agonized and clear.*

VIII

Some things that fly there be,—
Birds, hours, the bumble-bee:
Of these no elegy.

Some things that stay there be,—
Grief, hills, eternity:
Nor this behooveth me.

There are, that resting, rise.
Can I expound the skies?
How still the riddle lies!

IX

Much madness is divinest sense
To a discerning eye;
Much sense the starkest madness.
'Tis the majority

* First printed anonymously in A *Masque of Poets* (1878).

In this, as all, prevails.
Assent, and you are sane;
Demur,—you're straightway dangerous,
And handled with a chain.

x

The brain within its groove
Runs evenly and true;
But let a splinter swerve,
'Twere easier for you
To put the water back
When floods have slit the hills,
And scooped a turnpike for themselves,
And blotted out the mills!

xi

I asked no other thing,
No other was denied.
I offered Being for it;
The mighty merchant smiled.

Brazil? He twirled a button.
Without a glance my way:
"But, madam, is there nothing else
That we can show to-day?"

xii

Is Heaven a physician?
    They say that He can heal;
But medicine posthumous
    Is unavailable.

Is Heaven an exchequer?
   They speak of what we owe;
But that negotiation
   I'm not a party to.

XIII

To fight aloud is very brave,
But gallanter, I know,
Who charge within the bosom,
The cavalry of woe.

Who win, and nations do not see,
Who fall, and none observe,
Whose dying eyes no country
Regards with patriot love.

We trust, in plumed procession,
For such the angels go,
Rank after rank, with even feet
And uniforms of snow.

XIV

I took my power in my hand
And went against the world;
'Twas not so much as David had,
But I was twice as bold.

I aimed my pebble, but myself
Was all the one that fell.
Was it Goliath was too large,
Or only I too small?

XV

For each ecstatic instant
We must an anguish pay
In keen and quivering ratio
To the ecstasy.

For each beloved hour
Sharp pittances of years,
Bitter contested farthings
And coffers heaped with tears.

[handwritten annotation in margin: You may have Your ecstasy but you will pay! pay pay?]

XVI

Pain has an element of blank;
It cannot recollect
When it began, or if there were
A day when it was not.

It has no future but itself,
Its infinite realms contain
Its past, enlightened to perceive
New periods of pain.

XVII

Remorse is memory awake,
Her companies astir,—
A presence of departed acts
At window and at door.

Its past set down before the soul,
And lighted with a match,
Perusal to facilitate
Of its condensed despatch.

Remorse is cureless,—the disease
Not even God can heal;
For 'tis his institution,—
The complement of hell.

XVIII

I had no time to hate, because
The grave would hinder me,
And life was not so ample I
Could finish enmity.

[handwritten annotation: Hate can go along for a long time but stops at the grave.]

Nor had I time to love; but since
Some industry must be,
The little toil of love, I thought,
Was large enough for me.

[handwritten annotation: But have no Time for either and if you have to choose one, choose Love.]

XIX

He ate and drank the precious words,
His spirit grew robust;
He knew no more that he was poor,
Nor that his frame was dust.
He danced along the dingy days,
And this bequest of wings
Was but a book. What liberty
A loosened spirit brings!

XX *(Transcendental)*

He preached upon "breadth" till it argued him narrow,—
The broad are too broad to define;
And of "truth" until it proclaimed him a liar,—
The truth never flaunted a sign.

[handwritten annotation: You don't get truth in a Sermon. Some preachers,—preach things they don't understand, makes simple things hard.]

Simplicity fled from his counterfeit presence
As gold the pyrites would shun.
What confusion would cover the innocent Jesus
To meet so enabled a man!

XXI

BELSHAZZAR

Belshazzar had a letter,—
He never had but one;
Belshazzar's correspondent
Concluded and begun
In that immortal copy
The conscience of us all
Can read without its glasses
On revelation's wall.

Daniel + writing on the wall

XXII

Surgeons must be very careful
When they take the knife!
Underneath their fine incisions
Stirs the culprit,—Life!

XXIII

Faith is a fine invention
For gentlemen who see;
But microscopes are prudent
In an emergency!

Faith is fine in its place but science has its place in this world

XXIV

Prayer is the little implement
Through which men reach

definition of prayer

Where presence is denied them.
They fling their speech

By means of it in God's ear;
If then He hear,
This sums the apparatus
Comprised in prayer.

XXV

A shady friend for torrid days
Is easier to find
Than one of higher temperature
For frigid hour of mind.

The vane a little to the east
Scares muslin souls away;
If broadcloth breasts are firmer
Than those of organdy,

Who is to blame? The weaver?
Ah! the bewildering thread!
The tapestries of paradise
So notelessly are made!

XXVI

Just lost when I was saved!
Just felt the world go by!
Just girt me for the onset with eternity,
When breath blew back,
And on the other side
I heard recede the disappointed tide!

Therefore, as one returned, I feel,
Odd secrets of the line to tell!

Some sailor, skirting foreign shores,
Some pale reporter from the awful doors
Before the seal!

Next time, to stay!
Next time, the things to see
By ear unheard,
Unscrutinized by eye.

Next time, to tarry,
While the ages steal,—
Slow tramp the centuries,
And the cycles wheel.

She is looking forward to death & eternity

XXVII

mourning poem over 3rd death. She too outlived three people. Gods a burglar banker, Father

I never lost as much but twice,
And that was in the sod;
Twice have I stood a beggar
Before the door of God!

burglar – takes love
banker – leaves money
father – God – father of all men

Angels, twice descending,
Reimbursed my store.
Burglar, banker, father,
I am poor once more!

XXVIII

Your love memory but not the actual thing

I held a jewel in my fingers
And went to sleep.
The day was warm, and winds were prosy;
I said: " 'Twill keep."

I woke and chid my honest fingers,—
The gem was gone;

And now an amethyst remembrance
Is all I own.

XXIX

Love poem

Poem

There came a day at summer's full
Entirely for me;
I thought that such were for the saints,
Where revelations be.

The sun, as common, went abroad,
The flowers, accustomed, blew,
As if no soul the solstice passed
That maketh all things new.

The time was scarce profaned by speech;
The symbol of a word
Was needless, as at sacrament
The wardrobe of our Lord.

Each was to each the sealéd church,
Permitted to commune this time,
Lest we too awkward show
At supper of the Lamb.

The hours slid fast, as hours will,
Clutched tight by greedy hands;
So faces on two decks look back,
Bound to opposing lands.

And so, when all the time had failed,
Without external sound,
Each bound the other's crucifix,
We gave no other bond.

Sufficient troth that we shall rise—
Deposed, at length, the grave—
To that new marriage, justified
Through Calvaries of Love!

XXX

Of all the souls that stand create
I have elected one.
When sense from spirit files away,
And subterfuge is done;

When that which is and that which was
Apart, intrinsic, stand,
And this brief tragedy of flesh
Is shifted like a sand;

When figures show their royal front
And mists are carved away,—
Behold the atom I preferred
To all the lists of clay!

XXXI

If you were coming in the fall,
I'd brush the summer by
With half a smile and half a spurn,
As housewives do a fly.

If I could see you in a year,
I'd wind the months in balls,
And put them each in separate drawers,
Until their time befalls.

If only centuries delayed,
I'd count them on my hand,
Subtracting till my fingers dropped
Into Van Diemen's land.

If certain, when this life was out,
That yours and mine should be,
I'd toss it yonder like a rind,
And taste eternity.

*There is no
certainty, not
even in all
eternity*

But now, all ignorant of the length
Of time's uncertain wing,
It goads me, like the goblin bee,
That will not state its sting.

XXXII

"Going to him! Happy letter! Tell him—
Tell him the page I didn't write;
Tell him I only said the syntax,
And left the verb and the pronoun out.
Tell him just how the fingers hurried,
Then how they waded, slow, slow, slow;
And then you wished you had eyes in your pages,
So you could see what moved them so.

"Tell him it wasn't a practised writer,
You guessed, from the way the sentence toiled;
You could hear the bodice tug, behind you,
As if it held but the might of a child;
You almost pitied it, you, it worked so.
Tell him— No, you may quibble there,
For it would split his heart to know it,
And then you and I were silenter.

"Tell him night finished before we finished,
And the old clock kept neighing 'day!'
And you got sleepy and begged to be ended—
What could it hinder so, to say?
Tell him just how she sealed you, cautious,
But if he ask where you are hid
Until to-morrow,—happy letter!
Gesture, coquette, and shake your head!"

XXXIII

Love poem

Wild nights! Wild nights!
Were I with thee,
Wild nights should be
Our luxury!

Futile the winds
To a heart in port,—
Done with the compass,
Done with the chart.

Rowing in Eden!
Ah! the sea!
Might I but moor
To-night in thee!

XXXIV

I like a look of agony,
Because I know it's true;
Men do not sham convulsion,
Nor simulate a throe.

The eyes glaze once, and that is death.
Impossible to feign

The beads upon the forehead
By homely anguish strung.

XXXV

If I should die, and you should live,
    And time should gurgle on,
And morn should beam, and noon should burn,
    As it has usual done;
If birds should build as early,
    And bees as bustling go,—
One might depart at option
    From enterprise below!

'Tis sweet to know that stocks will stand
    When we with daisies lie,
That commerce will continue,
    And trades as briskly fly.
It makes the parting tranquil
    And keeps the soul serene,
That gentlemen so sprightly
    Conduct the pleasing scene!

XXXVI

I dreaded that first robin so,
    But he is mastered now,
And I'm accustomed to him grown,—
    He hurts a little, though.

I thought if I could only live
    Till that first shout got by,
Not all pianos in the woods
    Had power to mangle me.

I dared not meet the daffodils,
For fear their yellow gown
Would pierce me with a fashion
So foreign to my own.

I wished the grass would hurry,
So when 'twas time to see,
He'd be too tall, the tallest one
Could stretch to look at me.

I could not bear the bees should come,
I wished they'd stay away
In those dim countries where they go:
What word had they for me?

They're here, though; not a creature failed,
No blossom stayed away
In gentle deference to me,
The Queen of Calvary.

Each one salutes me as he goes,
And I my childish plumes
Lift, in bereaved acknowledgment
Of their unthinking drums.

[margin annotation: the Picture of grace]

XXXVII

A bird came down the walk:
He did not know I saw;
He bit an angle-worm in halves
And ate the fellow, raw.

And then he drank a dew
From a convenient grass,

[margin annotations: significance - Lost / Sad lines set in his / element - The Air - / 1st 6 lines on / ground - doesn't / fit situation / goes back too Dickinson - / she was in her element / when writing & left / alone. / out of her element / like the bird, for / she in society she / did not fit.]

And then hopped sidewise to the wall
To let a beetle pass.

He glanced with rapid eyes
That hurried all abroad,—
They looked like frightened beads, I thought;
He stirred his velvet head

Like one in danger; cautious,
I offered him a crumb,
And he unrolled his feathers
And rowed him softer home

Than oars divide the ocean,
Too silver for a seam,
Or butterflies, off banks of noon,
Leap, plashless, as they swim.

XXXVIII

THE HUMMINGBIRD

A route of evanescence
With a revolving wheel;
A resonance of emerald,
A rush of cochineal;
And every blossom on the bush
Adjusts its tumbled head,—
The mail from Tunis, probably,
An easy morning's ride.

XXXIX

The grass so little has to do,—
A sphere of simple green,

With only butterflies to brood,
And bees to entertain,

And stir all day to pretty tunes
The breezes fetch along,
And hold the sunshine in its lap
And bow to everything;

And thread the dews all night, like pearls,
And make itself so fine,—
A duchess were too common
For such a noticing.

And even when it dies, to pass
In odors so divine,
As lowly spices gone to sleep,
Or amulets of pine.

And then to dwell in sovereign barns,
And dream the days away,—
The grass so little has to do,
I wish I were the hay!*

XL

The mushroom is the elf of plants,
At evening it is not;
At morning in a truffled hut
It stops upon a spot

As if it tarried always;
And yet its whole career

---

* The poet wrote "I wish I were a hay!" but the definite article was substituted at Higginson's insistence.

Is shorter than a snake's delay,
And fleeter than a tare.

'Tis vegetation's juggler,
The germ of alibi;
Doth like a bubble antedate,
And like a bubble hie.

I feel as if the grass were pleased
To have it intermit;
The surreptitious scion
Of summer's circumspect.

Had nature any outcast face,
Could she a son contemn,
Had nature an Iscariot,
That mushroom,—it is him.

XLI
THE SNAKE

A narrow fellow in the grass
Occasionally rides;
You may have met him—did you not,
His notice instant is.
The grass divides as with a comb,
A spotted shaft is seen;
And then it closes at your feet,
And opens further on.

He likes a boggy acre,
A floor too cool for corn.
Yet when a boy, and barefoot,
I more than once, at noon,

Have passed, I thought, a whip-lash
Unbraiding in the sun,—
When, stooping to secure it,
It wrinkled, and was gone.

Several of nature's people
I know, and they know me;
I feel for them a transport
Of cordiality;
Yet never met this fellow,
Attended or alone,
Without a tighter breathing,
And zero at the bone.*

XLII

I think the hemlock likes to stand
Upon a marge of snow;
It suits his own austerity,
And satisfies an awe

That men must slake in wilderness,
Or in the desert cloy,—
An instinct for the hoar, the bald,
Lapland's necessity.

The hemlock's nature thrives on cold;
The gnash of northern winds
Is sweetest nutriment to him,
His best Norwegian wines.

To satin races he is nought;
But children on the Don

* First printed in the *Springfield Republican*, February 14, 1866. Changes
later made in the text of the poem were presumably due to Higginson.

Beneath his tabernacles play,
And Dnieper wrestlers run.

XLIII

I started early, took my dog,
And visited the sea;
The mermaids in the basement
Came out to look at me,

And frigates in the upper floor
Extended hempen hands,
Presuming me to be a mouse
Aground, upon the sands.

But no man moved me till the tide
Went past my simple shoe,
And past my apron and my belt,
And past my bodice too,

And made as he would eat me up
As wholly as a dew
Upon a dandelion's sleeve—
And then I started too.

And he—he followed close behind;
I felt his silver heel
Upon my ankle,—then my shoes
Would overflow with pearl.

Until we met the solid town,
No man he seemed to know;
And bowing with a mighty look
At me, the sea withdrew.

[handwritten marginalia: Whimsical poem about death — Never feared death, sort of looked forward to it, yet wasn't quite ready for it,]

XLIV

THE LOCOMOTIVE

I like to see it lap the miles,
And lick the valleys up,
And stop to feed itself at tanks;
And then, prodigious, step

Around a pile of mountains,
And, supercilious, peer
In shanties by the sides of roads;
And then a quarry pare

To fit its sides, and crawl between,
Complaining all the while
In horrid, hooting stanza;
Then chase itself down hill

And neigh like Boanerges;
Then, punctual as a star,
Stop—docile and omnipotent—
At its own stable door.

XLV

How happy is the little stone
That rambles in the road alone,
And doesn't care about careers,
And exigencies never fears;
Whose coat of elemental brown
A passing universe put on;
And independent as the sun,
Associates or glows alone,

Fulfilling absolute decree
In casual simplicity.

XLVI

It sounded as if the streets were running,
And then the streets stood still.
Eclipse was all we could see at the window,
And awe was all we could feel.

By and by the boldest stole out of his covert,
To see if time was there.
Nature was in her beryl apron,
Mixing fresher air.

XLVII

The leaves, like women, interchange
    Sagacious confidence;
Somewhat of nods, and somewhat of
    Portentous inference,

The parties in both cases
    Enjoining secrecy,—
Inviolable compact
    To notoriety.

XLVIII

THE CRICKETS

Farther in summer than the birds,
Pathetic from the grass,
A minor nation celebrates
Its unobtrusive mass.

No ordinance is seen,
So gradual the grace,
A pensive custom it becomes,
Enlarging loneliness.

Antiquest felt at noon
When August, burning low,
Calls forth this spectral canticle,
Repose to typify.

Remit as yet no grace,
No furrow on the glow,
Yet a druidic difference
Enhances nature now.

XLIX

These are the days when birds come back,
A very few, a bird or two,
To take a backward look.

Indian Summer Poem

These are the days when skies put on
The old, old sophistries of June,—
A blue and gold mistake.

Oh, fraud that cannot cheat the bee.
Almost thy plausibility
Induces my belief,

Till ranks of seeds their witness bear,
And softly through the altered air
Hurries a timid leaf!

Oh, sacrament of summer days,
Oh, last communion in the haze,
Permit a child to join,

Thy sacred emblems to partake,
Thy consecrated bread to break,
Taste thine immortal wine!

L

The sky is low, the clouds are mean,
A travelling flake of snow
Across a barn or through a rut
Debates if it will go.

A narrow wind complains all day
How some one treated him;
Nature, like us, is sometimes caught
Without her diadem.

LI

The gentian weaves her fringes,
The maple's loom is red.
My departing blossoms
Obviate parade.

A brief, but patient illness,
An hour to prepare;
And one, below this morning,
Is where the angels are.

It was a short procession,—
The bobolink was there,
An aged bee addressed us,
And then we knelt in prayer.

We trust that she was willing,—
We ask that we may be.

Summer, sister, seraph,
Let us go with thee!

In the name of the bee
And of the butterfly
And of the breeze, amen!

LII

There's a certain slant of light,
On winter afternoons,
That oppresses, like the weight
Of cathedral tunes.

Heavenly hurt it gives us;
We can find no scar,
But internal difference
Where the meanings are.

None may teach it anything,
'Tis the seal, despair,—
An imperial affliction
Sent us of the air.

When it comes, the landscape listens,
Shadows hold their breath;
When it goes, 'tis like the distance
On the look of death.

LIII

I never saw a moor,
I never saw the sea;
Yet know I how the heather looks,
And what a wave must be.

you don't need prayer, preacher's or church because faith is transcendental

I never spoke with God,
Nor visited in heaven;
Yet certain am I of the spot
As if the chart were given.

LIV

Safe in their alabaster chambers,
Untouched by morning and untouched by noon,
Sleep the meek members of the resurrection,
Rafter of satin, and roof of stone.

Light laughs the breeze in her castle of sunshine;
Babbles the bee in a stolid ear;
Pipe the sweet birds in ignorant cadence,—
Ah, what sagacity perished here!

Grand go the years in the crescent above them;
Worlds scoop their arcs, and firmaments row,
Diadems drop and Doges surrender,
Soundless as dots on a disk of snow.

LV

The bustle in a house
The morning after death
Is solemnest of industries
Enacted upon earth,—

The sweeping up the heart,
And putting love away
We shall not want to use again
Until eternity.

LVI

Because I could not stop for Death,
He kindly stopped for me;
The carriage held but just ourselves
And Immortality.

We slowly drove, he knew no haste,
And I had put away
My labor, and my leisure too,
For his civility.

We passed the school where children played
At wrestling in a ring;
We passed the fields of gazing grain,
We passed the setting sun.

We paused before a house that seemed
A swelling of the ground;
The roof was scarcely visible,
The cornice but a mound.

Since then 'tis centuries; but each
Feels shorter than the day
I first surmised the horses' heads
Were toward eternity.

LVII

If I shouldn't be alive
When the robins come,
Give the one in red cravat
A memorial crumb.

If I couldn't thank you,
Being just asleep,
You will know I'm trying
With my granite lip!

LVIII

I died for beauty, but was scarce
Adjusted in the tomb,
When one who died for truth was lain
In an adjoining room.

He questioned softly why I failed?
"For beauty," I replied.
"And I for truth,—the two are one;
We brethren are," he said.

And so, as kinsmen met a night,
We talked between the rooms,
Until the moss had reached our lips,
And covered up our names.

LIX

One need not be a chamber to be haunted,
One need not be a house;
The brain has corridors surpassing
Material place.

Far safer, of a midnight meeting
External ghost,
Than an interior confronting
That whiter host.

Far safer through an Abbey gallop,
The stones achase,

Than, moonless, one's own self encounter
In lonesome place.

Ourself, behind ourself concealed,
Should startle most;
Assassin, hid in our apartment,
Be horror's least.

The prudent carries a revolver,
He bolts the door,
O'erlooking a superior spectre
More near.

LX

After a hundred years
Nobody knows the place,—
Agony, that enacted there,
Motionless as peace.

Weeds triumphant ranged,
Strangers strolled and spelled
At the lone orthography
Of the elder dead.

Winds of summer fields
Recollect the way,—
Instinct picking up the key
Dropped by memory.

ldison and Steele, SEL. FROM THE TATLER & THE SPECTATOR 87
MERICAN THOUGHT: CIVIL WAR TO WORLD WAR I 70
NTHOLOGY OF ENGLISH DRAMA BEFORE SHAKESPEARE 45
NTHOLOGY OF GREEK DRAMA: FIRST SERIES 29
NTHOLOGY OF GREEK DRAMA: SECOND SERIES 68
NTHOLOGY OF ROMAN DRAMA 101
nold, Matthew, SELECTED POETRY AND PROSE 62
sten, Jane, PRIDE AND PREJUDICE 22
lzac, Honoré de, PÈRE GORIOT 18
nét, S. V., SELECTED POETRY & PROSE 100
E BIBLE: SEL. FROM OLD & NEW TESTAMENTS 56
ontë, Charlotte, JANE EYRE 24
ontë, Emily, WUTHERING HEIGHTS 23
owning, Robert, SELECTED POETRY 71
nyan, John, THE PILGRIM'S PROGRESS 27
rke, Edmund, REFLECTIONS ON THE REVOLUTION IN FRANCE 84
tler, Samuel, THE WAY OF ALL FLESH 7
ron, George Gordon, Lord, SELECTED POETRY AND LETTERS 54
aucer, Geoffrey, THE CANTERBURY TALES 65
leridge, Samuel Taylor, SELECTED POETRY AND PROSE 55
LONIAL AMERICAN WRITING 43
nrad, Joseph, LORD JIM 85
oper, James Fenimore, THE PIONEERS 99
oper, James Fenimore, THE PRAIRIE 26
ane, Stephen, RED BADGE OF COURAGE, SEL'D PROSE & POETRY 47
ante, THE DIVINE COMEDY 72
foe, Daniel, MOLL FLANDERS 25
Forest, John William, MISS RAVENEL'S CONVERSION 74
ckens, Charles, GREAT EXPECTATIONS 20
ckens, Charles, HARD TIMES 95
eiser, Theodore, SISTER CARRIE 86
yden, John, SELECTED WORKS 60
iot, George, ADAM BEDE 32
IZABETHAN FICTION 64
nerson, Ralph Waldo, SELECTED PROSE AND POETRY 30
elding, Henry, JOSEPH ANDREWS 15
FTEEN MODERN AMERICAN POETS 79
aubert, Gustav, MADAME BOVARY 2
UR MODERN PLAYS: Ibsen, Shaw, O'Neill, Miller 90
anklin, Benjamin, AUTOBIOGRAPHY AND SELECTED WRITINGS 12
rland, Hamlin, MAIN-TRAVELLED ROADS 66
dwin, William, CALEB WILLIAMS 103
ethe, Johann Wolfgang von, FAUST: PART I 75
ethe, SORROWS OF YOUNG WERTHER, NEW MELUSINA, NOVELLE 13
gol, Nikolai, DEAD SOULS 5
EAT ENGLISH AND AMERICAN ESSAYS 34
rdy, Thomas, FAR FROM THE MADDING CROWD 98
rdy, Thomas, THE MAYOR OF CASTERBRIDGE 9
rdy, Thomas, THE RETURN OF THE NATIVE 39
uptmann, THREE PLAYS: The Weavers, Hannele, The Beaver Coat 52
wthorne, Nathaniel, THE HOUSE OF THE SEVEN GABLES 89
wthorne, Nathaniel, THE SCARLET LETTER 1
wthorne, Nathaniel, SELECTED TALES AND SKETCHES 33
wells, William Dean, THE RISE OF SILAS LAPHAM 19

*Rinehart
Editions*

Ibsen, THREE PLAYS: Ghosts, Enemy of the People, Wild Duck 4
Irving, Washington, SELECTED PROSE 41
James, Henry, THE AMBASSADORS 104
James, Henry, THE AMERICAN 16
James, Henry, SELECTED SHORT STORIES 31
Johnson, Samuel, RASSELAS, POEMS, & SELECTED PROSE 57
Keats, John, SELECTED POETRY AND LETTERS 50
Lincoln, Abraham, SELECTED SPEECHES, MESSAGES, AND LETTERS 82
LITERATURE OF THE EARLY REPUBLIC 44
London, Jack, MARTIN EDEN 80
MASTERPIECES OF THE SPANISH GOLDEN AGE 93
Melville, Herman, MOBY DICK 6
Melville, Herman, SELECTED TALES AND POEMS 36
Milton, John, PARADISE LOST AND SELECTED POETRY AND PROSE 35
MODERN AMERICAN LITERATURE 53
Newman, John Henry, THE IDEA OF A UNIVERSITY 102
Norris, Frank, MC TEAGUE 40
Parkman, Francis, THE DISCOVERY OF THE GREAT WEST: LA SALLE 77
PLUTARCH—EIGHT GREAT LIVES 105
Poe, Edgar Allan, SELECTED PROSE AND POETRY, Rev. 42
POETRY OF THE NEW ENGLAND RENAISSANCE, 1790–1890 38
Pope, Alexander, SELECTED POETRY AND PROSE 46
THE RINEHART BOOK OF SHORT STORIES 59
THE RINEHART BOOK OF VERSE 58
Robinson, E. A., SEL. EARLY POEMS AND LETTERS 107
Roosevelt, F. D., SPEECHES, MESSAGES, PRESS CONFERENCES, & LETTERS 83
Scott, Sir Walter, THE HEART OF MIDLOTHIAN 14
SELECTED AMERICAN PROSE, 1841–1900 94
SELECTIONS FROM GREEK AND ROMAN HISTORIANS 88
Shakespeare, FIVE PLAYS: Hamlet; King Lear; Henry IV, Part I; Much Ado
    about Nothing; The Tempest 51
Shakespeare, AS YOU LIKE IT, JULIUS CAESAR, MACBETH 91
Shakespeare, TWELFTH NIGHT, OTHELLO 92
Shaw, Bernard, SELECTED PLAYS AND OTHER WRITINGS 81
Shelley, Percy Bysshe, SELECTED POETRY AND PROSE 49
SIR GAWAIN AND THE GREEN KNIGHT 97
Smollett, Tobias, HUMPHRY CLINKER 48
SOUTHERN STORIES 106
Spenser, Edmund, SELECTED POETRY 73
Sterne, Laurence, TRISTRAM SHANDY 37
Stevenson, Robert Louis, MASTER OF BALLANTRAE 67
Swift, Jonathan, GULLIVER'S TRAVELS 10
Swift, Jonathan, SELECTED PROSE AND POETRY 78
Tennyson, Alfred, SELECTED POETRY 69
Thackeray, William Makepeace, VANITY FAIR 76
Thoreau, Henry David, WALDEN, ON THE DUTY OF CIVIL DISOBEDIENCE 8
Trollope, Anthony, BARCHESTER TOWERS 21
Turgenev, Ivan, FATHERS AND CHILDREN 17
Twain, Mark, THE ADVENTURES OF HUCKLEBERRY FINN 11
Twain, Mark, ROUGHING IT 61
Vergil, THE AENEID 63
VICTORIAN POETRY: Clough to Kipling 96
Whitman, Walt, LEAVES OF GRASS AND SELECTED PROSE 28
Wordsworth, THE PRELUDE, SEL'D SONNETS & MINOR POEMS, Rev. & Enl. 3